THE NEW
PARENTS' MAGAZINE
FAMILY COOKBOOK

BY BLANCHE M. STOVER
Former Food Editor, Parents' Magazine

PARENTS' MAGAZINE ENTERPRISES, INC.
PUBLISHERS OF PARENTS' MAGAZINE
52 VANDERBILT AVENUE, NEW YORK

Parents' Magazine Books

BABY CARE BOOK

FAMILY COOKBOOK

GUIDING YOUR CHILD

FAMILY HEALTH

BETTER LIVING AND HOME

MANAGEMENT GUIDE

1970 EDITION

Preface

This book is planned for every mother who wants her family to be well fed and to enjoy nutritious, appetizing meals. It is neither a basic cookbook nor a gourmet's delight. Rather it is a practical guide to better family meals. The recipes selected are all within the ability of the average cook and the budget of the average household. Every recipe has been tested by families with children or by the food staff of *Parents' Magazine*.

Many of these are basic recipes using standard ingredients and methods of preparation, followed by suggestions for simple variations. Once the basic technique is mastered, it is easy to make minor changes and substitutions to provide a variety of interesting dishes.

Short cuts and simplified methods make a mother's work easier and give her more time to spend with her children and on other phases of homemaking. For this reason, many helpful tips are interspersed throughout the recipe section. Suggestions for pleasing food combinations and attractive garnishes accompany many of the recipes.

Special features include chapters on family health and nutrition, wise spending of the family dollar, frozen foods, packing children's lunch boxes, special diets and food for parties, picnics and barbecues. An added feature, which makes this cookbook different from others, is a memo to mothers who want to help their children learn to cook and a cookbook for children. To it, in the most recent revision, we have added suggestions which will increase your childs cooking creativity.

Because studies show that in many homes lunches are hit-or-miss affairs, we have included well-balanced lunch menus for every weekday of the year. It is not expected that these menus will be used just as they are. Adjustments can be made easily to suit family tastes.

Good meals served in a pleasant atmosphere strengthen family ties and give children a feeling of security. We hope this book will help many mothers to feed their families with both greater confidence and greater pleasure.

In this book we have not attempted to cover the preservation of food by canning, freezing or pickling. Excellent food-preservation booklets are available from manufacturers of the equipment used in preserving food and also from the Superintendent of Documents, Department of Agriculture, Washington 25, D.C. Nor have we included directions for using special equipment such as pressure cookers and electric blenders, feeling that the instructions and recipes accompanying such equipment are adequate for their use.

We wish to thank Jean MacGregor Whelan, nutritionist and mother of five children, for her help in selecting and testing many of the recipes in this book. Our appreciation also goes to the many mothers who have family-tested recipes for us and to the home economists in business who have provided us with the most recent information in their special food fields. Carol Brock, present Food Editor of Parents', and her assistants, who worked on this 1969 edition, have added a new quick and easy chapter right in step with the times.

Blanche M. Stover
Former Food Editor, *Parents' Magazine*

Contents

Food for
a Healthy Family

One of the most important jobs you as a woman can have, and one of the most rewarding, is the raising of a healthy, happy family.

Health, of course, depends upon many things but its basis is good nutrition. Success here requires a working knowledge of nutrition, an understanding of the changing needs of growing children, and the ability to plan and prepare appetizing, attractive, well-balanced meals.

If you keep the Basic 4 Food Groups in mind, you'll find planning well-balanced meals simple. Foods within each group are similar in food value and can be used interchangeably in menu planning. Everyone needs some foods from each group daily.

Basic 4 Food Groups

1. Milk, Cheese, Ice Cream

Need daily—3 to 4 cups milk or its equivalent for children; 2 or more cups for adults, more for expectant and nursing mothers

Milk is one of the best sources of calcium and riboflavin. It is also valuable for high-quality protein and other nutrients including vitamin A from the butterfat in milk. Calcium is essential for building and maintaining strong bones, teeth and blood, and for proper functioning of the entire body. Riboflavin, a B vitamin, promotes general well being.

Part of the milk may be drunk and part eaten in such foods as cream soups and puddings. It may be whole, skim, evaporated or dry. Cheddar-style cheese (1⅓ ozs.), cream cheese (1 lb.), cottage cheese (¾ lb.) and ice cream (1 scant pint) provide about the same amount of calcium as 1 cup of milk.

2. Meat, Poultry, Fish, Eggs

Need daily—2 or more servings, if possible, including 1 egg a day or at least 4 a week.

These foods are important for protein, B vitamins (thiamine, riboflavin and niacin) and iron. Eggs also provide a little vitamin A and D. Protein's primary job is building and repairing tissues. The B vitamins are primarily regulators. Iron is needed for building good red blood. (Young children, adolescent girls and pregnant women need extra servings of iron-rich foods.)

Dry peas and beans, lentils, soy beans, peanut butter, peanuts and other nuts may be used occasionally as alternates for meat, poultry, fish or eggs.

3. Fruits and Vegetables

Need daily—4 or more servings including 1 rich in vitamin C and at least 1 of a dark green or deep yellow vegetable.

Citrus fruits such as oranges and lemons, strawberries, cantaloupe and tomatoes provide large amounts of vitamin C (ascorbic acid). Raw cabbage, cauliflower, green peppers, turnips and salad greens are also good sources of vitamin C. This vitamin is needed for healthy gums and blood vessels.

Green and yellow vegetables are rich in vitamin A for good eyesight, healthy mucous membranes and resistance to infection. Among the best vegetable sources of vitamin A are carrots, sweet potatoes, yellow squash, asparagus, Brussels sprouts and peas. White potatoes contain worth-while amounts of several vitamins and minerals, including vitamin C and iron.

4. Grain Products

Need daily—4 or more servings

Breads, cereals and other grain products such as macaroni and noodles are primarily carbohydrates—starches and sugars— and provide energy for work and play. When whole grain, en- riched or restored, they also provide iron and B vitamins needed for good appetite and general well-being.

Mothers please note—

Why is it vital that every member of your family eat the right foods in the right amounts every day? Because when they do, they feel better, look better—and often act better.

Nutritionists agree that it is best to satisfy ¼ to ⅓ of daily food needs at breakfast time. In general, breakfast should supply citrus fruit, cereal, eggs and milk. Dinner, the largest meal of the day, should be built around a protein food from Group 2 supplemented with vegetables, bread, milk, dessert, preferably fruit. Lunch or supper is a good spot to make up for weaknesses in the other two meals of the day.

Use foods not included in the Basic 4, such as butter and other fats, sugar and other sweets, to round out meals and satisfy ap- petite. Snacks can be nutritionally significant.

The Major Nutrients: Functions and Food Sources

FUNCTIONS	PRINCIPAL FOOD SOURCES	

Proteins

Essential for building body tissues	Cheese	Peanuts
Help balance alkali-acid in body	Eggs	Poultry
Help in disease resistance	Fish	Soybeans
Furnish energy	Legumes	Wheat germ
	Meats, lean	Whole grain
	and organ	cereals
	Milk	Yeast

Carbohydrates (starches and sugars)

Essential for energy and work	Bananas	Macaroni
Essential for body warmth	Bread	Potatoes
Help in metabolism of other foods	Candy	Preserves
Aid digestive tract by adding bulk	Cereals	Sugar
	Fruit, dried	Vegetables,
	Honey	starchy

Fats

Furnish energy: as body fat they are	Butter	Meats, fat
an energy reserve	Cheese	Nuts
Act as insulators against heat loss and	Cream	Oils, edible
for body tissues	Egg yolk	Salad dressing
Help in metabolism of other foods	Lard	Shortening
Help in utilization of vitamins	Margarine	Soybeans

Calcium

Essential for development of strong	Beans	Milk
bones and teeth	Bread	Molasses
Essential for maintaining functions of	Broccoli	Nuts
nerves, muscles and heart	Cabbage	Oranges
Essential for blood clotting	Carrots	Peas
Essential for nursing	Cauliflower	Salad greens
Helps prevent rickets	Cheese	Salmon
	Egg yolk	Sardines
	Figs, dried	Strawberries
	Ice cream	Sugar, brown
	Kale	Turnips

Phosphorus

Essential for development of strong bones and sound teeth
Essential for good development and functioning of all body cells
Helps in formation and function of several important enzymes
Helps balance alkali-acid in body
Helps prevent rickets

Bread
Cantaloupe
Cheese
Corn
Egg yolk
Fish
Grapefruit
Ice cream
Legumes

Meats, lean and organ
Milk
Oatmeal
Potatoes
Poultry
Shellfish
Soybeans
Whole grains

Iron

Essential for the production of hemoglobin and red blood cells
Essential for functioning of all body cells
Essential for the respiration of tissues and the transportation of oxygen

Apricots, dried
Bananas
Beets
Bread
Dates
Egg yolks
Fish
Legumes
Liver
Meats, lean

Molasses
Potatoes
Poultry
Prunes
Raisins
Shellfish
Vegetables, green and leafy
Whole grains

Iodine

Promotes normal growth
Essential for the regulation of thyroid and basal metabolism
Helps prevent simple goiter

Cod-liver oil
Fish, salt water
Iodized salt
Sea foods

Vitamin A

Promotes growth in general
Contributes to normal formation of bones and teeth
Helps maintain disease resistance by keeping mucous membranes in good condition
Essential for ability to see in dim light
Is important in bearing and nursing children

Asparagus
Beans, green
Butter or margarine
Carrots
Cheese, Cheddar
Corn, yellow
Cream
Egg yolks

Kidneys
Liver
Milk, whole
Peaches
Peas
Peppers
Prunes
Squash, yellow
Sweet potatoes
Tomatoes

Vitamin B₁ (Thiamine)

Promotes normal growth

Promotes good muscle tone of the digestive tract, necessary for normal digestion and elimination

Essential for normal utilization of carbohydrates for energy

Promotes good appetite

Helps maintain healthy nerve structure and normal nerve function

Helps prevent beri-beri

Helps in bearing and nursing children

Beef	Legumes
Bread,	Liver
enriched	Milk
white and	Nuts
whole-	Oysters
wheat	Pork
Chard	Potatoes
Corn	Prunes
Egg yolk	Turnip greens
Fish	Variety meats
Kale	Veal
Lamb	Yeast

Vitamin B₂ (Riboflavin)

Promotes mental and physical growth and development

Essential for respiration of body cells

Necessary for normal skin tone and vision

Helps prolong the prime of life

Helps in bearing and nursing children

Promotes well-being and vitality

Asparagus	Legumes
Bread,	Meats, lean
enriched	and organ
and whole	Milk
wheat	Nuts
Cheese	Oysters
Corn	Peppers
Eggs	Prunes
Fish	Tomatoes
Greens	Whole grains
Ice cream	Yeast

Niacin

Essential for maintaining health of skin and tongue

Helps maintain normal function of gastro-intestinal tract

Helps prevent pellagra

Contributes to the proper functioning of nervous system

Bread,	Meats
enriched	Oysters
and whole	Peaches
wheat	Peanuts
Buttermilk	Peanut butter
Fish	Potatoes
Greens	Rice
Legumes	Wheat
Liver	Yeast

Vitamin B₆ (Pyridoxine)

Essential for growth
Essential for health of skin
Aids in proper functioning of muscles
and nervous system
Helps prevent anemia

Fish
Meats, lean
and organ

Milk
Whole-grain
cereals

Pantothenic Acid

Essential for growth
Essential for healthy skin
Helps in normal hair growth and
may retard graying hair

Eggs
Kidney
Liver
Meats

Milk
Nuts
Whole-grain
cereals

Vitamin B₁₂

Promotes blood regeneration
Helps prevent pernicious anemia

Cheese
Eggs
Kidney

Liver
Meats
Milk

Vitamin C (Ascorbic Acid)

Essential for normal growth
Maintains strong bones and walls of
blood vessels
Promotes good teeth structure,
soundness of jawbones and gums
Increases ability to resist infections
Essential for tissue respiration
Helps prevent scurvy

Beans, green
Broccoli
Cabbage, raw
Cantaloupe
Grapefruit
Greens
Lemons
Liver

Oranges
Peas
Peppers
Pineapples
Potatoes
Strawberries
Tomatoes
Turnips

Vitamin D

Essential for development of sound
teeth, strong straight bones
Aids in regulating utilization of calcium and phosphorus
Helps prevent rickets

Butter
Egg yolk
Enriched
bread and
cereals

Fat fish
Liver
Milk or cream
with vita-
min D

Vitamin E

Essential for growth and normal
reproduction
Presumed essential to cell nuclei
Essential for functioning of glands
Helps prevent sterility

Egg yolk
Legumes
Nuts
Pork liver
Seed-germ oils

Soybean oil
Tomatoes
Vegetables,
green and
leafy

Family Meal Plan for 1 Week

	BREAKFAST	DINNER	SUPPER
Sunday	Grapefruit (1/2 each) * Waffles Maple flavored syrup Coffee Milk	* Stuffed lamb shoulder Creamed spinach Baked potato Lettuce and tomato salad * Chocolate cake Coffee Milk	Grilled cheese and bacon sandwiches Carrot and celery sticks Assorted fresh fruit * Oatmeal raisin cookies Tea Cocoa

	BREAKFAST	LUNCH	DINNER
Monday	Orange juice * Scrambled eggs * Cinnamon toast Coffee Milk	Broiled hamburger sandwiches Catsup Pickles Chocolate cake (leftover) Canned peaches Milk	* Corned beef hash Green beans Raw garden salad * Basic French dressing Apples and cheese Coffee Milk
Tuesday	Orange sections Ready-to-serve cereal with bananas Coffee Milk	Tomato soup Deviled ham sandwiches Fruited gelatin Milk	* Swiss steak O'Brien potatoes Corn Green salad * Hot gingerbread Coffee Milk

Wednesday	Tomato juice
	* Poached eggs
	Toast and honey
	Coffee Milk
		Frankfurters, wrapped in
		   bacon and broiled
		Green beans
		Fresh or canned fruit
		* Hermits Milk
			* Braised veal with
			   vegetables
			Coleslaw and raisins
			* Apple betty
			Coffee Milk

Thursday	Orange juice
	Cream of rice or other
	   hot cereal
	Coffee Milk
		Tiny meat balls with
		   chili sauce dip
		Broccoli
		Potato chips
		Chocolate pudding
		Milk
			* Beef stew
			Lettuce wedges with
			   French dressing
			Garlic bread
			* Strawberry shortcake
			Tea Milk

Friday	Prunes
	* Soft-cooked eggs
	Biscuits (from a mix)
	Grape jelly
	Coffee Milk
		Vegetable soup
		Assorted crackers
		Cottage cheese and fresh
		   fruit in season
		* Brownies Milk
			* Macaroni tuna
			   casserole
			* Molded vegetable salad
			Honey-broiled grape-
			   fruit
			* Sugar cookies
			Coffee Cocoa

Saturday	Orange juice
	* French toast with syrup
	Coffee Milk
		Bologna on soft buns
		Celery stalks stuffed with
		   peanut butter
		Fresh butter
		* Toll House cookies
		Coffee Milk
			* Pan fried calf's liver
			Fluffy mashed potatoes
			Frozen mixed vegeta-
			   bles
			Crackers and assorted
			   spreads
			Coffee Milk

* See index for recipe

Food for the Very Young

Feeding the family starts long before your baby takes his first spoonful of solid food, even before he gets his first bottle or his first feeding at the breast. While he lies snug and warm in the womb, the food elements he needs—proteins, carbohydrates, fat, vitamins, minerals—filter through your tissues into his blood stream. That's why it's so important for you to choose your food wisely during your pregnancy. You must eat plenty of meat, eggs, cheese and milk, lots of fruits and vegetables and whole-grain or enriched cereals. Only by eating body-building, vitamin-rich foods can you be sure that your baby is getting the food elements he needs.

As soon as your baby is born, he must eat and digest food for himself. The job is new to him and it's a big one, for he grows more rapidly in the first months of life than he ever will again. (A baby doubles his weight the first six months.)

Most pediatricians believe that mother's milk is the best possible food for the newborn baby. If you are breast-feeding your infant, remember that his food supply depends upon yours. The same foods recommended during pregnancy—protein foods such as meat, fish and eggs; dairy products; fruits and vegetables; and cereals—offer the best guarantee that your milk will contain the food elements your baby needs to grow and develop properly. If you do not nurse your baby, the pediatrician will advise a formula.

Solid foods are given to babies at much earlier ages these days, some doctors suggesting cereal diluted with milk as early as three weeks. Make the cereal very thin at first, only a little thicker than the formula or milk with which it is mixed. Offer a single spoonful the first day and increase the amount gradually.

Precooked cereals especially prepared for infant feeding are a great convenience during the first months.

Today, some doctors start babies on strained fruit. Apples, apricots, prunes, pears, peaches, pineapples and bananas are all suitable. Jars of fruits prepared especially for babies can save you much time and work. However, if you wish to prepare the fruit yourself, cook it well and force it through a strainer. Banana need not be cooked but it should be thoroughly ripe. Just mash it well with a fork. Offer a tiny amount of any fruit the first time.

When your baby has become accustomed to cereals and fruits, he is ready to try vegetables. You may use the strained vegetables prepared for babies or cook and strain fresh vegetables at home. Green beans, peas, squash, beets, carrots and spinach are all good choices. As with any new food, go slowly at first, increasing only as the baby is ready for it. Since cooked vegetables spoil quickly, store any uneaten portion in the refrigerator and use within two days.

When the doctor says your baby may have meat, you will find on your grocer's shelves a wide variety of canned baby meats already cooked and strained. If you prefer to prepare the meat yourself, buy lean meat, scrape it with a very sharp knife, then cook the scrapings quickly in the least possible amount of butter or margarine. Some mothers use an electric blender to prepare family foods for the baby.

During the second half of the baby's first year, you will be adding a variety of protein foods to his diet: eggs, meat and cheese. Give your baby strained egg yolk at first. It should be thoroughly cooked and forced through a strainer. Some babies like it with a smidgen of salt and a little milk or formula added; some prefer it with their cereal or vegetable. Egg yolks, and egg and cereal combinations, are among the prepared baby foods.

Most babies take to cheese right away—softened cream cheese or cottage cheese fed from a spoon, or pieces of mild Cheddar or Swiss to eat out of hand. A baby likes to take food in his hands long before he can manage a spoon. As soon as the first teeth begin to come through, he may have dry toast, zwieback or a cracker at the end of his meals.

During the second half of the first year, a number of other foods may be added to your baby's diet. Baked potato, noodles, spaghetti, soups and puddings will broaden his knowledge of food and supply the energy he needs for active play. Mash the baked potato with a fork and mix it with salt, butter or margarine and a little milk or make a small serving of instant mashed potato. Mash noodles and spaghetti or serve pastina, made especially for babies. Strained soups and puddings for babies are available in jars, or you can make them at home. Custard, cornstarch and gelatin puddings are all good desserts for this age.

Before he is a year old your baby should have at least a nodding acquaintance with nearly every group of food. He will be eating three meals a day, with the big meal at noon. His daily menus will be similar to this:

BREAKFAST Precooked cereal mixed with milk
Strained peaches
Milk—either bottle or cup
MIDMORNING SNACK Orange juice (with vitamin drops)
Zwieback
DINNER Strained beef liver
Baked potato   Strained carrots
Chocolate custard   Milk
SUPPER Soft-cooked egg with cereal
Zwieback or baby cookie   Milk

Most pediatricians start babies on coarse foods before the end of the first year. Make the change from strained to junior foods gradually. Mash foods fine with a fork the first few times you offer them, then mash less and less as your baby learns to handle larger pieces. Let him pick up lumps of food with his fingers. It's messy but a step toward self-feeding.

Today's thinking is to continue with baby cereal with its vital iron content. Later you can substitute the cereal cooked for the rest of the family. Whole-grain or enriched cereals are best, although others may be served for variety.

Your baby may have any of the junior meats that come canned or he may eat the meat you cook for the rest of the family, cut up in fine pieces. He will like crisp bits of cooked bacon too. A one-year-old doesn't require meat every day, if he has a daily egg and drinks plenty of milk. But meat adds variety to his meals and most babies like it.

Milk remains an important item in baby's diet. He should get at least a pint a day, but no more than a quart. And don't worry if he doesn't always drink that pint a day. You can use other means of getting milk into his diet: cream soups, milk puddings, cereals cooked in milk, and dishes like scalloped potatoes, creamed vegetables and baked macaroni and cheese.

A one-year-old may have non-oily fish like cod, haddock, flounder, sole and halibut. It may be baked, poached or broiled. Mash it for him, removing any bones, and serve with salt and butter or margarine. He may also have eggs other than soft-cooked: hard-cooked and chopped, scrambled, cooked into foods or beaten into eggnogs.

Besides the chopped baby vegetables that come in cans and jars, your baby may now have all vegetables you cook for the rest of the family except whole kernel corn, as long as you cut them fine. Mash peas a little so he cannot swallow them whole. Even Lima beans, broccoli, cabbage, cauliflower and parsnips are all right if they agree with him, but offer small amounts at first. When you prepare a highly seasoned vegetable dish for adults in the family, reserve some of the vegetable plain for the baby.

A one-year-old may share the fruits you cook for the rest of the family. Just chop up his portion. Raw fruits, except berries and melons, may be given if they are thoroughly ripe. Peel apples, pears, plums and peaches and slice for out-of-hand eating.

Here are some menus, one-year-old style:

BREAKFAST Applesauce (canned or homemade)
Oatmeal   Toast
Scrambled egg   Milk

DINNER Chopped chicken livers
Buttered noodles   Chopped green beans
Fruit gelatin   Milk

SUPPER Meat and vegetable soup with crackers
Sliced peaches or bananas
Plain cookies   Milk

BREAKFAST Orange juice   Whole wheat cereal
Toast   Milk

DINNER Minced cooked lamb
Mashed baked potato   Chopped beets
Strawberry rennet custard   Milk

SUPPER Hard-cooked egg with toast
Chopped stewed apricots   Milk

Feeding the baby becomes easier now that he can eat the same foods as the rest of the family. At breakfast he may have some of the family cereal, fruit, toast, and even some of the eggs, if you scramble or hard-cook them. At noon, since he still eats his big meal in the middle of the day, you may want to rely on canned baby foods, or you may give him some of the meat and vegetables left from last night's dinner. (Each evening put aside a little meat, a little vegetable, perhaps a bit of pudding for the baby's dinner next day.) For supper he may have an egg, if he did not have one for breakfast, or soup (perhaps some left from the older children's lunch), or scalloped potato or macaroni and cheese (prepared for the family dinner), fruit, milk and a cracker or two.

By the time a child is three he will be eating family meals with only a few minor changes. It will still be a while before he can manage to feed himself all adult foods without help: you will have to butter his bread, scoop out his grapefruit, open and butter his baked potato, and cut meat and some vegetables into pieces small enough for him to handle with fork or spoon.

A child who eats some foods from each of the Basic 4 Food Groups each day is certain of getting the food elements he needs for proper growth. The "extra" foods in adult diets, the sweets and refined starches, are the foods he does *not* need. Rich cookies, frosted cakes, pastries and candies fill him up and take away his appetite for more essential foods.

It's a good idea to avoid oversweetening any food for children. Make stewed fruits and applesauce a little less sweet than you and Dad like them; you can always add more sugar to yours. Many children like cereal without sugar, especially if they have always had it that way.

Children do better without highly seasoned foods such as hot chilies, curries and sauces. A child's sense of taste is more acute than an adult's and he doesn't need as much seasoning to make foods appealing. If he becomes accustomed to spicy foods, there is a possibility that he will find the natural, delicate flavors of fruits, vegetables and milk less interesting.

Between-meal eating can be a problem throughout childhood. Because of the tremendous energy they use in active play, children are often unable to eat enough at one meal to carry them through to the next. Most children really need between-meal snacks and there is no harm in such a snack if it consists of the right food eaten at the right time. Fruit, fruit juice, bread, crackers and milk are the best foods for snack time. Given not less than 1½ hours before the next meal, they are unlikely to spoil the mealtime appetite. When a child gets very hungry just before lunch or dinner and you know the meal will not be ready for fifteen minutes or more, a glass of tomato or fruit juice will tide him over and help keep peace in the kitchen.

Ten Tips for Encouraging Good Eating Habits

1. Set the stage for happy mealtimes from the very beginning. Cuddle the infant as he nurses or gets his bottle so that he associates food with a feeling of love and security. When he is ready for strained foods, try only one new food at a time and serve it with a familiar well-liked food. If the new food is refused, don't make an issue of it, try again another day.

2. Be sure a child is comfortable while eating and that he has the proper utensils. His chair should be the right height for the eating surface and there should be support for his feet so they won't dangle. A bowl-like dish, for easy scooping of food, and short, straight-handled spoons and forks are best for beginners.

3. Serve small portions to the child who is graduating to junior foods. Anything larger than a tablespoon looks mountainous from a tot's-eye-view and may discourage him from eating. After all, he can always have a second helping.

4. Encourage your learning-to-eat child to feed himself but help him if he gets tired. Praise him for his efforts and try to ignore the mess he makes in the process. He needs to gain confidence in himself. Expect—and tolerate—some dawdling; time means nothing to a child. Hovering over a child, prompting him to eat, causes him to rebel instinctively. And if you are always there to feed him, he may take the path of least resistance and let you.

5. Refrain from trying to force or coerce a child to eat when he doesn't want to. That rules out all forms of coaxing, bribing, threatening and rewarding. Respect the child's ability to judge how much he can eat. If, after a reasonable length of time, he shows no interest in the appetizing food set before him, remove his plate *without comment* but don't give him anything to eat until the next meal. He'll surely be ready to

eat then. And he'll think twice before refusing food again.

6. Don't compare your child's eating habits with others, and certainly not in his hearing. While most children go through similar stages of development, the timing varies. And so do children's temperaments. One child has a hearty appetite and cleans his plate in no time. Another equally healthy and happy child may be more interested in other things and hence a slow eater. Furthermore, the same child's appetite can fluctuate from day to day and it's best not to show concern unless a child appears ill.

7. Make light of food fads. They'll pass quickly unless your child senses they're cause for concern. Above all, don't let him know that he is getting under your skin by refusing to eat or "acting up" at the table. If you do, you're asking for trouble.

8. Give your child the security of a few rules about eating. Insist that he come to the table clean, that he try new foods before deciding he doesn't like them, that he ask to be excused from the table. But don't expect or demand perfect manners from a child. If you are overly concerned with how your child eats, he may refuse to eat. Consider how you would feel if your husband constantly reminded you to "take smaller bites," "keep your elbows off the table," "don't talk with your mouth full." Wouldn't you rebel?

9. Enlist the aid of all in setting a good example for the young child·at the family table. A child learns by imitating others and he copies the person he most admires. If daddy refuses to eat vegetables, what can you expect of his son? Of course, all of us are entitled to a few food dislikes!

10. Plan to make family mealtimes fun times. Having pleasant— and regular—mealtimes to look forward to is important to young children. Center the family conversation around topics of interest to all. The dining table is no place to settle scraps or dish out discipline. Happy children are likely to be good eaters.

Food Shopping for the Family

Shopping for the family food can be a pleasure or a burden. It depends entirely upon the way you go about it. If you buy haphazardly, chances are it will be a burden—an ever-present duty which must be performed if the family is to eat. But if you plan the spending of your food dollar wisely, for better nourishment and more eating pleasure for your family, you will find that marketing can be a satisfying experience.

The best place to begin your marketing venture is right in your own kitchen or favorite easy chair. Look over the food columns in the local papers and note what foods are listed as good buys. Make tentative menu plans for the following week, including as many of these food bargains as is practicable. Check menus for nutritional adequacy.

Then make out a marketing list. Check the supplies you have on hand, and list those that are needed. Be sure to include staples. Many a cook has come to grief when, halfway through a recipe, she discovered that she lacked a necessary ingredient. It is also easier on the budget to replace staple products as they are used rather than to restock all at once.

How Do You Rate as a Food Shopper?

Do you sometimes wonder if you are a good family food shopper? If you do, perhaps a quick check of these shopping tips will help you decide how good you really are.

You're a good food shopper if . . .

1. You keep a pad handy in the kitchen for listing items that are running low.
2. You plan tentative menus ahead and use them as a guide when making a shopping list.
3. You divide your list according to food types (canned, frozen, fresh, staples, baked goods) to save you steps when shopping.
4. You list quantities, sizes and brands you prefer.
5. You keep up to date on foods in season when they are usually less expensive and hence good buys.
6. You watch newspaper ads and store window displays for food specials and seasonal sales.
7. You encourage other members of the family to help with the shopping. (They will be flattered.)
8. You give yourself more time to shop, thereby reducing hasty and unwise buying decisions.
9. You try to shop when the stores are least crowded.
10. You buy according to your family's needs and preferences, considering how much money you have to spend and how much space you have for storage.
11. You buy for longer periods, if groceries are delivered, to cut down on delivery costs.
12. You compare prices of the same food in various forms—fresh, frozen, canned, dried—and buy accordingly.
13. You note the weight on packages because the size may not be a true guide to amount of contents.
14. You know that nutritive value does not depend on price. For example, beef liver, while high in nutritive value, is low in price and a good meat buy.
15. You consider the amount of edible meat per pound rather

than price alone; some cuts have more waste than others.

16. You recognize the signs of quality in foods. For example, you avoid wilted, bruised or over-ripe fruits and vegetables.

17. You buy economical large-size containers when you can use the quantity conveniently.

18. You know that ready-to-bake goods are usually more expensive than homemade products, but their convenience may make them well worth the extra cost.

19. You keep your eyes open for new foods and your mind open for trying them.

20. You know the store personnel and are courteous to them.

Ways to Stretch Your Food Dollar

If it is necessary for you to cut your food bill, here are ways you can do it and still give your family a healthful diet:

1. Buy fruits and vegetables when they are most plentiful and therefore cheapest.

2. Use all the edible portions of the food you buy, such as the leafy tops of vegetables.

3. Compare prices of fresh, frozen and canned foods and buy whichever gives you most for the money.

4. Use more evaporated milk and nonfat dry milk in place of fluid milk for cooking, on cereals and in milk drinks.

5. Buy cheaper cuts and grades of meat. They are as nutritious as the more expensive cuts. Use variety meats such as liver.

6. Use protein foods other than meat—fish, cheese, eggs, dry beans and peas—when they cost less per pound. Buy grades B and C eggs instead of grade A. They are just as nutritious.

7. Limit the purchase of more expensive ready-baked items. If you have time, do more home baking.

8. Watch the markets for reductions on foods which the grocer does not want to hold over a weekend and buy whatever food you can use before it spoils.

Guide to Buying Canned Foods

Some foods are packed only in one size container. Others come in small, medium or family size cans or jars. The following chart, prepared by the National Canners Association, is designed to help you select the can size best suited to the used planned.

FOODS PACKED	NET WEIGHT OR FLUID MEASURE*	CUPS	SERVINGS
Fruits, vegetables, † specialties for small families	8 ozs.	1	2
Condensed soups mainly. Some fruits, vegetables, meat, fish, † specialties	10½ to 12 ozs.	1¼	3
Corn, vacuum pack	12 ozs.	1½	3 to 4
Pork and beans, baked beans, meat products, cranberry sauce, blueberries, † specialties	14 to 16 ozs.	1¾	3 to 4
Fruits and vegetables (principal size). Some meat products, ready-to-serve soups, † specialties	16 to 17 ozs.	2	4
Juices, ready-to-serve soups, pineapple, apple slices, † specialties	1 lb. 4 ozs. or 1 pt. 2 fl. ozs.	2½	5
Fruits, some vegetables (pumpkin, sauerkraut, spinach, other greens, tomatoes)	1 lb. 13 ozs.	3½	7
Fruit and vegetable juices, pork and beans (economy family size). Condensed soups, some vegetables	3 lbs. 3 ozs. or 1 qt. 14 fl. ozs.	5¾	10 to 12

Meats, fish and seafood are sold almost entirely by weight.

Infant and junior foods come in small jars suitable for the smaller servings used. Content is given on label.

---

* Approximate. The labels of cans of identical size may show a net weight for one product that differs slightly from the net weight on the label of another product, due to a difference in the density of the foods.

† Specialties: Usually a food combination such as macaroni and cheese, Spanish-style rice, Mexican-type foods, Chinese foods, tomato aspic, etc.

2 EGGS
1 CUP milk
1 Teaspoo

Cook's Guide and Recipes

How to Get Best Results from Recipes

The recipes in this book have all been tested carefully for accuracy and appetite appeal either in the Parents' Magazine Better Homemaking Center or in the homes of families with children. For best results, follow these basic rules:

1. Read the recipe through carefully.
2. Assemble the ingredients. Use only ingredients called for or substitutions, page 25.
   a. Use all-purpose flour unless the recipe calls for cake flour.
   b. Use granulated sugar unless otherwise specified.
   c. Butter or margarine may be used interchangeably.
3. Assemble utensils; this makes work easier

and more efficient. Use standard measuring cups and spoons.

4. Set oven 5 to 10 minutes ahead of baking time if a preheated oven is suggested in the recipe.

5. Measure accurately.

   a. Use level measurements for dry ingredients unless otherwise stated. Level measure means to fill to overflowing, then level off with straight edge of knife.

   b. Sift flour once before measuring.

   c. If sugar is lumpy, roll and sift before measuring.

   d. Measure liquids at eye level.

6. Prepare baking dish as directed before combining ingredients. Use pan or dish of recommended size, keeping in mind that all pan sizes are rounded to the nearest whole number.

7. Follow directions for combining ingredients. If you are not sure of the meaning of terms used, check Cookery Terms and What They Mean, page 23.

8. Place food to be baked on center rack in oven, unless otherwise stated in recipe. Leave at least two inches of space around container. Overcrowding causes uneven cooking.

9. Follow baking time to the letter unless you know that your range is not accurate. Then test for doneness toward end of stated baking time.

10. Do not increase oven heat to speed cooking. Cooking just can't be hurried.

NOTE: For latest information on cooking meat and poultry, see Roast Meat Timetable, page 158; Roast Poultry Timetable, page 176.

Oven Temperature Guide		Common Cookery Measurements		
Very slow	250-275°F.	3 teaspoons	=	1 tablespoon
Slow	300-325°F.	4 tablespoons	=	¼ cup
Moderate	350-375°F.	5⅓ tablespoons	=	⅓ cup
Hot	400-425°F.	8 tablespoons	=	½ cup
Very hot	450-475°F.	16 tablespoons	=	1 cup
Extremely hot	500-525°F.	2 cups	=	1 pint
		2 pints	=	1 quart

Cookery Terms and What They Mean

Bake—to cook by dry heat in an oven.

Barbecue—to roast or broil, usually basting with a special sauce.

Baste—to moisten foods while cooking, usually with a melted fat or flavored sauce.

Beat—to mix with a quick, even motion until light and creamy; also to incorporate air.

Blanch—to dip in boiling water in order to loosen the skin, remove or set color.

Blend—to thoroughly mix two or more ingredients.

Boil—to cook in boiling liquid (212°F. at sea level) in which bubbles constantly rise to surface and break.

Braise—to brown in a little hot fat and then cook slowly in a closely covered utensil, usually adding a small amount of liquid to prevent burning.

Broil—to cook by direct heat, as in a broiler.

Caramelize—to heat sugar slowly in a skillet until melted and brown.

Chop—to cut into small pieces.

Coat—to cover all sides of a food with another ingredient.

Cream—to make smooth and creamy; usually applied to blending fat and sugar.

Crisp—to make firm and brittle in cold water, as for celery; to heat in a moderate oven, as for potato chips.

Cut—to combine shortening and dry ingredients by means of two knives or a pastry blender, to distribute shortening evenly.

Devil—to combine with hot seasonings.

Dice—to cut into very small cubes, about ¼-inch in size.

Dot—to scatter bits of food over surface of another food.

Dredge—to coat with some dry ingredients, as flour or sugar.

Dust—to sprinkle with another ingredient such as flour.

Fold—to combine ingredients by cutting vertically down through the mixture with spoon or other utensil, sliding it across bottom of bowl, then bringing it up and over.

Fry—to cook in hot fat.

Grate—to cut into fine particles, by rubbing against a grater.

Julienne—food cut into long, slender strips.

Knead—to work dough with hands until smooth and shiny—folding it toward you, then pressing down and pushing away.

Lard—to cover meat with strips of fat or to insert fat in meat to add flavor and prevent dryness.

Marinate—to let stand in liquid, usually an oil-acid mixture.

Melt—to use heat to make a solid food liquid.

Mince—to cut into very fine pieces.

Mix—to combine ingredients until evenly blended.

Panbroil—to cook uncovered in a skillet without added fat.

Parboil—to boil food in water until partially cooked.

Poach—to cook gently in hot liquid just below boiling point.

Purée—to press through fine sieve.

Sauté—to cook in small amount of hot fat.

Scald—to heat a liquid to a point just below boiling.

Scallop—to bake food in a casserole with a liquid or sauce, and crumbs sprinkled over the top until browned.

Score—to make shallow criss-cross cuts in the surface of a food.

Sear—to brown the surface of meat by the quick application of intense heat, usually in a hot pan or hot oven.

Shred—to cut into thin strips or pieces with a knife or shredder.

Sift—to put through a flour sifter or sieve.

Simmer—to cook slowly in liquid over low heat, the liquid surface barely rippling.

Skewer—to fasten with wooden or metal pins.

Steam—to cook directly over boiling water in tightly covered container.

Steep—to extract color and flavor by allowing to stand in water just below boiling point.

Stew—to cook slowly in just enough water to cover.

Stir—to mix with a circular motion for uniform consistency.

Toast—to brown in a hot oven or roaster.

Whip—to beat rapidly to incorporate air and cause expansion.

How to Make Food Substitutions

Isn't it exasperating to discover, after you've decided to prepare a recipe for dinner, that one of the necessary ingredients is missing? If you're the adventurous type, you'll probably go ahead and use a similar ingredient without a qualm. But for most of us it's reassuring to know that the right amounts of substitutes for commonly used foods have been scientifically worked out for us. So, if in doubt, better check with this chart.

FOOD	AMOUNT	SUBSTITUTION
Baking powder	1 teaspoon	¼ teaspoon baking soda *plus* ½ teaspoon cream of tartar
Butter	1 cup	1 cup margarine or 1 cup (scant) hydrogenated fat *plus* ½ teaspoon salt or ⅞ cup lard *plus* ½ teaspoon salt
Chocolate, unsweetened	1 square (1 oz.)	3 tablespoons cocoa *plus* 1 tablespoon fat
Cream, heavy	1 cup (not for whipping)	¾ cup sweet milk *plus* ⅓ cup butter
Cream, light	1 cup	⅞ cup sweet milk *plus* 3 tablespoons butter
Flour, all purpose	2 tablespoons (for thickening)	1 tablespoon cornstarch or 1⅓ tablespoons quick-cooking tapioca
Flour, cake	1 cup sifted	1 cup minus 2 tablespoons (⅞ cup) all-purpose flour, sifted
Honey	1 cup	1 to 1¼ cups sugar *plus* ¼ cup liquid
Milk, sour	1 cup	1 cup sweet milk *plus* 1 tablespoon vinegar or lemon juice
Milk, sweet	1 cup	½ cup evaporated milk *plus* ½ cup water or 1 cup reconstituted nonfat dry milk *plus* 2 teaspoons butter
Syrup, corn	1 cup	1 cup sugar *plus* ¼ cup liquid.
Yeast	1 cake, compressed	1 package, active dry

Guide to Common Food Yields

How often do you read a recipe and wonder if you have enough of a required ingredient on hand? Will that quart of berries make 3½ cups when washed and hulled? Does a half-pint of cream yield a cup when whipped? How much rice must be cooked to get the three cups called for in the recipe? You'll find the answers to these and similar questions *below*.

FOOD	RECIPE CALLS FOR	YOU WILL NEED
Apples	3 medium *or* 2½ to 3 cups sliced	1 pound
Bananas	3 medium *or* 2 cups sliced	1 pound
Berries	3½ cups hulled	1 quart
Beans, Lima	2½ cups cooked	1 cup uncooked
Beans, navy	2½ cups uncooked *or* 6 cups cooked	1 pound
Bread	12 to 16 slices	1 pound loaf
Bread crumbs, soft	1 cup	1 to 2 slices
Bread crumbs, dry	1 cup	3 to 4 slices
Butter; margarine	1 cup *or* 2 sticks	½ pound
Cabbage	3½ to 4 cups shredded	1 pound
Cheese, American	1 cup shredded	¼ pound
Cheese, cottage	1 cup	½ pound
Cheese, cream	6 tablespoons	3 ounces
Corn	1 cup cut off cob	4 ears
Corn meal	1 cup cooked	¼ cup uncooked

FOOD	RECIPE CALLS FOR	YOU WILL NEED
Cream, whipped	1 cup	½ cup heavy cream
Dates	2½ cups sliced	1 pound
Eggs	1 cup	4 to 6 whole
Egg whites	1 cup	8 to 10
Egg yolks	1 cup	12 to 14
Flour, all-purpose	3½ cups (3¾ sifted)	1 pound
Flour, cake	4¾ cups (5 sifted)	1 pound
Graham crackers	1 cup finely rolled	12 to 15 square
Lemon juice	3 tablespoons	1 medium
Lemon peel	2 tablespoons	1 medium
Macaroni	4½ cups	8 ounces uncooked
Noodles	2¼ cups cooked	4 ounces uncooked
Nuts in general (average)	1 cup chopped 2 cups shelled	¼ pound shelled 1 pound in shell
Orange juice	½ cup	1 medium
Orange peel	¼ cup	1 medium
Peas	1 cup cooked	1 pound unshelled
Potatoes	3 medium or 2½ cups sliced	1 pound
Prunes	2 cups cooked and pitted	1 pound
Raisins	3 to 3½ cups	1 pound
Rice	1 cup cooked	⅓ cup uncooked
Spaghetti	2½ cups cooked	4 ounces uncooked
Sugar, brown	2¼ cups packed	1 pound
Sugar, confectioners'	4½ cups sifted	1 pound
Sugar, granulated	2¼ cups	1 pound
Tomatoes	3 medium	1 pound
Vanilla wafers	1 cup finely rolled	24 to 25 small

A Guide to Fine Seasoning

The American Spice Trade Association has prepared this handy chart to acquaint you with a variety of spices and their uses. Until familiar with a spice, it's best to start with ¼ teaspoon (less for the red pepper spices) to a pint of sauce, soup or vegetable, or to a pound of meat, fish or fowl.

SPICE	APPETIZER	SOUP	MEAT & EGGS	FISH & POULTRY	SAUCES	VEGETABLES	SALAD & DRESSING	DESSERTS
ALLSPICE	Cocktail Meatballs	Pot Au Feu	Hamsteak	Oyster Stew	Barbecue	Eggplant Creole	Cottage Cheese Dressing	Apple Tapioca Pudding
BASIL,	Cheese Stuffed Celery	Manhattan Clam Chowder	Ragout of Beef	Shrimp Creole	Spaghetti	Stewed Tomatoes	Russian Dressing	
BAY LEAF	Pickled Beets	Vegetable Soup	Lamb Stew	Simmered Chicken	Bordelaise	Boiled New Potatoes	Tomato Juice Dressing	
CARAWAY Seed	Mild Cheese Spreads		Sauerbraten		Beef à la Mode Sauce	Cabbage Wedges		
CINNAMON	Cranberry Juice	Fruit Soup	Pork Chops	Sweet and Sour Fish	Butter Sauce for Squash	Sweet Potato Croquettes	Stewed Fruit Salad	Chocolate Pudding
CAYENNE	Deviled Eggs	Oyster Stew	Barbecued Beef	Poached Salmon Hollandaise	Bearnaise	Cooked Greens	Tuna Salad	
CELERY Salt and Seed	Ham Spread (Salt)	Cream of Celery (Seed)	Meat Loaf (Seed)	Chicken Croquettes (Salt)	Celery Sauce (Seed)	Cauliflower (Salt)	Coleslaw (Seed)	
CHERVIL	Fish Dips	Cream Soup	Omelet	Chicken Sauté	Vegetable Sauce	Peas Française	Caesar Salad	
CHILI Powder	Sea Food Cocktail Sauce	Pepper Pot	Chili con Carne	Arroz con Pollo	Meat Gravy	Corn Mexicali	Chili French Dressing	
CLOVES	Fruit Punch	Mulligatawney	Boiled Tongue	Baked Fish	Sauce Madeira	Candied Sweet Potatoes		Stewed Pears
CURRY Powder	Curried Shrimp	Cream of Mushroom	Curry of Lamb	Chicken Hash	Orientale or Indienne	Creamed Vegetables	Curried Mayonnaise	
DILL, Seed	Cottage Cheese	Split Pea	Grilled Lamb Steak	Drawn Butter for Shellfish	Dill Sauce for Fish or Chicken	Peas and Carrots	Sour Cream Dressing	

GARLIC Salt, Powder	Clam Dip	Vegetable Soup	Roast Lamb	Bouillabaisse	Garlic Butter	Eggs and Tomato Casserole	Tomato and Cucumber Salad	
GINGER	Broiled Grapefruit	Bean Soup	Dust lightly over Steak	Roast Chicken	Cocktail	Buttered Beets	Cream Dressing for Ginger Pears	Stewed Dried Fruits
MACE	Quiche Lorraine	Petite Marmite	Veal Fricassee	Fish Stew	Creole	Succotash	Fruit Salad	Cottage Pudding
MARJORAM	Fruit Punch Cup	Onion Soup	Roast Lamb	Salmon Loaf	Brown	Eggplant	Mixed Green Salad	
MINT	Fruit Cup	Sprinkle over Split Pea	Veal Roast	Cold Fish	Lamb	Green Peas	Cottage Cheese	Ambrosia
MUSTARD Powdered Dry	Ham Spread	Lobster Bisque	Virginia Ham	Deviled Crab	Cream Sauce for Fish	Baked Beans	Egg Salad	Gingerbread Cookies
NUTMEG	Chopped Oysters	Cream DuBarry	Salsbury Steak	Southern Fried Chicken	Mushroom	Glazed Carrots	Sweet Salad Dressing	Sprinkle over Vanilla Ice Cream
ONION Powder, Salt, Flakes and Instant Minced Onion	Avocado Spread (Powder)	Consommé (Flakes)	Meat Loaf (Instant Minced Onion)	Fried Shrimp (Salt)	Tomato (Powder)	Broiled Tomatoes (Salt)	Vinaigrette Dressing (Instant Minced Onion)	
OREGANO	Sharp Cheese Spread	Beef Soup	Swiss Steak	Court Bouillon	Spaghetti	Boiled Onions	Sea Food	
PAPRIKA	Creamed Sea Food	Creamed Soup	Hungarian Goulash	Oven Fried Chicken	Paprika Cream	Baked Potato	Coleslaw	
PARSLEY Flakes	Cheese Balls	Cream of Asparagus	Irish Lamb Stew	Broiled Mackerel	Chasseur	French Fried Potatoes	Tossed Green Salad	
ROSEMARY	Deviled Eggs	Mock Turtle	Lamb Loaf	Chicken à la King	Cheese	Sautéed Mushrooms	Meat Salad	
SAGE	Cheese Spreads	Consommé	Cold Roast Beef	Poultry Stuffing	Duck	Brussels Sprouts	Herbed French Dressing	
SAVORY	Liver Paste	Lentil Soup	Scrambled Eggs	Chicken Loaf	Fish	Beets	Red Kidney Bean Salad	
TARRAGON	Mushrooms à la Greque	Snap Bean Soup	Marinated Lamb or Beef	Lobster	Green	Buttered Broccoli	Chicken Salad	
THYME	Artichokes	Clam Chowder	Use sparingly in Fricassees	Poultry Stuffing	Bordelaise	Lightly on Sautéed Mushrooms	Tomato Aspic	

Leftovers Better Than Ever

Occasionally every homemaker, no matter how carefully she plans, has food leftovers too good to throw away. Fortunately, most of them can be returned to the table in a new guise, tasting better than ever. Here are some common food leftovers with suggestions for ways to use them. See index for recipes.

BREAD

Basic Bread Pudding
Bread and Onion Stuffing
Company Meat Roll
French Toast
Milk Toast
Panned Scallops
Taffy Toast
Tomato Egg Delight

BREAD CRUMBS

Apple Betty
Baked Eggs with Cheese
Baked Chicken Croquettes
Baked Fish Fillets with Dressing
Breaded Veal Cutlet
Cauliflower Au Gratin
Chili Noodle Pie
Curry-stuffed Veal Birds
Family Meat Loaf
Fried Oysters
Grilled Tomatoes
Liver Patties
Macaroni in Cheese Sauce
Macaroni Tomato Pie
Macaroni Tuna Casserole
Meat and Onion Pie
Noodle Beef Casserole
Oven-baked Chicken Maryland
Panned Scallops
Salmon Rice Patties
Sautéed Fish
Scalloped Cabbage and Apples
Scalloped Onions
Spinach Au Gratin
Spinach Ring
Stuffed Spareribs
Tuna or Salmon Loaf

FISH AND MEAT

Basic Fish Salad
Fish Dinner Casserole
Flaked Fish Ring
American Chop Suey
Baked Chicken Croquettes
Chef's Salad Bowl
Chicken à la King
Chicken and Rice Ring
Chicken Broccoli Pie
Chicken Chow Mein
Chicken, Meat or Fish Mousse
Chicken Salad
Corned Beef Hash
Ham Supper Casserole
Pork Pancake Special
Roast Beef Hash
Shepherd's Pie
Stuffed Peppers
Veal-stuffed Cabbage Rolls

RICE

Chicken and Rice Ring
Custard Rice Pudding
Salmon Rice Patties
Strawberry Pilau
Veal-stuffed Cabbage Rolls

VEGETABLES

Chicken Broccoli Pie
Cream of Celery Soup
Cream of Cheese Soup
Macaroni Tuna Casserole
Molded Beet Salad
Pork Pancake Special
Shepherd's Pie
Shrimp Creole

Beverages and Hors d'Oeuvres

What is more inviting than a frosty lemonade on a hot summer day—or more welcome than a cup of hot chocolate on a cold winter evening? Beverages are first-rate refreshers and morale boosters in any weather, and they go hand in hand with easy hospitality.

Many beverages can boast more solid virtues as well. Milk and milk drinks provide protein, minerals and vitamins; fruit and vegetable juices supply vitamins and minerals. Such nutritious beverages, along with crackers or bread and a spread, make good between-meal snacks for hungry youngsters. And they are a boon to mothers who must cater to a child's finicky appetite when hot weather or illness makes him indifferent to solid food. A variety of glasses, fancy straws, colored ice cubes and garnishes make summer beverages even more tempting.

 Roll lemons and limes on a hard surface with the heel of the hand before cutting. This softens the fruit and makes squeezing easier.

31

Hot Cocoa

½ cup cocoa
6 tablespoons sugar
¼ teaspoon salt
1½ cups boiling water

4 cups milk *or* 2 cups
  evaporated milk and
  2 cups water
6 marshmallows

1. Mix together cocoa, sugar and salt in a saucepan.
2. Add boiling water and blend to a smooth paste.
3. Place over low heat for 5 minutes, stirring until mixture boils
4. Slowly stir in milk and heat thoroughly.
5. Remove from heat and beat 1 minute.
6. Serve at once, topping each serving with a marshmallow.
Makes 6 servings.

Quick Hot Cocoa: Stir 1 to 2 tablespoons Cocoa Syrup (recipe below) into each cup hot milk.
Iced Cocoa: Follow basic recipe for Hot Cocoa. Chill thoroughly and serve over ice cubes.
Minted Cocoa: Add 1 teaspoon peppermint flavoring or 2 drops oil of peppermint to iced cocoa just before serving. Garnish with sprigs of fresh mint.

Cocoa Syrup

1 cup cocoa
1 cup sugar
½ teaspoon salt

1⅓ cups water
½ teaspoon vanilla
  extract

Mix together cocoa, sugar and salt in a saucepan. Add water gradually, stirring to blend. Place over low heat and simmer 5 minutes, stirring constantly. Remove from heat; add vanilla. Pour into a jar and store, tightly covered, in refrigerator. Use as a dessert sauce or for making cocoa beverages. Makes 2 cups.

Hot Chocolate

2 squares (2 ozs.) un-
  sweetened chocolate
1 cup water
3 tablespoons sugar

Dash of salt
3 cups milk *or* 1½ cups
  evaporated milk and
  1½ cups water

1. Put chocolate, water, sugar and salt in top of double boiler.
2. Place over direct heat and heat slowly until chocolate melts, stirring constantly.
3. Bring to the boiling point and boil 3 minutes, stirring constantly.
4. Place over boiling water; gradually stir in milk.
5. Cover and heat thoroughly.
6. Beat 1 minute just before serving.

Makes 6 servings.

Variation of Hot Chocolate

Honey Chocolate: Follow basic Hot Chocolate recipe substituting 2 tablespoons honey for sugar.

Flavored Milk Drinks

Chocolate Milk: Blend 2 tablespoons canned chocolate-flavored syrup or Cocoa Syrup, page 32, into 1 cup cold milk.

Molasses Milk: Blend 1 tablespoon molasses into 1 cup cold milk.

Maple Milk: Stir 1 or 2 tablespoons maple syrup (or ½ teaspoon maple flavoring and 1 or 2 teaspoons sugar) into 1 cup cold milk.

Banana Milk Shake: Beat together ½ ripe, mashed banana, 1 cup cold milk and ¼ teaspoon vanilla extract.

Spiced Milk 'n' Honey: Blend 2 tablespoons liquid honey into 1 cup cold milk. Top with a dash of cinnamon or nutmeg.

Honey Peanut Butter Milk Shake: Blend together 2 tablespoons peanut butter and 1 tablespoon honey. Slowly add 1 cup cold milk, stirring constantly. Beat until smooth.

Hula Milk Shake

2 large, ripe bananas   Juice of 1 lime
⅔ cup evaporated milk   Dash of salt
⅔ cup pineapple juice   Crushed ice

Mash bananas and add cold evaporated milk, fruit juices and salt. Pour liquid mixture into a quart bottle and add crushed ice. Shake vigorously and serve at once. Makes 2 servings.

Eggnog

2 eggs, beaten   2 cups cold milk
2 tablespoons confectioners'   ½ teaspoon vanilla extract
   sugar or honey   Dash of nutmeg

Combine eggs with sugar or honey and mix well. Beat in milk and vanilla. Sprinkle lightly with nutmeg. Makes 2 servings.

Frosted Milk Drinks

Orange Frosted: For each serving, beat together ⅔ cup cold milk, ⅓ cup orange juice, 1 tablespoon sugar and 1 scoop vanilla ice cream.

Strawberry Frosted: For each serving, beat together 1 cup cold milk, 2 tablespoons strawberry preserves and 1 scoop vanilla ice cream.

Raspberry Frosted: For each serving, beat together ⅔ cup cold milk, ⅓ cup frozen raspberries and 1 scoop vanilla ice cream.

Mocha Frosted: For each serving, beat together ¾ cup chocolate-flavored whole milk, ¾ teaspoon instant coffee and 1 scoop vanilla ice cream.

Root Beer Frosted: For each serving, beat together ½ cup cold milk, ½ cup root beer and 1 scoop vanilla ice cream.

Chocolate Frosted: For each serving, beat together 1 cup cold milk, 2 tablespoons canned chocolate syrup or Cocoa Syrup, page 32, and 1 scoop vanilla ice cream.

Ice Cream Sodas

Chocolate Soda: Blend 2 tablespoons canned chocolate syrup or Cocoa Syrup, page 32, with 2 tablespoons milk in a tall glass. Add a scoop of ice cream and fill with carbonated water.

Pineapple Soda: Blend 2 tablespoons crushed pineapple with 1 tablespoon sugar in a tall glass. Add a scoop of ice cream and fill with carbonated water.

Fruit Drinks

Lemonade

1 cup sugar	1 cup lemon juice
7 cups water	(5 or 6 lemons)

Combine sugar and 1 cup water in saucepan. Simmer 5 minutes, or until sugar is dissolved. Cool. Add remaining water and lemon juice. Sweeten to taste with additional sugar, if desired. Pour over ice. Garnish with cherries, strawberries or sprigs of fresh mint. Makes about 8 cups.

Orangeade

¾ cup sugar	3 cups orange juice
4 cups water	⅓ cup lemon juice

Make according to directions for lemonade.

Limeade

¾ cup sugar	1 cup lime juice
6 cups water	(6 to 8 limes)

Make according to directions for lemonade.

Pineapple Punch

1 can (46 ozs.) pineapple
    juice
1 cup fresh or reconstituted
    lemon juice

1 pint bottle cranberry juice
1 cup sugar (or to taste)
Ice cubes
2 quarts ginger ale, chilled

Combine first four ingredients and chill well. Just before serving, pour fruit mixture over ice cubes in large punch bowl and add ginger ale. Garnish with pineapple chunks and maraschino cherries. Makes 32 punch cups (4 oz.-size).

Grape Juice Punch

1 cup sugar
1 cup water
2 cups grape juice

1 cup orange juice
1 pint chilled ginger ale
Ice cubes

Boil sugar and water until clear, then cool. Add fruit juices and chill. Just before serving, add ginger ale and pour over ice cubes. Makes 6 to 8 servings.

Party Punch (for adults)

1 cup sugar
1 cup water
1 quart orange juice

1 cup lemon juice
1 cup strong tea
2 quarts ginger ale

Boil sugar and water together 10 minutes. Mix with fruit juices. Add tea and chill. When ready to serve, pour into punch bowl containing ice. Add ginger ale. Float thin slices of orange and lemon and some maraschino cherries or strawberries on top. Add a few mint leaves, if desired. Makes 4 quarts.

Hot Spiced Cider

1 teaspoon allspice
2 sticks cinnamon
10 whole cloves
2 quarts cider

⅔ cup brown sugar, firmly
  packed
Dash of nutmeg

Tie allspice, cinnamon and cloves in a cheesecloth bag. Heat together cider and sugar. Add spice bag and simmer 10 minutes or until cider is spicy enough to suit taste. Remove bag and discard. Serve steaming hot in mugs, each topped with a dash of nutmeg. Makes 8 servings.

Fruit Juice Drinks

Canned fruit juice concentrates and fruit juice drinks enriched with vitamin C offer a world of healthful and satisfying beverages for the whole family. Many mothers keep a supply in the freezer and refrigerator to use for breakfast appetizers, midday thirst-quenchers and quick party punches.

 Use a large hollowed-out pumpkin as a punch bowl for Halloween or a watermelon shell to hold summer party punches.

Hors d'Oeuvres

Appetizing tidbits, served with a glass of fruit or vegetable juice, are a pleasing first course for family or company dinners.

Shrimp-pets

Arrange small cooked shrimp on lightly buttered Melba toast rounds. Top each shrimp with ½ teaspoon chili sauce and a ½-inch square of cheese cut from a slice of process American or pimiento cheese. Place on cookie sheet and broil three inches below heat until cheese melts. Serve hot.

Peanut Butter Pips

Blend ¼ cup peanut butter with 2 tablespoons mayonnaise. Stir in 2 slices of crisp cooked bacon, crumbled, and 1 teaspoon minced green pepper or onion. Spread on crackers. Place on cookie sheet and broil three inches below heat until bubbly.

Spiced Ham Roll-ups

1 tablespoon grated onion	Milk
1 package (3 ozs.) cream cheese	6 to 8 slices spiced ham

Blend onion into softened cream cheese, with enough milk to make a mixture of good spreading consistency. Spread on ham slices, roll up as for jelly roll and secure with wooden picks. To serve, slice each roll into 4 or 5 pieces; serve on picks.

Minced Clam Dunk

1 can (7½ ozs.) minced clams	1 teaspoon Worcestershire sauce
1 package (3 ozs.) cream cheese	¼ teaspoon celery salt
1 tablespoon minced onion	¼ teaspoon garlic salt

Drain clams, reserving juice. Combine clams with remaining ingredients and blend. Thin mixture to good dipping consistency with clam juice. Serve with potato or corn chips.

Breads

What homemaker would deny that there's a special satisfaction in taking a pan of fragrant rolls from the oven to place before an appreciative family? Home-baked rolls, coffee cakes, biscuits and muffins give everyday meals a lift that makes the extra effort well worth while.

When time is short, packaged mixes and refrigerated dough products provide short cuts not only to biscuits and muffins but also to a variety of rolls and coffee cakes, waffles, pancakes, corn bread and popovers. With such mixes and partially prepared products on hand, home-baked breads can come from your oven or griddle as easily as rabbits from a magician's hat.

Whether plain or fancy, bread is an important food because we eat so much of it. Made with whole-grain or enriched flour, it supplies not only energy but also some of the iron and B vitamins we need each day.

Yeast Breads and Rolls

Coolrise White Bread
One-Bowl

5½ to 6½ cups all-purpose
    flour
2 packages active dry
    yeast
2 tablespoons sugar

1 tablespoon salt
¼ cup margarine or
    shortening, softened
2¼ cups hot tap water
Salad oil

1. Combine 2 cups flour, undissolved yeast, sugar and salt in large mixing bowl; blend well.
2. Add softened margarine.
3. Add hot tap water; beat with electric mixer at medium speed 2 minutes. Scrape bowl occasionally.
4. Add 1 cup more flour. Beat at high speed for 1 minute or until thick and elastic. Scrape bowl occasionally.
5. Gradually stir in enough of remaining flour with a wooden spoon to make a soft dough which leaves sides of bowl.
6. Turn dough onto floured board or pastry cloth and knead for 5 to 10 minutes or until dough is smooth and elastic.
7. Cover with saran then a towel. Let rest on board 20 minutes.
8. Punch down dough. Divide into 2 equal portions.
9. Roll each portion into an 8 x 12-inch rectangle. Roll up tightly beginning with 8-inch side. Seal lengthwise edge and ends well. Place each in a greased 9 x 5 x 3-inch loaf pan.
10. Brush lightly with oil. Cover loosely with saran. Refrigerate 2 to 24 hours.
11. When ready to bake, remove from refrigerator; uncover; let stand 10 minutes. Puncture any surface bubbles before baking.
12. Bake in hot oven (400°F.) 30 to 40 minutes or until loaf sounds hollow when thumped.
13. Remove from pans immediately. Cool on racks. Makes 2 loaves.

Cheddar Cheese Bread

1 cup milk
3 tablespoons sugar
1 tablespoon shortening
1 tablespoon salt
2 packages or cakes yeast, active dry or compressed

1 cup very warm water
1 cup shredded sharp Cheddar cheese
4½ cups sifted flour
½ teaspoon ground sage (optional—but adds a haunting fragrance)

Scald milk. Stir in sugar, shortening and salt, and let stand until lukewarm. Meanwhile dissolve yeast in the very warm water in a large bowl. To it, add milk mixture, cheese, flour and sage. Mix well, cover with a dish towel and set in a warm place 1 hour or until the batter is double in bulk. Then stir batter down, beat about 30 strokes and turn into a greased 9 x 5 x 3-inch loaf pan or a 2-quart casserole. Bake in moderate oven (375°F.) 55 minutes or until top springs back when firmly tapped.

Lora Stover's Oatmeal Bread

2 cups rolled oats
1 cup sugar
2 teaspoons salt
3 tablespoons butter
1 quart boiling water

2 packages or cakes yeast, active dry or compressed
¼ cup very warm water
9 to 10 cups sifted flour

Place oats, sugar, salt and butter in a mixing bowl. Add boiling water, stir to dampen and allow to stand until mixture is lukewarm. Meanwhile dissolve yeast in the very warm water. Add to lukewarm oats mixture and mix well. Add half of flour and stir well. Then add remaining flour and mix thoroughly. Cover, set in warm place and let rise 1 hour or until dough has doubled in bulk. Stir down, cover and let dough rise again until light, 30 to 40 minutes. Shape into 3 loaves and place in 9 x 5 x 3-inch pans. Cover and keep warm until doubled in bulk, about 30 minutes. Bake in slow oven (300°F.) 1 hour or until done.

Plaited Christmas Bread

2 packages or cakes yeast, active dry or compressed
¼ cup very warm water
1 cup milk, scalded and cooled to lukewarm
½ cup melted shortening
¾ cup sugar
½ teaspoon salt
2 eggs, beaten
5½ cups sifted flour
¼ cup raisins or currants
¼ cup chopped candied citron or mixed glacéed fruits
¼ cup chopped walnuts
1 egg yolk, slightly beaten with 1 tablespoon water
1 to 2 tablespoons hot milk
1 cup sifted confectioners' sugar
1 teaspoon vanilla extract

Sprinkle or crumble yeast into very warm water. Stir and let stand 5 minutes. Meanwhile, combine milk, shortening, sugar and salt in a large bowl. Add dissolved yeast and mix well. Beat in eggs and 3 cups of the flour; beat until smooth. Stir in raisins, citron and walnuts. Add all or part of remaining flour to make the dough stiff enough to handle. Turn out onto a floured board and knead until smooth and elastic. Shape into a ball. Place in a greased bowl and grease top of dough lightly. Cover, place in a draft-free warm area (about 85°F.) and let rise 1½ to 2 hours or until doubled in bulk. Punch down dough and divide in half. Divide each half into three equal parts. Roll each part of dough into an 18-inch strip. Place strips on greased cookie sheet in two groups of three each. Pinch one end of three strips together and form into braid. Repeat with second group. Let rise again until doubled in bulk. Brush top with a mixture of egg yolk and water. Bake in moderate oven (375°F.) until golden brown, about 30 minutes. Cool on a rack. Meanwhile, blend hot milk with confectioners' sugar, stir in vanilla and dribble over braids. Decorate with glacéed fruits.

Refrigerator Rolls

¾ cup milk
¼ cup sugar
¼ cup shortening or salad
  oil
1½ teaspoons salt

1 package or cake yeast,
  active dry or com-
  pressed
¼ cup very warm water
1 egg
3½ cups sifted flour

1. Scald milk.
2. Combine sugar, shortening and salt in mixing bowl.
3. Add scalded milk and stir until sugar dissolves. Cool to luke-warm.
4. Soften yeast in the water and blend; add to milk mixture.
5. Beat egg; add to milk mixture.
6. Add flour and mix to form a soft dough.
7. Turn dough onto floured board and knead 3 or 4 minutes.
8. Place dough in greased bowl; cover and let rise in a warm place (85 to 90°F.) until double in bulk, about 1 hour.
9. Punch dough in center, fold edges over, turn upside down in bowl. Grease top of dough; cover tightly and store in refrigerator until needed. Dough may be kept 3 days.
10. To make rolls, cut off amount of dough needed and return remainder to refrigerator. Shape as desired (see directions below and on following page) and place in greased pans.
11. Cover rolls with a cloth and let rise in a warm place (85 to 90°F.) until double in bulk, about 1 hour.
12. Bake in hot oven (400°F.) 15 to 20 minutes.
Makes 24 medium or 36 small rolls.

How to Shape Rolls

Pan Rolls: Pinch off pieces of roll dough and shape into 2-inch balls. Place each ball in section of greased muffin pan or place close together in greased baking pan.

Clover Leaf Rolls: Pinch off small pieces of roll dough and shape into 1-inch balls. Place 3 balls in each greased muffin pan cup.

Parker House Rolls: Pat or roll dough ¼-inch thick on floured board; cut into rounds with 2½-inch biscuit cutter. Crease each round through the center with a dull knife; fold over, pressing edges together. Place on greased baking sheet.

Crescent Rolls: Divide dough into three equal parts. Roll each third of the dough into a circle ¼-inch thick. Cut into 8 pie-shaped wedges with a sharp knife. Roll up each piece, starting at the wide end. Place on greased baking sheet, point side down, and curve ends toward point to form crescents.

Sticky Refrigerator Rolls: Grease an 8-inch round cake pan; sprinkle 4 tablespoons brown sugar over the bottom and dot with 2 tablespoons butter or margarine. After first rising, roll ⅓ of Refrigerator Roll dough into an oblong ¼-inch thick. Brush with 2 tablespoons melted butter or margarine and sprinkle on 4 tablespoons brown sugar. Roll as for jelly roll and cut 1-inch slices with a sharp knife. Lay flat in prepared pan. Let rise in a warm place until double in bulk, about 1 hour. Bake in moderate oven (375°F.) 20 minutes. Makes 8 to 10 rolls.

Peanut Cinnamon Refrigerator Rolls: After first rising, roll ⅓ of Refrigerator Roll dough into an oblong ¼-inch thick. Brush with 2 tablespoons melted butter or margarine and sprinkle with 4 tablespoons sugar, ¼ cup chopped peanuts and 1 teaspoon cinnamon. Roll as for jelly roll and cut 1-inch slices with a sharp knife. Lay flat in greased 8-inch round cake pan or in greased muffin tins. Let rise in a warm place until double in bulk, about 1 hour. Bake in moderate oven (375°F.) 20 minutes. Makes 8 to 10 rolls.

Quick Breads

Basic Baking Powder Biscuits

2 cups sifted flour
3 teaspoons baking
   powder

1 teaspoon salt
¼ cup shortening
⅔ to ¾ cup milk

1. Sift first three ingredients together into mixing bowl.
2. Cut in shortening with pastry blender or two knives until mixture resembles coarse corn meal.
3. Add ⅔ cup milk and stir with a fork until all ingredients are dampened.
4. Stir in enough more milk to form a soft dough which comes away from the sides of the bowl.
5. Turn dough onto lightly floured board or pastry cloth and knead gently ½ minute.
6. Pat or roll out dough ½-inch thick; cut into rounds with floured 2-inch biscuit cutter, and place on a lightly greased baking sheet.
7. Bake in hot oven (425 to 450°F.) 12 to 15 minutes. (Longer baking at the lower temperature gives crustier biscuits.)

Makes 14 to 16 biscuits.

Variations of Basic Baking Powder Biscuits

Drop Biscuits: Follow basic recipe for Baking Powder Biscuits through Step 3, using ¾ cup milk. Drop dough by spoonfuls

When biscuits are ready for the oven, brush tops with milk to get a rich, golden brown crust.

Add finely chopped chives to biscuit dough to make delicious biscuits to serve with meat or poultry dishes.

onto greased baking sheet or fill greased muffin tins two-thirds full. Bake in very hot oven (450°F.) 12 to 15 minutes.

Cheese Biscuits: Follow basic recipe, increasing baking powder to 4 teaspoons and adding 1 cup shredded American process cheese with the first addition of milk in Step 3. Place biscuits on greased baking sheet and brush tops with melted butter or margarine. Bake in hot oven (425°F.) 12 minutes. Makes 18 to 20.

Cheese Purses: Follow basic recipe. Roll out dough ¼-inch thick; cut into rounds with floured 3-inch biscuit cutter or into rectangles 2 x 4 inches with floured knife. Cut ¼ pound Cheddar cheese into ¼-inch cubes; place a cheese cube on each piece of biscuit dough, fold over, and crimp edges together with a fork. Place close together on baking sheet so edges overlap. Bake in very hot oven (450°F.) 10 to 12 minutes. Makes 24.

Cinnamon Pinwheels: Follow basic recipe. Roll out dough into a rectangle ¼-inch thick. Spread with 4 tablespoons softened butter or margarine and sprinkle with 2 tablespoons sugar mixed with 1½ teaspoons cinnamon. Roll up as for jelly roll; cut ½-inch slices with a sharp knife. Place, cut side down, on greased baking sheet or in greased muffin pans. Bake in very hot oven (450°F.) 12 to 15 minutes. Makes 14 to 16 pinwheels.

Butterscotch Pecan Rolls: Follow basic recipe. Roll out dough into a rectangle about 8 x 12 inches. Cream together ⅓ cup butter or margarine and ¾ cup brown sugar. Spread about 3 tablespoons of this mixture on biscuit dough; roll lengthwise as tightly as possible, and cut slices ½-inch thick. Divide remaining creamed mixture into 24 greased 2-inch muffin tin cups; press 3 pecan halves into each. Place pinwheels, cut side down, in muffin tins. Bake in hot oven (400°F.) 15 to 20 minutes. To remove from pans, invert pans so that sugar mixture will adhere to rolls.

 Save cutting time when making biscuits. Roll dough into a rectangle to fit baking pan; place in greased pan and cut into squares with a sharp greased knife.

Basic Muffins

2 cups sifted flour
3 teaspoons baking powder
½ teaspoon salt
3 tablespoons sugar

1 egg
1 cup milk
¼ cup melted shortening or
    salad oil

1. Sift first four ingredients together into mixing bowl.
2. In another bowl, beat egg with milk and shortening.
3. Pour liquid into dry ingredients all at once, and stir just enough to moisten all dry ingredients. Batter will be lumpy.
4. Fill well-greased muffin pans two-thirds full.
5. Bake in hot oven (425°F.) 20 to 25 minutes.

Makes 10 to 12 muffins.

Variations of Basic Muffin Recipe

Corn Meal Muffins: Follow basic recipe for Muffins, substituting 1 cup yellow corn meal for 1 cup of the flour.

Bacon Corn Meal Muffins: Fry 3 slices bacon until crisp; break into small pieces. Make Corn Meal Muffins, using 3 tablespoons melted bacon fat for shortening and adding bacon bits with liquid ingredients in Step 3.

Blueberry Muffins: Follow basic recipe, adding 1 cup fresh blueberries to dry ingredients. Makes 14 to 16 muffins.

Bran Muffins: Follow basic recipe, decreasing flour to 1 cup and blending 1 cup bran into sifted dry ingredients.

Date Bran Muffins: Make bran muffins as directed above and add ½ cup chopped dates to dry ingredients.

 Quick mixing of dry and liquid ingredients is the secret of light muffins. Stir only until all flour is moistened, even though the batter may look lumpy.

Peanut Butter Bran Muffins

¼ cup peanut butter
⅓ cup molasses
1 egg
1½ cups milk
1½ cups bran flakes
1 cup raisins
1½ cups sifted flour

1 teaspoon salt
4 teaspoons baking
    powder
2 tablespoons sugar
2 tablespoons melted
    shortening

Cream peanut butter and gradually blend in molasses; beat in egg; add milk, bran and raisins; mix and let stand until most of the milk is absorbed by the bran flakes. Sift together flour, salt, baking powder and sugar. Make a hollow in the center of the dry ingredients; add first mixture and the melted shortening (slightly cooled). Stir only until all the flour is dampened. Bake in greased muffin tins in moderate oven (375°F.) about 25 minutes. Makes 12 large muffins.

Banana Tea Muffins

1¾ cups sifted cake flour
2 teaspoons baking
    powder
¼ teaspoon baking soda
¾ teaspoon salt

¼ cup shortening
⅓ cup sugar
1 egg, beaten
1 cup mashed ripe
    bananas (2-3)

Sift together flour, baking powder, soda and salt. Beat shortening until creamy. Add sugar gradually and continue beating until light and fluffy. Add egg and beat well. Add flour mixture alternately with bananas, mixing until batter is smooth. Turn into well-greased, small muffin pans and bake in hot oven (425°F.) about 20 minutes, or until muffins are done. Makes 16.

 Add flavor and color to muffins by nesting ½ teaspoon of jelly in top of each muffin before baking.

Popovers

1 cup sifted flour   2 eggs
¼ teaspoon salt   1 teaspoon melted butter
1 cup milk   or margarine

Sift together flour and salt. Add milk gradually, beating until
smooth. Beat eggs until thick; then add to mixture. Add shortening and beat for 2 minutes. Pour into hot, greased muffin pans
until two-thirds full. Bake in hot oven (425°F.) 30 minutes.
Makes 10 to 12 popovers.

Corn Bread

1 cup sifted flour   1 egg
3½ teaspoons baking   1 cup milk *or* ½ cup
   powder   evaporated milk and
1 teaspoon salt   ½ cup water
3 tablespoons sugar   ¼ cup melted shortening or
1 cup yellow corn meal   salad oil

1. Sift together first five ingredients into a mixing bowl.
2. Beat egg in a small bowl; add milk and shortening.
3. Pour liquid into dry ingredients all at once, stirring just enough
   to moisten all dry ingredients.
4. Pour into a greased 8 x 8-inch pan and bake in hot oven
   (425°F.) 25 to 30 minutes.
5. Cut into 2-inch squares and serve hot.
Makes 16 corn bread squares.

Variation of Corn Bread

Bacon Corn Bread: Follow basic recipe for Corn Bread, folding
4 slices crisp cooked bacon, crumbled, into batter just before
pouring into pan.

Quick Loaf Breads

Orange Pecan Bread

2 tablespoons butter or margarine
1 cup honey
1 egg, beaten
1½ tablespoons grated orange peel
2½ cups sifted flour

2½ teaspoons baking powder
½ teaspoon baking soda
½ teaspoon salt
¾ cup orange juice
¾ cup chopped pecans

Cream butter and honey together thoroughly. Add egg and orange peel. Sift flour with baking powder, soda and salt. Add the flour mixture to the creamed mixture alternately with the orange juice. Add pecans. Bake in a greased 9 x 5 x 3-inch loaf pan in moderate oven (350°F.) 70 minutes. Makes 1 loaf.

Peanut Butter Bread

2 cups sifted flour
⅓ cup sugar
3 teaspoons baking powder
1 teaspoon salt

¾ cup peanut butter
1 egg
1 cup milk *or* ½ cup evaporated milk and ½ cup water

Sift together first four ingredients and cut in peanut butter with pastry blender or two knives. Beat egg with milk. Add to dry mixture and blend well. Pour into a greased 9 x 5 x 3-inch loaf pan and bake in moderate oven (350°F.) 1 hour. Makes 1 loaf.

 Quick breads improve in flavor and slice more easily the day after baking. Use to vary the children's lunch-box sandwiches or to serve with fruit for dessert.

Pineapple Walnut Bread

2 cups sifted flour
½ cup sugar
2 teaspoons baking powder
¼ teaspoon baking soda
1 teaspoon salt
½ cup chopped walnuts
⅔ cup whole bran cereal

⅔ cup pineapple syrup, from canned fruit
⅔ cup well-drained crushed pineapple
1 egg, well beaten
2 tablespoons melted shortening or oil

Sift together first five ingredients; mix in nuts. Combine cereal, pineapple syrup and drained fruit; let stand 15 minutes and then add egg and shortening. Combine with the flour mixture and mix only until blended. Turn into a greased 9 x 5 x 3-inch loaf pan. Bake in moderate oven (350°F.) 1 to 1¼ hours.

Banana Bread

1¾ cups sifted flour
2 teaspoons baking powder
¼ teaspoon baking soda
½ teaspoon salt

⅓ cup butter or margarine
⅔ cup sugar
2 eggs, well beaten
1 cup mashed ripe bananas (2-3)

Sift together flour, baking powder, soda and salt. Beat butter until creamy. Add sugar gradually and continue beating until light and fluffy. Add eggs and beat well. Add flour mixture alternately with bananas, a small amount at a time, beating after each addition until smooth. Turn into a well-greased 9 x 5 x 3 inch loaf pan, and bake in moderate oven (350°F.) about 1 hour and 10 minutes or until bread is done. Makes 1 loaf.

Steamed Brown Bread

1 cup yellow corn meal	1¼ teaspoons salt
1 cup whole wheat flour	1 cup raisins
1 cup sifted flour	¾ cup molasses
2 teaspoons baking soda	2 cups buttermilk

Sift together corn meal, flours, soda and salt. Add raisins and mix thoroughly. Add molasses and buttermilk, mixing only until blended. Turn mixture into 3 well-greased 2½-cup molds. (No. 2 cans—1 pound, 4 ounces—make excellent molds when tops are removed smoothly.) Fill molds two-thirds full; cover with two thicknesses of wax paper and one of brown paper; tie firmly with string. Set the molds on a rack in a large kettle. Pour in boiling water to half the depth of the mold; cover and steam 2¼ hours. Keep the water boiling gently, add additional water when necessary. When done, remove from water; cut string and discard paper. Shake to remove from mold or can, invert on a cake cooler. Serve hot. Makes 3 loaves.

Quick Fruit Coffee Cake

1 cup sifted flour	½ cup milk
2 teaspoons baking powder	3 tablespoons melted shortening
½ teaspoon salt	3 tablespoons grated orange peel
½ teaspoon cinnamon	¼ cup brown sugar
1 egg, beaten	½ cup broken nutmeats
½ cup sugar	

Sift together first four ingredients. Combine egg, sugar, milk, 2 tablespoons of the shortening and 1 tablespoon of the orange peel. Add dry ingredients and mix thoroughly. Pour into greased 8 x 8 x 2-inch pan and sprinkle evenly with a topping made of the remaining shortening and peel, and the brown sugar and nutmeats. Bake in hot oven (400°F.) 20 to 25 minutes.

Doughnuts

4 cups flour
4 teaspoons baking
  powder
1 teaspoon salt
¼ teaspoon cinnamon
¼ teaspoon ground cloves

⅛ teaspoon mace
3 tablespoons shortening
⅔ cup sugar
2 eggs, well beaten
⅔ cup milk
Confectioners' sugar

Sift together flour, baking powder, salt and spices. Cream shortening and add sugar gradually. Stir in eggs and add dry ingredients alternately with milk, stirring well after each addition. Roll dough ½-inch thick on lightly floured board and cut with floured doughnut cutter. Fry in deep, hot fat (370°F.) 2 to 3 minutes or until lightly browned, turning doughnuts during cooking. Fat is at right temperature when a cube of day-old bread browns in 1 minute. Drain on absorbent paper and sprinkle with confectioners' sugar. Makes 2 dozen doughnuts.

 Watch fat temperature when frying doughnuts. If temperature is too high, doughnuts will not bake through; if too low, they will soak up fat and be less digestible as well as less tasty.

 To renew stale doughnuts, split crosswise, spread with softened butter or margarine, sprinkle with sugar and cinnamon, and heat in the oven.

Orange Tea Doughnuts

1 cup sugar	3 eggs
3 cups sifted flour	1 tablespoon salad oil
3 teaspoons baking powder	1 cup orange juice
½ teaspoon baking soda	1 tablespoon grated
½ teaspoon salt	orange peel

Sift together dry ingredients. Beat eggs until very light; add salad oil, orange juice and peel. Add to dry ingredients and mix only until blended. Drop by teaspoonfuls into 4 inches of hot fat (365°F.). Fat is at right temperature when a cube of day-old bread browns in 1 minute. Fry until golden brown on both sides, turning only once. Drain on absorbent or brown paper. Serve plain or sugared. To sugar-coat, place in paper bag with 1 cup sugar and shake. Makes 3 dozen.

Waffles and Pancakes

Waffles

2 cups sifted cake flour	2 eggs, separated
3 teaspoons baking powder	1⅔ cups milk
½ teaspoon salt	½ cup melted shortening
2 tablespoons sugar	or salad oil

Sift together first four ingredients into mixing bowl. Beat egg yolks in another bowl; add milk and shortening. Pour liquid into dry ingredients all at once and stir until smooth. Beat egg whites until stiff peaks form; fold gently into batter. Bake batter in pre-heated waffle iron. Waffle is done when steam no longer appears. Makes 6 four-sectioned waffles.

NOTE: For fluffier waffles decrease milk to 1⅓ cups; for crispier waffles increase milk to 2 cups.

Corn Meal Waffles

1 cup corn meal	½ cup melted butter or
¾ cup sifted flour	margarine
3 teaspoons baking powder	2 eggs, well beaten
1 teaspoon salt	1 cup milk

Sift together dry ingredients. Stir butter into eggs. Add milk. Stir in dry ingredients, all at once, beating only until smooth. Bake in hot waffle iron until no steam escapes from iron. Makes 4 four-sectioned waffles.

Chocolate Dessert Waffles

1½ cups sifted cake flour	½ teaspoon vanilla extract
2 teaspoons baking powder	½ cup butter or margarine
½ teaspoon salt	2 squares (2 ozs.) unsweetened chocolate
6 tablespoons sugar	
2 egg yolks	2 egg whites, stiffly beaten
¾ cup milk	

Sift together first four ingredients. Beat egg yolks; add milk and vanilla. Pour liquid into dry ingredients and stir until smooth. Melt butter and chocolate together in top of double boiler over boiling water; blend into batter. Fold in egg whites. Bake batter in preheated waffle iron. Waffle is done when steam no longer appears. Serve hot with ice cream and chocolate sauce. Makes 5 four-sectioned waffles.

 Pour waffle or pancake batter from a pitcher. It's easier and quicker than dropping by spoonfuls.

Pancakes

1½ cups sifted flour
¾ teaspoon salt
3 teaspoons baking powder
2 tablespoons sugar
1 egg

1 cup milk *or* ½ cup
    evaporated milk plus
    ½ cup water
3 tablespoons melted
    shortening or salad oil

1. Sift together first four ingredients into a mixing bowl.
2. Beat egg in a small bowl; add milk.
3. Pour liquid into dry ingredients all at once, stirring just enough to moisten all dry ingredients. Batter will be lumpy.
4. Stir in melted shortening or salad oil.
5. Spoon batter or pour from pitcher onto hot griddle or frying pan, using 2 to 3 tablespoons batter for each cake. Cook only as many cakes at a time as griddle will hold without crowding.
6. Cook over low heat until tops of cakes are covered with broken bubbles. Turn cakes with spatula and continue cooking to brown other sides.

Makes 12 to 14 pancakes, about 4 inches in diameter.

Variation of Pancakes

Corn Meal Pancakes: Follow basic recipe for Pancakes, substituting ½ cup yellow corn meal for ½ cup of the flour.

For Animal Pancakes, drop batter in circles for the body and add smaller amounts of batter for head, legs and tail as fancy dictates.

For dessert pancakes, fold 1 cup well-drained, fresh, frozen or canned blueberries into the batter. Sprinkle baked cakes with a mixture of cinnamon and sugar, or top with sour cream.

Toast

Milk Toast

½ cup milk
1 teaspoon sugar
Dash of salt

1 tablespoon butter or
margarine
1 slice hot toast

Heat first four ingredients together. Place toast in soup bowl; pour on hot milk mixture. Serve at once. Makes 1 serving.

Taffy Toast

2 tablespoons softened
butter or margarine
3 tablespoons molasses

6 slices white or whole
wheat bread

Mix together butter and molasses, blending well. Toast bread slices on one side; spread untoasted side with molasses mixture. Broil 5 minutes or until topping is bubbly.

Orange Toast

¼ cup orange juice
1 teaspoon grated
orange peel

½ cup sugar
6 slices hot buttered
toast

Mix together first three ingredients. Spread on toast. Place in hot oven (400°F.) or under broiler until golden brown.

See recipe for Cinnamon Toast, page 333; for French Toast, page 338.

Save toast left from breakfast to use in cooking. Crumble to sprinkle over luncheon soups and casseroles or to use in stuffing poultry, tomatoes and peppers.

*For soft bread crumbs, cut the crust from one side
of a slice of bread. Then hold the slice flat on a bread
board and tear away crumbs with a fork, starting at
cut edge. For dry bread crumbs, crisp bread in a slow
oven, put in a paper bag and crush with a rolling pin.*

Cakes, Frostings and Fillings

There's been a revolution in cake making in the past few years. New streamlined recipes are replacing the time-honored ones which called for creaming the shortening and sugar, beating the eggs before adding and then beating again, and finally adding the dry ingredients and milk alternately a little at a time. Today, all ingredients except eggs and part of the milk are beaten together, then beaten once more after the eggs and remaining milk are added. Mixing time is cut in half, yet cakes are as feather-light and delicious as grandmother's finest. A few cakes such as sponge cake and angel food do not lend themselves to this method but chiffon cakes, which are very similar, do.

Even quicker are cakes made from packaged mixes which need only the addition of milk, and sometimes an egg or two, plus three or four minutes of beating. Packaged frosting mixes are also available, as are colored icings in tubes and aerosol cans with decorating heads—a joy for junior cooks.

One-egg Cake

1⅓ cups sifted cake flour
2 teaspoons baking
  powder
½ teaspoon salt
⅔ cup sugar

¼ cup hydrogenated
  shortening
½ cup milk
1 egg
1 teaspoon vanilla extract

All ingredients must be at room temperature.

1. Grease 8 x 8 x 2-inch square or 9-inch round cake pan and line with wax paper.
2. Set oven for moderate heat (350°F.).
3. Sift first four ingredients together in mixing bowl.
4. Add shortening and milk; blend.
5. Beat for 2 minutes with electric mixer at medium speed or 300 strokes by hand, scraping bowl and spoon often.
6. Add egg and vanilla; blend.
7. Beat 2 minutes longer. Batter will be thin.
8. Pour into pan and bake in moderate oven (350°F.) 30 to 35 minutes or until top of cake springs back when lightly touched with the finger.
9. Cool cake on rack 5 minutes before removing from pan.

IMPORTANT NOTE: The quick-mix (no creaming) method of cake making is based on the use of hydrogenated (emulsifier-type) shortening. This shortening is simply solidified oil which has been treated so it will mix readily with other ingredients. Because cakes using this hydrogenated shortening require a higher proportion of liquid and sugar to flour than standard cakes, no other fat can be substituted successfully for the hydrogenated shortening.

 Sift dry ingredients onto a square of wax paper to save washing an extra bowl.

Pineapple Upside-down Cake

6 tablespoons butter or
   margarine
⅔ cup brown sugar

1 can (1 lb. 4 ozs.) crushed
   pineapple
Maraschino cherries and
   pecans

Melt butter in 8 x 8 x 2-inch square or 9-inch round cake pan and sprinkle with brown sugar. Drain crushed pineapple and spoon over sugar mixture. Decorate with cherries and nuts. Cover this topping with One-egg Cake batter, page 60, or cake mix for one layer prepared according to package directions. Bake in moderate oven (350°F.) 40 to 50 minutes. Let stand 5 minutes and then turn out on plate bottom side up. Serve warm with whipped cream or fluffy marshmallow garnish. Makes 6 to 8 servings.
NOTE: Other drained canned fruits such as sliced cling peaches may be substituted for the pineapple.

Apricot Prune Upside-down Cake

¼ cup water
½ cup sugar
¼ cup butter or margarine,
   melted

1 cup cooked, dried
   apricots
1 cup cooked, dried
   prunes, pitted

Combine water, sugar and butter, and stir to blend. Pour into greased 8 x 8 x 2-inch cake pan. Arrange fruits over mixture, alternating apricots and prunes. Cover fruit with One-egg Cake batter, page 60, or cake mix for one layer prepared according to directions. Bake in moderate oven (350°F.) 40 to 50 minutes. Allow to stand 5 minutes, then turn out on plate. Serve warm with whipped cream. Makes 6 to 8 servings.

 To prevent cake from sticking to plate, dust with confectioners' sugar before placing cake on plate.

White Cake

2¼ cups sifted cake flour

4 teaspoons baking powder

1 teaspoon salt

1½ cups sugar

½ cup hydrogenated shortening

1 cup milk

4 egg whites (½ cup)

1½ teaspoons vanilla extract

All ingredients must be at room temperature.

1. Grease 8 x 12 x 2-inch or 10 x 10 x 2-inch pan or two 8-inch layer cake pans and line with wax paper.
2. Set oven for moderate heat (350°F.).
3. Sift first four ingredients together into mixing bowl.
4. Add shortening and ⅔ cup milk; blend.
5. Beat 2 minutes with electric mixer at medium speed or beat 300 strokes by hand, scraping bowl and spoon often.
6. Add egg whites, remaining milk and vanilla; blend.
7. Beat 2 minutes longer.
8. Pour into prepared pan and bake in moderate oven (350°F.) 35 to 40 minutes (30 to 35 for layer cakes) or until top of cake springs back when lightly touched with the finger.
9. Cool cake on rack 5 minutes before removing from pan.

Variation of White Cake

Spice Cake: Follow basic recipe for White Cake or Gold Cake, sifting ½ teaspoon cloves, 1½ teaspoons nutmeg and 1½ teaspoons cinnamon with dry ingredients in Step 3. Bake as directed in basic recipe.

 To test cake for doneness, insert wire cake tester or wooden pick in center of cake. If tester comes out clean, cake is done.

Gold Cake

2¼ cups sifted cake
   flour
3 teaspoons baking
   powder
1 teaspoon salt
1½ cups sugar

½ cup hydrogenated
   shortening
1 cup milk
2 eggs *or* 5 yolks
1½ teaspoons vanilla
   extract

All ingredients must be at room temperature.
1. Grease 12 x 8 x 2-inch or 9 x 9 x 2-inch pan and line with wax paper.
2. Set oven for moderate heat (350°F.).
3. Sift first four ingredients into mixing bowl.
4. Add shortening and ⅔ cup milk; blend.
5. Beat 2 minutes with electric mixer at medium speed or beat 300 strokes by hand, scraping bowl and spoon often.
6. Add eggs, remaining milk and vanilla; blend.
7. Beat 2 minutes longer.
8. Pour into prepared pan and bake in a moderate oven (350°F.) 35 to 40 minutes, or until top of cake springs back when lightly touched with the finger.
9. Cool cake on rack 5 minutes before removing from pan.

 When making cupcakes from cake recipes, fill cups about two-thirds full and bake 18-20 minutes in a hot oven (400°F).

 The following pans may be used interchangeably: two 8-inch round layer cake pans or one 9 x 9 x 2-inch square pan or one 12 x 8 x 2-inch oblong pan or three 8-cup cupcake tins;
   two 9-inch round layer cake pans or two 8-inch square layer pans or one 13 x 9 x 2-inch oblong pan.

Angel Food Cake

1 cup sifted cake flour	1 teaspoon cream of
1½ cups sugar	tartar
½ teaspoon salt	1 teaspoon vanilla extract
1½ cups egg whites	½ teaspoon almond
(about 12)	extract

All ingredients must be at room temperature.

1. Set oven for slow heat (325°F.).
2. Sift flour with ¾ cup sugar three times.
3. Add salt to egg whites and beat until foamy.
4. Sprinkle cream of tartar on egg whites and continue beating until peaks formed are stiff but not dry.
5. Carefully fold remaining ¾ cup sugar into egg whites, 2 tablespoons at a time; fold in vanilla and almond extracts.
6. Sift flour mixture over top a few tablespoons at a time, folding in gently.
7. Pour into an ungreased 10-inch tube pan and bake in slow oven (325°F.) 60 to 70 minutes, or until top of cake is golden brown.
8. Invert pan immediately and allow cake to cool 1 hour before removing from pan.

 When using oven glassware in cake baking, decrease the oven temperature called for in the recipe by 25°F. because glass absorbs more heat than metal.

 When using an odd-shaped cake pan, different from that called for in the recipe, fill the cake pan ½ by volume. The easiest way to do this is to fill the cake pan with water, pour water into quart measure and divide by two. Then use that amount of cake batter.

Sponge Cake

6 eggs, separated
2 tablespoons cold water
1 cup sugar
2 teaspoons lemon peel

1 tablespoon lemon juice
¼ teaspoon salt
1 cup sifted cake flour

1. Set oven for slow heat (325°F.).
2. Combine egg yolks, water and sugar in a small bowl and beat until thick and custard-colored.
3. Stir in lemon peel and lemon juice.
4. Beat egg whites until foamy.
5. Add salt and continue beating until egg whites stand in stiff but not dry peaks.
6. Gently fold egg yolk mixture into egg whites.
7. Sift flour over mixture a few tablespoons at a time, folding in gently after each addition.
8. Pour into ungreased 9-inch tube cake pan and bake in slow oven (325°F.) 40 to 50 minutes, or until top of cake is light brown.
9. Invert pan and let cake cool 1 hour before removing from pan.

Variation of Sponge Cake

Cocoa Sponge Cake: Follow basic recipe for Sponge Cake, increasing water to 3 tablespoons, omitting lemon peel and juice, and using ⅔ cup cake flour sifted with 6 tablespoons cocoa.

For packed lunches, fill cupcakes instead of frosting them. Cut off top third, scoop out center of cupcake and fill with jam, frosting or instant pudding.

Chocolate Cake

2 squares (2 ozs.) un-
   sweetened chocolate
1¾ cups sifted cake flour
1 teaspoon baking
   powder
½ teaspoon baking soda
1 teaspoon salt
⅔ cup sugar

⅔ cup brown sugar
½ cup hydrogenated
   shortening
1 cup milk
2 eggs
1 teaspoon vanilla
   extract

Shortening, milk and eggs must be at room temperature.

1. Grease 12 x 8 x 2-inch or two 8-inch layer-cake pans and line with wax paper.
2. Set oven for moderate heat (350°F.).
3. Melt chocolate in top of double boiler over hot water.
4. Sift next five ingredients into large mixing bowl; add brown sugar forced through coarse strainer.
5. Add shortening and ⅔ cup milk; blend.
6. Beat 2 minutes with electric mixer at medium speed or beat 300 strokes by hand, scraping bowl and spoon often.
7. Add eggs, remaining milk and vanilla; blend.
8. Beat 1 minute with electric mixer or 150 strokes by hand.
9. Add melted chocolate and beat 1 minute longer.
10. Pour into prepared pan and bake in moderate oven (350°F.) 35 to 45 minutes (30 to 35 minutes for layer cakes) or until top of cake springs back when lightly touched with the finger.
11. Cool cake on cake rack 5 minutes before removing from pan.

 When a cake sticks to the bottom of the pan, wring a cloth out of hot water and place over bottom of inverted pan until cake loosens.

Devil's Food Cake

3 squares (3 ozs.) un-
sweetened chocolate

1½ cups sifted cake flour

1 teaspoon baking
powder

1 teaspoon baking soda

1 teaspoon salt

1⅓ cups sugar

½ cup hydrogenated
shortening

1 cup buttermilk or
sour milk

2 eggs

1½ teaspoons vanilla
extract

Shortening, milk and eggs must be at room temperature.

1. Grease 12 x 8 x 2-inch or 9 x 9 x 2-inch pan and line with wax paper.
2. Set oven for moderate heat (350°F.).
3. Melt chocolate in top of double boiler over hot water.
4. Sift next five ingredients together into mixing bowl.
5. Add shortening and ⅔ cup milk; blend.
6. Beat 2 minutes with electric mixer at medium speed or beat 300 strokes by hand, scraping bowl and spoon often.
7. Add eggs, remaining milk and vanilla; blend.
8. Beat 1 minute with electric mixer or 150 strokes by hand.
9. Add melted chocolate and beat 1 minute longer.
10. Pour into prepared pan and bake in moderate oven (350°F.) 35 to 45 minutes, or until top of cake springs back when lightly touched with the finger.
11. Cool cake on rack 5 minutes before removing from pan.

For an easy chocolate mint topping, arrange 24 large chocolate mints on top of an 8-inch layer cake immediately after removing from oven. Return to oven for 2 minutes or until mints melt. Leave as is or spread over cake before the topping cools.

Rich Loaf Cake

1 cup softened butter or margarine	¼ teaspoon salt
1½ cups sifted cake flour	4 eggs, separated
¾ teaspoon baking powder	1⅓ cups sugar
	1 teaspoon vanilla extract

1. Grease 9 x 5 x 3-inch loaf pan and line bottom with wax paper.
2. Set oven for moderate heat (350°F.).
3. Cream butter until fluffy in a mixing bowl.
4. Sift together flour, baking powder and salt.
5. Add flour mixture to shortening a little at a time, blending well after each addition.
6. Beat egg yolks in a second bowl; stir in sugar and vanilla.
7. Add yolks to flour mixture; blend well.
8. Beat egg whites until stiff but not dry and fold thoroughly into batter.
9. Pour into pan and bake in moderate oven (350°F.) 55 minutes or until top of cake springs back when lightly pressed with the finger.

Variations of Rich Loaf Cake

Nut Loaf Cake: Follow basic recipe for Rich Loaf Cake, folding 1 cup broken nutmeats into batter before pouring into pan.

Raisin Loaf Cake: Follow basic recipe for Rich Loaf Cake, folding 1 cup raisins into batter just before pouring into pan.

Chocolate Marble Loaf Cake: Follow basic recipe for Rich Loaf Cake. To ⅓ of the batter add 1 square unsweetened chocolate, melted, mixed with 1 tablespoon boiling water and ¼ teaspoon baking soda. Spoon light and dark batters alternately into pan and cut through with a knife to "marble" it.

Jelly Roll

¾ cup sifted cake flour	4 eggs
1 teaspoon baking powder	¾ cup sugar
¼ teaspoon salt	1 teaspoon vanilla extract

Grease 10 x 15 x 1-inch pan and line with paper. Set oven for high heat (400°F.). Sift first three ingredients together onto wax paper. Beat eggs until thick; add sugar, a few tablespoons at a time, beating well after each addition. Stir in vanilla. Sift dry ingredients over egg-sugar mixture and fold in gently but thoroughly. Pour batter into pan, spreading evenly over pan. Bake 12 to 14 minutes. Loosen edges with spatula and turn hot cake at once onto a cloth dusted with confectioners' sugar. Remove wax paper; trim crisp edges. Roll cake in cloth and let cool about 10 minutes on cake rack. Unroll; spread with tart jelly or other filling such as whipped cream, chocolate cream or soft ice cream; roll up again. Wrap rolled cake in cloth and place on rack until thoroughly cooled. Makes 8 servings.

 To make alphabet block cakes for the children, frost a pound cake, cut into squares, and add letters with a pastry tube, using a variety of colored frostings.

 Grease inside of cup before measuring molasses, honey or syrup to prevent sticking and make it easier to wash the cup.

 If a recipe calls for greasing and flouring cake pans, use about ½ tablespoon of fat and 1 tablespoon of flour per pan. Do not grease sides of pan.

Gingerbread

¼ cup shortening
¼ cup sugar
1 egg, well beaten
½ cup molasses
1¼ cups sifted flour
¾ teaspoon baking
    powder

¼ teaspoon salt
½ teaspoon cinnamon
½ teaspoon ginger
¼ teaspoon ground
    cloves
½ cup hot water

Line the bottom of a 9 x 5 x 3 or 8 x 8 x 2-inch pan with wax paper. Cream shortening, add sugar gradually, mixing until light and fluffy. Add egg and molasses; blend well. Sift together dry ingredients. Add sifted dry ingredients alternately with hot water to the molasses mixture. Turn batter into pan and bake in moderate oven (350°F.) 30 to 35 minutes. Makes 8 servings.

Applesauce Cake

½ cup shortening
½ cup sugar
¼ cup brown sugar
1 egg, beaten
1 cup applesauce
2 cups sifted flour
½ teaspoon baking soda

½ teaspoon salt
2 teaspoons baking powder
½ teaspoon cinnamon
¼ teaspoon nutmeg
1 teaspoon ground cloves
½ cup raisins

Cream together shortening and sugars. Add egg and applesauce, stirring until well blended. Sift together remaining ingredients, except raisins; add to applesauce mixture and beat until smooth. Stir in raisins. Pour into a greased and floured 8 x 8 x 2-inch pan and bake in moderate oven (350° F.) 35 minutes.

Easy-does-it Fruit Cake

1 cup shortening
1¼ cups brown sugar
4 eggs
2 cups sifted flour
1 teaspoon salt
1 teaspoon baking soda
1 teaspoon cinnamon
1 teaspoon ground cloves
¼ cup orange juice

1 pound mixed, candied
   fruits (cherries,
   citron, etc.)
1 pound raisins
1 pound pitted dates,
   chopped
1 cup walnuts, chopped
1 cup Brazil nuts,
   chopped

Cream shortening and sugar; add eggs, one at a time, beating until batter is smooth. Sift 1¾ cups flour and other dry ingredients together twice and add to creamed mixture alternately with orange juice. Sift ¼ cup flour over the chopped fruits and nuts, mixing well with floured hands. Add to creamed mixture, mixing until well blended. Pour batter, until three-fourths full, into a large loaf pan or five 1-pound coffee tins which have been greased, lined with wax paper and greased again. Bake in very slow oven (275°F.) for 2½ to 3 hours, keeping a shallow pan filled with water on the bottom of oven during baking. Remove from oven ½ hour before end of baking time. Brush top with Confectioners' Sugar Glaze, page 77, and decorate with fruits and nuts. Return to oven to finish baking and to set decorations. Store in an airtight container in a cool, dry place. Makes about 5 pounds cake.

When using quick cake mixes, add a personal touch:
1. Fold 3 tablespoons grated orange peel into lemon cake mix batter.
2. Fold ½ cup finely chopped walnuts into devil's food or chocolate mint cake mix batter.
3. Fold ½ cup flaked coconut into white or cherry cake mix batter.

Zolita's Cheese Cake

1 cup heavy cream
½ cup fresh lemon juice
1 envelope unflavored
　　gelatin
¼ cup cold water
8 ounces cream cheese *or*
　　1 cup sieved cottage
　　cheese

1 can (14 or 15 ozs.)
　　sweetened condensed
　　milk
½ teaspoon vanilla
　　extract
24 graham crackers
½ cup butter, melted

Pour cream into large mixing bowl; add lemon juice, stirring constantly until well mixed. Let stand 10 minutes. Put gelatin to soak in cold water 5 minutes; then stir over hot water until dissolved. Mash cream cheese and work condensed milk into it until smooth. Beat the cream and lemon mixture until it begins to stiffen. Add cream cheese mixture and dissolved gelatin. Continue beating until smooth and thick. Stir in vanilla. Pour into graham cracker shell made by crushing graham crackers, mixing thoroughly with the melted butter, pressing into a 9-inch pie plate and chilling 1 hour before filling. Chill until firm.

Cheese Cakelets

¾ cup graham cracker
　　crumbs
2 tablespoons soft butter
8 ounces cream cheese

1 egg
¼ cup sugar
½ teaspoon vanilla
　　extract

Set fluted paper baking cups in small muffin pan cups. Mix together graham cracker crumbs and butter. Press 1 teaspoonful in bottom of each paper cup. Combine cream cheese, egg, sugar and vanilla; beat until smooth. Pour over crumbs until cups are three-fourths full. Bake in moderate oven (350°F.) 10 to 12 minutes. Cool and top each with a bit of red raspberry jam, chocolate syrup or ginger marmalade. Makes 16 small cupcakes.

Frostings

Confectioners' Sugar Frosting

6 tablespoons butter or
margarine
3 cups sifted confectioners'
sugar

4 to 6 tablespoons cream
or evaporated milk
1/8 teaspoon salt
1 1/2 teaspoons vanilla extract

1. Cream butter until fluffy.
2. Add confectioners' sugar and 4 tablespoons cream alternately in several portions, blending well after each addition.
3. Add salt and vanilla and beat until creamy.
4. Add more cream if softer frosting is desired.

Makes enough to fill and frost two 8 or 9-inch layers of cake. To frost an 8 x 12-inch or 10 x 10-inch loaf cake, or 18 cupcakes, halve the recipe.

Variations of Confectioners' Sugar Frosting

Cocoa Frosting: Make Confectioners' Sugar Frosting using 2 1/2 cups confectioners' sugar sifted with 1/2 cup cocoa.

Lemon Frosting: Make Confectioners' Sugar Frosting substituting 1 tablespoon lemon juice for 1 tablespoon of the cream and 1 teaspoon grated lemon peel for the vanilla extract.

Banana Frosting: Make Confectioners' Sugar Frosting substituting 1/3 cup mashed banana (1 small banana) for cream and 1/2 teaspoon lemon juice for the vanilla extract.

Molasses Frosting: Make Confectioners' Sugar Frosting substituting 2 tablespoons molasses for 2 tablespoons of the cream and 2 teaspoons lemon juice for the vanilla extract.

 Cool cake and remove any crumbs before spreading with frosting.

Seven-minute Frosting

2 egg whites
1½ cups sugar
¼ teaspoon salt
⅓ cup cold water

1 tablespoon light corn
   syrup
1 teaspoon vanilla
   extract

1. Combine first five ingredients in top of double boiler.
2. Place over rapidly boiling water and beat 7 minutes or until frosting stands in stiff but not dry peaks.
3. Remove from heat; add vanilla and continue beating until frosting is thick enough to spread.

Makes enough to fill and frost two 8 or 9-inch layers of cake. To frost an 8 x 12-inch or 10 x 10-inch loaf cake, or 18 cupcakes, halve the recipe using 3 tablespoons water and decrease cooking time to 5 minutes.

Variations of Seven-minute Frosting

Chocolate Seven-minute Frosting: Follow basic recipe folding in 2 or 3 squares (2 or 3 ozs.) melted unsweetened chocolate just before spreading frosting.

Peppermint Frosting: Follow basic recipe substituting 2 or 3 drops oil of peppermint for vanilla extract.

Coconut Frosting: Frost cake with Seven-minute Frosting, then immediately sprinkle top and sides of cake with 1½ cups moist shredded, flaked or finely grated coconut.

Chocolate Shadow Frosting: Frost cake with Seven-minute Frosting. When frosting has set, melt 2 squares (2 ozs.) unsweetened chocolate and 2 teaspoons butter or margarine over hot water; blend thoroughly. Cool mixture slightly; then pour from tip of spoon over cake, letting chocolate run down over the sides.

Lord Baltimore Frosting: Follow basic recipe. Fill 8-inch cake layers with ⅓ cup each chopped maraschino cherries, chopped raisins and chopped figs mixed with enough frosting to spread easily. Frost top and sides of cake with remaining plain frosting.

Caramel Frosting

1 cup sugar	⅔ cup milk
1 cup brown sugar	1½ teaspoons butter
1 tablespoon light corn syrup	1 teaspoon vanilla extract
¼ teaspoon salt	

Combine first 5 ingredients in saucepan. Bring to boiling point, stirring until sugars dissolve; continue to cook without stirring to 234°F. on candy thermometer or until a little of the mixture forms a soft ball when dropped into cold water. Remove from heat; add butter and vanilla. Cool to lukewarm (110°F.); then beat until thick enough to spread. If frosting becomes too thick to spread easily, thin with 1 or 2 teaspoons milk. Makes enough to fill and frost two 8-inch layers of cake.

Variation of Caramel Frosting

Fudge Frosting: Make Caramel Frosting, adding 2 squares (2 ozs.) unsweetened chocolate before cooking.

Hurry-up Chocolate Frosting

1 package (6 ozs.) semi-sweet chocolate pieces	½ teaspoon vanilla extract
⅓ cup evaporated milk	1 cup sifted confectioners' sugar

Melt chocolate in top of double boiler over hot, not boiling, water. Blend in evaporated milk and vanilla. Add confectioners' sugar and beat until smooth. Spread on cooled cake *immediately*. Makes enough to cover sides and top of two 8-inch layers.

 For quick cake decoration, place paper doily or strips of paper on cooled, baked cake. Dust with confectioners' sugar and remove doily or paper strips.

Peanut Butter Frosting

½ cup peanut butter
2 tablespoons honey
⅛ teaspoon salt
2 to 4 tablespoons light
   cream

2½ cups sifted confec-
   tioners' sugar
½ teaspoon vanilla
   extract

Cream together peanut butter and honey. Add salt and blend thoroughly. Add cream alternately with sugar, a small amount at a time. Add vanilla and mix until smooth. Makes about 1½ cups, enough to frost two 8 or 9-inch layers of cake.

Cream Cheese Frosting

1 package (3 ozs.) cream
   cheese
½ teaspoon vanilla extract
2 tablespoons cream

1 cup sifted confectioners'
   sugar
½ cup nonfat dry milk

Cream together cream cheese, vanilla and cream. Sift sugar and dry milk together. Gradually add to cheese mixture, beating until smooth and creamy. Tint with vegetable coloring if desired. Makes about 1½ cups frosting, or enough for two 9-inch layers of cake, or 2 dozen cupcakes. Very good on gingerbread or spice cupcakes.

Jam Frosting

1 cup jam
2 teaspoons lemon juice

1 cup heavy cream, stiffly
   beaten

Fold jam and lemon juice into stiffly beaten cream. Makes enough to fill and frost two 8 or 9-inch layers of cake.

Confectioners' Sugar Glaze

Gradually add 4 to 5 teaspoons water to 1 cup sifted confectioners' sugar until desired consistency. Use on cookies, fruit cake, apple turnovers, etc., for an attractive sheen.

Boiled Frosting

1½ cups sugar
⅓ cup water
1 tablespoon light corn
  syrup

2 egg whites, stiffly beaten
Dash of salt
1 teaspoon vanilla
  extract

Combine sugar, water and corn syrup in saucepan and stir over low heat until sugar is dissolved. Cover saucepan and boil for 3 minutes. Uncover and continue cooking without stirring to 236°F. or until a small amount of syrup forms a soft ball when dropped into cold water. Remove syrup from heat and pour in fine stream over egg whites, beating constantly. Add salt and vanilla, beating until frosting is of spreading consistency. Makes enough frosting for tops and sides of two 8 or 9-inch layers or an 8 x 8 x 2-inch cake or 2 dozen cupcakes.

Variations of Boiled Frosting

Caramel Frosting: Substitute 1 cup brown sugar for 1 cup of the sugar.

Mocha Frosting: Substitute strong coffee for water and, before spreading, fold in 2 squares (2 ozs.) unsweetened chocolate, melted and cooled.

Pineapple Frosting: Substitute syrup from canned pineapple for water. Omit vanilla and add 1 teaspoon grated lemon peel.

Orange Frosting: Substitute orange juice for water. Omit vanilla extract and add 1 teaspoon grated orange peel.

Strawberry Frosting: Substitute syrup from canned or frozen strawberries for water.

Speedy Baked-on Frosting

⅓ cup brown sugar
1 tablespoon flour
⅓ cup chopped nutmeats

3 tablespoons butter or
   margarine, melted
1 tablespoon water

Combine all ingredients and mix thoroughly. When cake is done, spread this mixture over top of cake in pan. Return to oven and bake 5 minutes longer. Makes enough to frost one 8 x 8-inch cake or one 9-inch layer.

NOTE: When planning to use this frosting, grease and flour cake pan but do *not* line with paper. This makes it easier to cut and serve cake directly from pan.

Cake Fillings

Custard Filling

1¼ cups milk
2 tablespoons cornstarch
¼ cup sugar

2 egg yolks, slightly
   beaten
½ teaspoon vanilla extract

1. Scald 1 cup of the milk in double boiler over boiling water.
2. Combine cornstarch and sugar, and blend to a smooth paste with remaining ¼ cup milk. Add to hot milk and stir until smooth.
3. Gradually add egg yolks, stirring until mixture thickens.
4. Cool and flavor with vanilla.
5. When cold, spread between layers of cake.

Makes about 2 cups, enough to fill two 8 or 9-inch layers of cake.

Variations of Custard Filling

Butterscotch Custard: Substitute 6 tablespoons brown sugar for ¼ cup sugar and add 1 tablespoon butter to cooked filling.
Chocolate Custard: Add 2 squares (2 ozs.) melted, unsweetened chocolate to hot milk and beat well before adding egg yolks. Increase sugar to ½ cup.

Pineapple Custard: Substitute ½ teaspoon lemon juice for vanilla extract and add ½ cup crushed pineapple to cooled filling.
Coconut Custard: Add ½ cup coconut to filling.
Banana Custard: Substitute ½ teaspoon lemon juice for vanilla extract. Add 1 medium-size banana, diced, to cooled filling.

Lemon Filling

¾ cup sugar
¼ cup flour
¼ teaspoon salt
1 egg yolk
¾ cup water

¼ cup lemon juice
1 teaspoon grated lemon
  peel
2 tablespoons butter or
  margarine

1. Combine sugar, flour and salt in top of double boiler.
2. Beat egg yolk slightly; add water and lemon juice. Add to dry ingredients, stirring to blend.
3. Cook over boiling water, stirring constantly, until thick, about 10 minutes.
4. Remove from heat; stir in lemon peel and butter.
5. Cool thoroughly before spreading on cake.
Makes about 2 cups, enough to fill two 8 or 9-inch layers of cake or a 10 x 15-inch jelly roll.

Variations of Lemon Filling

Lime Filling: Follow basic recipe, substituting ¼ cup lime juice and 1 teaspoon grated lime peel for lemon juice and peel.
Orange Filling: Follow basic recipe, decreasing sugar to ½ cup, using 1 cup orange juice for combined lemon juice and water, and using orange peel for lemon peel.
Orange Coconut Filling: Follow recipe for Orange Filling adding ½ cup shredded coconut.
Pineapple Filling: Follow recipe for Orange Filling adding ½ cup crushed pineapple to cooled mixture.

Marshmallow Fig Filling

14 marshmallows
¼ cup chopped figs
1 tablespoon cream

⅓ cup chopped nutmeats
½ teaspoon grated orange
   peel

Cut marshmallows into quarters with scissors dipped in hot water. Place in top of double boiler; add figs and steam over hot water until marshmallows are melted. Remove from heat and stir in cream. Add nutmeats and orange peel, and mix well. Makes about 1¼ cups filling, enough for two 8 or 9-inch layers.

 Prepared pudding mixes make good cake fillings. Follow directions on package.

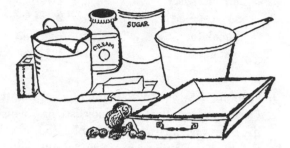

Candies and Confections

Many modern homemakers overlook the opportunity to create family fun and save money, too, by making candy at home.

Children just naturally like candy, occasionally crave it, as adults do. And there is no reason why a child who eats three well-balanced meals a day should not be allowed a reasonable amount of sweets—after meals, not between meals. When these sweets are made at home, mother can put her knowledge of nutrition to good use, choosing simple candies such as butterscotch and molasses taffy, cereal confections, and recipes which use dried fruits such as figs, dates, raisins and prunes.

Children enjoy making candy almost as much as eating it. They love to stir and beat, to pull and pat, to mold popcorn balls and lick sticky fingers. The resulting concoctions may not take any prizes for appearance but they will taste just as good as blue ribbon winners. Furthermore, when candy making is a family affair, children and parents have shared a happy experience.

81

Basic Chocolate Fudge

¾ cup milk
2 squares (2 ozs.)
  unsweetened
  chocolate
2 cups sugar

¼ teaspoon salt
1 tablespoon corn syrup
2 tablespoons butter or
  margarine
1 teaspoon vanilla extract

1. Combine first five ingredients in a saucepan.
2. Place over low heat and cook, stirring constantly, until sugar dissolves and mixture is well blended.
3. Bring to the boiling point and boil gently, without stirring, until candy thermometer registers 236°F. or until a little of the mixture dropped into cold water forms a soft ball. Remove from heat.
4. Add butter. Cool to 110°F. or for about 10 minutes.
5. Add vanilla; then beat with a spoon until mixture thickens and loses its gloss.
6. Pour at once into a greased pan or platter, about 4 x 8 inches. (Do *not* scrape hardened fudge from sides of saucepan.)
7. Cool until firm; then cut into squares.

Makes 18 pieces, 1⅓-inches square.

Variations of Basic Chocolate Fudge

Marshmallow Fudge: Cut 9 marshmallows in half with scissors; place 18 halves cut side up on greased pan or platter, about 4 x 8 inches. Follow basic recipe for Chocolate Fudge, pouring beaten fudge over marshmallows.

Nut Fudge: Follow basic recipe, adding ¾ cup broken nutmeats to fudge just before pouring into greased pan or platter.

Peppermint Fudge: Follow basic recipe, adding 2 or 3 drops oil of peppermint to fudge before beating.

Coconut Fudge: Follow basic recipe, adding ¾ cup chopped coconut to fudge just before pouring into greased pan or platter.

Brown Sugar Fudge (Penuche): Follow basic recipe, omitting chocolate and substituting 2½ cups firmly packed brown sugar for the sugar.

Divinity

2½ cups sugar
½ cup light corn syrup
½ cup cold water

2 egg whites, stiffly beaten
1 teaspoon vanilla extract
1 cup chopped nutmeats

1. Combine sugar, syrup and water in saucepan and stir over low heat until sugar dissolves.
2. Cook until candy thermometer registers 260°F. or until a little of the mixture dropped into cold water forms a very hard ball.
3. Remove from heat and cool slightly.
4. Pour very slowly over egg whites, beating constantly.
5. Continue beating until mixture becomes very stiff and loses its gloss. A final beating with a hand whisk improves texture.
6. Add vanilla and nutmeats and pour into a greased 9 x 9 x 2-inch pan.
7. Cool and cut into squares.

Makes about 1½ pounds.

Variation of Divinity

Tutti Frutti: Follow Divinity recipe, substituting ¾ cup chopped candied fruits, such as cherries, pineapple and orange, for ¾ cup of nutmeats, just before pouring into pan in Step 6.

Never scrape the pan when making candies such as fudge and penuche. Sugar crystals from sides of the pan can make the whole batch turn grainy.

Vanilla Caramels

1 cup sugar	1 cup light cream
⅓ cup butter or margarine	1 teaspoon vanilla extract
¾ cup light corn syrup	⅛ teaspoon salt

1. Combine first four ingredients in a saucepan.
2. Bring to a boil and cook slowly, stirring, to 255°F. on candy thermometer or until a little of the mixture forms a hard ball when dropped into cold water.
3. Remove from heat; stir in vanilla and salt.
4. Pour at once into a greased 9 x 5 x 3-inch pan; cool until firm.
5. Turn out of pan onto wax paper and cut into ¾-inch squares with a sharp knife.
6. Wrap each caramel in wax paper; store in tightly closed container.

Makes about 3 dozen caramels.

Variations of Vanilla Caramels

Nut Caramels: Make Vanilla Caramels, stirring in ½ cup broken nutmeats along with vanilla and salt in Step 3.

Chocolate Caramels: Make Vanilla Caramels, adding 1 square (1 oz.) unsweetened chocolate before cooking in Step 1.

Butterscotch

½ cup sugar	2 tablespoons butter or margarine
½ cup brown sugar	
¼ cup light corn syrup	1 teaspoon vanilla extract
½ cup water	⅛ teaspoon salt

Combine first four ingredients in a saucepan. Bring to a boil, stirring until sugars dissolve. Cook without stirring to 265°F. on candy thermometer or until a little of the mixture forms a very hard ball when dropped into cold water. Add butter and cook to

285°F. or until a little of the mixture becomes brittle in cold water. Remove from heat; stir in vanilla and salt. Drop by teaspoonfuls onto greased baking sheet. Or pour into greased shallow pan and break into pieces when cool. Store in tightly closed container. Makes 2 to 3 dozen pieces.

Peanut Brittle

1½ cups sugar   ¾ cup salted peanuts

Stir sugar in heavy skillet over medium heat until sugar dissolves and becomes a golden brown syrup. Continue to cook, stirring, until all lumps dissolve. Remove from heat. Add peanuts and pour at once into a well-greased pan. When cool, turn from pan and break into pieces. Makes about ½ pound.

Cereal Nut Brittle

½ cup butter or margarine   4 cups cereal flakes
¾ cup brown sugar   ½ cup chopped nutmeats

Melt butter, add sugar and cook until smooth and thick, stirring constantly. Blend in cereal and nuts. Cook a few seconds longer, stirring constantly. Spread mixture in a thin layer on a cookie sheet. When cool, break into about twenty 2-inch pieces.

 You can make colored sugar by adding a drop or two of food coloring to ¼ cup sugar, blending well with a fork and drying on wax paper overnight.

Basic Fondant

2 cups sugar
1⅓ cups water

2 tablespoons light corn
syrup

1. Combine ingredients in a 2-quart saucepan.
2. Place over low heat and cook, stirring, until sugar dissolves.
3. Bring to boiling point and boil gently, without stirring, until candy thermometer registers 238°F. or until a little of the mixture dropped into cold water forms a soft ball. (To remove crystals which form during cooking, occasionally wipe side of pan with a damp cloth wrapped around the tines of a fork.)
4. Pour at once onto a cold, wet platter or porcelain table top rinsed with cold water. (Do not scrape sides of pan.)
5. Let cool to lukewarm.
6. Work fondant with spatula or wooden spoon until it whitens and becomes creamy; then knead until free from lumps.
7. Place in a bowl and cover tightly, or wrap in wax paper. Store in refrigerator for at least 24 hours before making into candies as suggested below. (Fondant may be stored in refrigerator as long as 4 weeks, if desired.)

Makes about 1 pound, enough for 2 dozen ¾-inch candies.

Variations of Basic Fondant

Bonbons: To make bonbons, divide fondant into several portions; knead each portion, flavor to taste with flavoring, extracts or oils, and tint with desired food coloring. Form into balls about ¾-inch in diameter. Press walnut or pecan half, whole almond or candied cherry into top of each; or roll at once in coconut or ground nutmeats; or let stand for 24 hours before coating with chocolate.

Almond Bonbons: Flavor fondant with 1 teaspoon almond extract, tint with green food coloring. Shape into ¾-inch balls; press whole almond into top of each. Makes 24.

Lemon Bonbons: Flavor fondant with 1 teaspoon lemon extract, tint with yellow food coloring. Shape into ¾-inch balls; flatten and decorate as desired. Makes 24.

Orange Bonbons: Flavor fondant with 1 teaspoon orange extract, tint with orange food coloring. Shape into ¾-inch balls; flatten and decorate as desired. Makes 24.

Fondant-stuffed Fruits: Knead fondant; flavor and tint if desired. Use to stuff dried figs, pitted dates or prunes.

Fondant Kisses: Melt fondant in top of double boiler over hot, not boiling, water. Flavor and tint as desired or leave plain. Fold in flaked coconut or chopped nutmeats (using ¾ cup nuts to 1 recipe fondant). Drop by teaspoonfuls onto wax paper. Cool until firm before removing from paper.

Fondant-dipped Fruits and Nuts: Melt fondant in top of double boiler over hot, not boiling, water. Flavor and tint as desired. Dip candied fruits or nuts into melted fondant, one at a time. Lift out with a fork, place on wax paper and let cool until firm. Use whole almonds or Brazil nuts, walnut or pecan halves, candied cherries or candied pineapple wedges.

Chocolate-dipped Confections

For best results, dip chocolates on a cool, dry day. Use at least one pound of chocolate at a time; buy the type expressly made for coating candies. Have centers prepared in advance; whole almonds, cashews or Brazil nuts, pecan or walnut halves, caramels, candied fruits, pitted dates or prunes, fondant bonbons which have been molded the day before.

1. Break dipping chocolate into pieces and place in top of double boiler over enough hot, not boiling, water to touch the bottom of the upper vessel.
2. Stir constantly until chocolate melts.
3. Empty hot water and replace with lukewarm water (about 90°F.).
4. Working quickly, dip one center at a time into chocolate, roll

tint with yellow food coloring. Shape into ¾-inch balls; flatten and decorate as desired. Makes 24.

Orange Bonbons: Flavor fondant with 1 teaspoon orange extract, tint with orange food coloring. Shape into ¾-inch balls; flatten and decorate as desired. Makes 24.

Fondant-stuffed Fruits: Knead fondant; flavor and tint if desired. Use to stuff dried figs, pitted dates or prunes.

Fondant Kisses: Melt fondant in top of double boiler over hot, not boiling, water. Flavor and tint as desired or leave plain. Fold in flaked coconut or chopped nutmeats (using ¾ cup nuts to 1 recipe fondant). Drop by teaspoonfuls onto wax paper. Cool until firm before removing from paper.

Fondant-dipped Fruits and Nuts: Melt fondant in top of double boiler over hot, not boiling, water. Flavor and tint as desired. Dip candied fruits or nuts into melted fondant, one at a time. Lift out with a fork, place on wax paper and let cool until firm. Use whole almonds or Brazil nuts, walnut or pecan halves, candied cherries or candied pineapple wedges.

Chocolate-dipped Confections

For best results, dip chocolates on a cool, dry day. Use at least one pound of chocolate at a time; buy the type expressly made for coating candies. Have centers prepared in advance; whole almonds, cashews or Brazil nuts, pecan or walnut halves, caramels, candied fruits, pitted dates or prunes, fondant bonbons which have been molded the day before.

1. Break dipping chocolate into pieces and place in top of double boiler over enough hot, not boiling, water to touch the bottom of the upper vessel.
2. Stir constantly until chocolate melts.
3. Empty hot water and replace with lukewarm water (about 90°F.).
4. Working quickly, dip one center at a time into chocolate, roll

Lollipops

1 cup sugar
⅔ cup water
⅓ cup light corn syrup
2 to 3 drops food coloring

2 to 3 drops wintergreen,
peppermint or lemon-oil
extract

Put sugar, water and corn syrup in a saucepan. Cook, stirring only until sugar is melted, until temperature reaches 290°F. or until a few drops of the mixture become brittle when dropped into cold water. Remove from heat, add coloring and flavoring. Stir only enough to mix color and extract or candy will sugar. Grease molds or bottom of level pan with mineral oil; it gives hard candy an excellent glaze. Make lollipops quickly by dropping syrup from a spoon into greased molds or flat pan. Press ends of wooden skewers or picks into lollipops immediately after pouring. As soon as they are firm, loosen lollipops from pan or mold. If allowed to remain on pan too long they may crack while being removed. Makes 10 to 12 small lollipops.

Molasses Taffy

1 cup molasses
1 cup sugar
1 teaspoon vinegar

1 tablespoon butter or
margarine

Combine all ingredients in saucepan and cook slowly over low heat, stirring constantly, until candy thermometer registers 265°F. or until a little of the mixture dropped into cold water forms a hard ball. Pour at once onto a greased platter or cookie sheet. Cool, turning edges toward center with spatula as they begin to harden. When cool enough to handle, grease hands and form mixture into a ball. Pull with fingertips until light yellow in color. Stretch taffy into a long rope; cut into 1-inch pieces with scissors. When cool, wrap each piece in wax paper. Makes about 1¼ pounds.

Taffy Apples

12 small, all-purpose
   apples
1 cup molasses
1 cup sugar
¼ cup water

1 teaspoon vinegar
⅓ teaspoon salt
2 tablespoons butter or
   margarine
2 teaspoons vanilla extract

Wash apples thoroughly and dry well. Remove stems and stick the end of a lollipop stick into the stem end of each apple. Boil molasses, sugar, water, vinegar and salt, without stirring, to 270°F. or until it becomes brittle when a little of the mixture is dropped into cold water. Remove from heat and add butter and vanilla. Dip apples into the syrup, being careful to cover the entire surface with the glaze. When well coated, place apples, stick end down, in slots cut in cover of an empty shoe box.

Popcorn Balls

½ cup corn kernels
½ cup molasses
1 teaspoon vinegar

¼ cup sugar
¼ teaspoon salt
2 tablespoons water

Pop the corn. It should make between 3 and 4 cups. Shake unpopped kernels to the bottom and remove. Pour popcorn into large greased mixing bowl. Keep popcorn warm while cooking the molasses syrup. Mix molasses, vinegar, sugar, salt and water. Cook to 240°F. or until the syrup collects in a mass and can be pushed into a soft ball between the thumb and forefinger when dropped into cold water. Cool slightly. Pour over corn, stirring to coat all kernels. With buttered hands shape into balls. Makes about eight 2-inch balls.

Candied Citrus Peels

6 oranges *or* 4 grapefruits	1½ cups orange juice
3 cups sugar	½ cup lemon juice
1 cup light corn syrup	Sugar

Remove fruit peel, cut into thin strips with scissors and soak overnight in cold water. Pour off water, pour on fresh water and bring to a boil. Pour off water, cover again with fresh water and let come to a boil. Repeat this 3 times, or until there is no bitterness left in the water. Drain thoroughly.

Make a syrup of the sugar, corn syrup and fruit juices. When syrup comes to a boil, drop in a few cooked peels and cook until transparent. Roll in sugar, cool and store in jars. The peels should be candied a few at a time and the syrup kept boiling.

Stuffed Dried Fruits

Cook dried figs, dates, prunes or apricots until plump and tender. Make lengthwise slits in fruit and remove pits from prunes and dates. Stuff with nuts, peanut butter, marshmallow, fondant, candied cherries, grapefruit and orange peel, citron, pineapple, preserved ginger or any candied fruit. Roll in mixture of cocoa or cinnamon and confectioners' sugar.

 Wrap popcorn balls in red cellophane paper for an effective Christmas tree decoration. For variety, add pieces of chocolate or candied fruit to the popcorn.

Fruit and Peanut Butter Balls

1 pound dried prunes	3 tablespoons light cream
6 tablespoons peanut butter	Dash of salt
½ cup chopped nutmeats	Sugar

Pit the prunes and put through food chopper. Add peanut butter, nutmeats, cream and salt, and mix well. Shape into small balls and roll in sugar. Wrap in wax paper. This recipe makes 30 to 35 balls. If desired, apricots may be used instead of prunes or use equal quantities of both and chop together.

Date and Nut Confections

½ pound pitted dates	Dash of salt
½ pound figs	½ teaspoon orange extract
1 cup chopped, mixed nuts	

Put dates and figs through food chopper. To the fruit add nuts, salt and orange extract. Mix well and shape into small balls. Insert a wooden pick in one side or through the center. Roll in flaked coconut or in colored sprinkles. Makes 3 dozen.

Blanched Almonds

Pour boiling water over almonds and keep at a simmering temperature for 3 minutes. Drain. The skins should come off when pressed between thumb and forefinger. Spread the blanched kernels on absorbent paper and dry at room temperature.

Cookies

It's no easy matter to keep a cookie jar well stocked when there are children in the house, for the youngsters have a way of making cookies disappear as if by magic. But homemade cookies are such a hit at mealtime, for between-meal snacks and in the lunch box that even the busiest mother makes a valiant effort.

Drop cookies and cookies which are cut into bars after baking are gaining in popularity. A batch may be stirred up in the morning to bake while the breakfast dishes are being washed. Refrigerator cookies also are easy to fit into a crowded schedule. And among the great baking time savers are the cookie mixes and refrigerated ready-to-bake cookie doughs now available in a variety of flavors.

Cookies which must be rolled out and cut with a cookie cutter, including gingerbread men so dear to children's hearts, are usually too time consuming except for special occasions. A rainy day when the children must stay indoors can be just such an occasion. For what could be more fun for a small boy or girl than helping mother roll and pat out cookie dough to be cut into fancy shapes with shiny cutters?

93

Rolled Cookies

Basic Sugar Cookie

2 cups sifted flour	1 egg
1½ teaspoons baking powder	1 teaspoon vanilla extract
½ teaspoon salt	1 tablespoon milk
½ cup butter or margarine	1 tablespoon sugar
¾ cup sugar	¼ teaspoon cinnamon

1. Sift together flour, baking powder and salt.
2. Cream together butter and sugar: add egg and beat until smooth and fluffy. Stir in vanilla and milk.
3. Add flour mixture and blend thoroughly.
4. Chill cookie dough until easy to handle.
5. Roll half of dough at a time. Roll out to ¼-inch thickness on lightly floured board. Cut with cookie cutter.
6. Place on a lightly greased cookie sheet and sprinkle with granulated sugar and cinnamon.
7. Bake in hot oven (400°F.) 6 to 10 minutes.
8. Remove cookies to wire racks to cool. Makes about 2½ dozen cookies (cut with 2½-inch cutter).

Variations of Basic Sugar Cookie

Butterscotch Sugar Cookies: Substitute ⅔ cup firmly packed brown sugar for the sugar.

Chocolate Sugar Cookies: Add 2 squares (2 ozs.) unsweetened chocolate, melted, just before adding flour mixture and milk.

Coconut Sugar Cookies: Add ½ cup moist finely grated, toasted or tinted coconut just before adding flour mixture and milk.

Filled Sugar Cookies: Place 1 teaspoon of filling in center of half of the cookies. Cover with remaining cookies and press edges together before baking. For filling use jam, jelly, marmalade, mincemeat or other fruit fillings. Bake 10 to 12 minutes.

Nut Sugar Cookies: Add ½ cup chopped nutmeats to flour mixture using pecans, almonds, walnuts or peanuts.

Fruit Sugar Cookies: Add ½ cup chopped fruit to flour mixture, using raisins, currants, dates, prunes or apricots.

Lemon Sugar Cookies: Substitute ¾ teaspoon lemon juice and 2 teaspoons grated lemon peel for vanilla extract.

Orange Sugar Cookies: Substitute 1½ teaspoons orange juice and 1 tablespoon grated orange peel for vanilla extract.

Molasses Cookies

¼ cup shortening
1 cup brown sugar,
   firmly packed
½ cup molasses
¼ cup sour milk or
   buttermilk
1¾ cups sifted flour

1 teaspoon baking
   powder
¼ teaspoon baking soda
½ teaspoon salt
1 teaspoon ginger
1 teaspoon cinnamon

Cream together shortening and sugar until light and fluffy. Add molasses and sour milk, and blend well. Sift flour, baking powder, baking soda, salt and spices onto the creamed mixture and mix thoroughly. Chill several hours or overnight. Roll half of dough at a time to ⅛-inch thickness. Cut with a variety of cookie cutters. Decorate with colored sugar, dried fruits or nuts before baking, or decorate with frosting after baking and cooling. Bake in moderate oven (350°F.) about 15 minutes. Makes 2 dozen 3-inch cookies.

 If the last cookies stick to the cookie sheet, return to oven for a minute. This softens bottom of cookies, making them easier to remove.

Hermits

3½ cups sifted flour
¼ teaspoon baking soda
3 teaspoons baking
   powder
½ teaspoon salt
1 teaspoon cinnamon
½ teaspoon nutmeg
½ teaspoon ground cloves

½ cup shortening
1½ cups brown sugar,
   firmly packed
2 eggs, well beaten
2 tablespoons milk
1 cup raisins, cut in
   pieces
1 cup chopped walnuts

Sift together flour, soda, baking powder, salt and spices. Cream shortening, add sugar slowly, and beat until fluffy. Stir in eggs. Add sifted dry ingredients alternately with milk. Stir in raisins and ¾ cup walnut meats. Roll ⅛-inch thick on lightly floured board. Cut into desired shapes. Bake on greased cookie sheet in hot oven (400°F.) about 12 minutes. Cool and top with Confectioners' Sugar Frosting, page 73. Sprinkle with remaining nutmeats. Makes about 9 dozen 2-inch cookies.

Four-way Refrigerator Cookies

½ cup shortening
1 cup sugar
1 egg
1 tablespoon milk
½ teaspoon almond extract
2 cups sifted flour
1 teaspoon baking powder

1 teaspoon salt
1 square (1 oz.) unsweet-
   ened chocolate, melted
1 tablespoon orange juice
1 tablespoon grated orange
   peel

Cream together shortening and sugar until light and fluffy. Add egg, milk and almond extract. Beat well. Sift together flour, baking powder and salt. Add to creamed mixture and blend thoroughly. Divide dough into thirds. To one-third add chocolate, mixing well. To another third add orange juice and peel, blending thoroughly. Leave remaining dough plain. Divide chocolate and plain dough in half. Shape one half of each and the orange-flavored dough into three rolls. Wrap 'in wax paper and chill until firm. Roll out remaining chocolate and plain dough separately to ⅛-inch thickness. Place chocolate layer on top of plain layer and roll up together. Wrap in wax paper and chill until firm. Cut the four rolls in ¼-inch slices and place on greased cookie sheet. Press a blanched almond into chocolate cookies, a bit of candied pineapple into the orange-flavored cookies, a bit of candied cherry in the plain cookies. Bake in hot oven (400°F.) 10 minutes. Makes about 4 dozen small cookies.

Peanut Cookies

3 tablespoons peanut
   butter
⅓ cup shortening
½ cup dark corn syrup
½ cup sugar
1 egg
2 cups sifted flour

½ teaspoon cream of tartar
½ teaspoon baking soda
⅛ teaspoon salt
½ teaspoon cinnamon
½ cup salted peanuts,
   chopped

Cream together peanut butter, shortening, dark corn syrup and sugar. Add egg and mix well. Sift together flour, cream of tartar, baking soda, salt and cinnamon; gradually add to creamed mixture. Add peanuts. Shape into rolls about 2 inches in diameter. Wrap in wax paper. Chill thoroughly. Slice ⅛-inch thick; place on greased cookie sheet. Bake in hot oven (400°F.) 8 to 10 minutes. Makes 6 dozen cookies.

 For best results when baking cookies, use cookie sheet or a pan with very low sides. Bake in the center or slightly above center of oven.

Scotch Shortbread

2 cups sifted flour
¼ teaspoon baking powder
¼ teaspoon salt

1 cup butter or margarine
½ cup sifted confectioners'
   sugar

Sift together flour, baking powder and salt. Cream together butter and sugar. Gradually add flour mixture, mixing until ingredients are completely blended. Chill mixture until firm enough for handling. Roll out on floured board to ¼-inch thickness. Cut into desired shapes and bake on ungreased cookie sheet in moderate oven (350°F.) 20 to 25 minutes or until delicate brown. Makes about 25 cookies, 2 inches in diameter.

Drop Cookies

Oatmeal Raisin Cookies

¾ cup raisins
1½ cups rolled oats
¾ cup brown sugar,
   firmly packed
½ cup melted shortening,
   cooled
1 egg, slightly beaten

¾ cup sifted flour
1½ teaspoons baking
   powder
¾ teaspoon salt
¼ teaspoon maple
   flavoring

Rinse raisins and drain. Combine oats and sugar. Stir in shortening and egg. Sift together flour, baking powder, and salt. Add to first mixture. Stir in maple flavoring and raisins. Drop by teaspoonfuls onto greased cookie sheet. Bake in hot oven (400°F.) 8 to 10 minutes. Remove to wire rack to cool. Makes 3 dozen cookies.

Whole Wheat Raisin Cookies

1 cup whole wheat or
   graham flour
1 cup flour
1 tablespoon baking
   powder
¼ teaspoon salt
¼ teaspoon baking soda

1 cup chopped raisins
⅓ cup shortening
½ cup brown sugar,
   firmly packed
1 egg
⅓ cup sour milk
1 teaspoon vanilla extract

Sift together flours, baking powder, salt and soda. Stir in raisins. Cream shortening. Add sugar and egg and blend thoroughly. Add dry ingredients alternately with the sour milk, then add vanilla and beat well. Drop by level tablespoonfuls onto greased cookie sheets. Bake in hot oven (400°F.) about 10 minutes. Makes 3 to 3½ dozen cookies.

NOTE: If sweet milk is used, increase baking powder to 4 teaspoons.

Wheat Germ Crunchies

½ cup flour
½ teaspoon baking soda
2 teaspoons baking
   powder
¼ teaspoon salt
½ cup shortening
1 cup brown sugar,
   firmly packed

1 egg
½ teaspoon vanilla
   extract
1 cup wheat germ
½ cup coconut
½ cup rolled oats
1½ cups corn or wheat
   flakes

Mix and sift together flour, soda, baking powder and salt. Cream shortening and sugar. Add egg and vanilla, and beat together. Then add dry ingredients and wheat germ, mixing well. Stir in coconut, rolled oats and corn or wheat flakes. Drop by teaspoonfuls onto greased cookie sheet (or roll into walnut-size balls with the fingers) and bake 12 to 15 minutes in moderate oven (350°F.). Makes about 3½ dozen cookies.

Old-fashioned Molasses Cookies

5 cups flour
2 teaspoons baking soda
2 teaspoons salt
2 teaspoons cinnamon
1 teaspoon ground cloves
1 teaspoon ginger

1 cup butter or margarine
1 cup sugar
2 eggs
1 cup molasses
1 cup boiling water or
   coffee

Sift together flour, soda, salt and spices. Cream together butter and sugar. Add eggs and molasses and beat well. Add flour mixture alternately with boiling water or coffee. Place in refrigerator for an hour. Drop by teaspoonfuls onto greased cookie sheet and place a nut or raisin in the center of each cookie. Sprinkle with granulated sugar. Bake in moderate oven (350°F.) 10 to 12 minutes. Makes 6 dozen cookies.

Toll House Cookies

½ cup butter or
   margarine
6 tablespoons sugar
6 tablespoons brown
   sugar
1 egg, well beaten
1⅛ cups sifted flour

½ teaspoon baking soda
½ teaspoon salt
Few drops of hot water
½ cup chopped nutmeats
1 package (6 ozs.) semi-
   sweet chocolate pieces
½ teaspoon vanilla extract

Cream butter; gradually add sugars and beat until light and fluffy. Add egg and beat well. Sift together flour, soda and salt. Gradually stir into creamed mixture. Add a few drops of water and mix until well blended. Stir in nutmeats, chocolate pieces and vanilla. Drop by half teaspoons onto greased cookie sheet. Bake in moderate oven (375°F.) 10 to 12 minutes. Makes 4 dozen cookies.

Honey Nuggets

⅓ cup shortening
½ cup honey
1 egg
½ teaspoon vanilla extract
1¼ cups sifted flour

½ teaspoon baking soda
½ teaspoon salt
1 package (6 ozs.) semi-
   sweet chocolate pieces
½ cup chopped nuts

Cream together shortening and honey. Add egg and vanilla. Beat until light and fluffy. Sift together flour, soda and salt. Add to first mixture along with chocolate pieces and nuts. Drop by teaspoonfuls onto greased cookie sheet. Bake in moderate oven (375°F.) 10 to 12 minutes. Makes 4 dozen cookies.

Date Nut Puffs

3 egg whites
½ teaspoon salt
1 teaspoon vanilla extract

1 pound brown sugar (2¼
   cups, packed)
1 cup chopped, pitted dates
1 cup broken nutmeats

Beat egg whites until frothy. Add salt and vanilla, and beat until egg whites hold peaks. Add sugar, a few tablespoons at a time, and continue beating until mixture forms glossy, pointed peaks. Fold in dates and nutmeats. Drop by teaspoonfuls onto unglazed brown paper on cookie sheet. Bake 20 to 25 minutes in slow oven (300°F.). Cool slightly before removing from paper. Makes about 4 dozen puffs.

Sugar sprinkled over tops of cookies before baking makes a sweeter crust and a richer cookie.

Corn Flake Macaroons

¼ cup shortening   1 cup finely chopped nuts
¾ cup sugar   ¼ teaspoon almond extract
1 egg   5 cups corn flakes

Cream shortening and sugar; add egg and beat well. Add nuts, almond extract and corn flakes, and mix thoroughly. Drop by tablespoonfuls onto lightly greased cookie sheet. Bake in moderate oven (350°F.) 12 to 15 minutes. Let cookies cool slightly before removing from pan. Makes 2½ dozen cookies, 2½ inches in diameter.

NOTE: Macaroon mixture is somewhat dry in appearance before baking. Do not add additional liquid.

Meringues (Kisses)

2 egg whites   1 teaspoon vanilla extract
8 tablespoons sugar

Beat egg whites until very stiff and dry. Beat in 6 tablespoons of the sugar, a spoonful at a time, until mixture holds its shape when beater is lifted out. Beat in vanilla, then carefully fold in remaining 2 tablespoons of sugar. Use a pastry tube or spoon to make desired shapes on a cookie sheet covered with unglazed paper. Bake in very slow oven (250°F.) 50 minutes. Remove from paper at once and cool. Makes 18 small meringues.

Variations of Basic Meringues

Nut Meringues: Fold ½ cup finely chopped nuts into mixture just before baking.

Meringue Shells: Shape with spoons into 6 three-inch circles, using spoon to hollow center. Bake and fill with ice cream.

Bar Cookies

Chocolate Brownies

2 squares (2 ozs.)	½ teaspoon salt
unsweetened chocolate	2 eggs
⅓ cup shortening	1 cup sugar
⅔ cup sifted flour	1 teaspoon vanilla extract
½ teaspoon baking powder	¾ cup broken nutmeats

Melt chocolate and shortening in top of double boiler over hot water. Sift together flour, baking powder and salt onto a piece of wax paper. Beat eggs; add sugar gradually, beating well; then stir in chocolate mixture. Add dry ingredients, mixing well; then stir in vanilla and nutmeats. Pour into a greased 8 x 8-inch pan and bake in moderate oven (350°F.) 35 minutes. Cut into 2-inch squares while warm. Makes 16 brownies.

Butterscotch Brownies

¾ cup sifted flour	¼ cup butter or margarine
1 teaspoon baking powder	1 cup packed brown sugar
½ teaspoon salt	1 egg
¼ cup chopped nutmeats	½ teaspoon vanilla extract

Sift together flour, baking powder and salt. Stir in nutmeats. Melt butter in top of double boiler, gradually add sugar and cook for 2 minutes. Remove from heat, and beat in egg and vanilla. Stir in flour-nut mixture. Turn into a greased 8 x 8-inch pan and bake in slow oven (300°F.) 30 minutes. Cut into 2-inch squares before removing from pan. Makes 16 brownies.

Date Squares

1 cup pitted, finely cut   ½ teaspoon cinnamon
   dates   (optional)
1 cup brown sugar   ¼ teaspoon salt
½ cup evaporated milk   ¼ teaspoon baking soda
1 cup sifted flour   ½ cup melted shortening
1¼ cups rolled oats

Combine dates, ½ cup of the brown sugar and evaporated milk.
Cook until thick, stirring constantly. Remove from heat and cool.
Mix together flour, oats, remaining ½ cup brown sugar, cinnamon, salt, soda and shortening. Press half of flour-oat mixture
onto the bottom of a greased, 8-inch square pan. Spread with
date mixture and cover with rest of flour-oat mixture. Press down
with spoon or fingers. Bake in moderate oven (350°F.) 25 minutes or until light brown. When cool, cut into 16 squares.

Raisin Bars

1 cup sifted flour   ½ cup molasses
¼ teaspoon baking soda   2 eggs, beaten
½ teaspoon salt   ¼ teaspoon vanilla
½ teaspoon ginger   extract
¼ cup butter or margarine   1 cup raisins
¼ cup packed brown sugar   ¼ cup chopped nuts

Sift together flour, soda, salt and ginger. Cream together butter
and sugar until light and fluffy; add molasses and blend well.
Add eggs and vanilla. Mix well. Gradually add flour mixture to
creamed mixture, blending well. Fold in raisins and nuts. Spread
batter in a greased 8 x 12 x 1-inch pan, and bake in moderate
oven (350°F.) 30 minutes. Cut into 1 x 3-inch bars. Makes 32.

Desserts and Fruit

Desserts should be considered an important part of a meal, not something thrown in for good measure. Hearty meals call for a light dessert—fruit, gelatins and so forth. Meals low in protein are better balanced by a richer dessert containing eggs.

It's no problem to find a dessert that suits the whole family, right down to the little fellow who can hardly handle a spoon. Fruit desserts—from sugared strawberries to apricot whip, from banana pudding to baked apple—are all good choices. So are most puddings—custard, tapioca, rice and gelatin. Served plain, they are fine for toddlers; a sauce makes them tempting to daddy's more sophisticated palate.

For days when five o'clock comes too soon and there's no dessert ready for dinner, it's good to have several speedy dessert mixes on hand. Tapioca and many other puddings can be made in a few minutes using packaged mixes. Canned plum puddings, canned nut rolls and canned fruit can all be counted on to make a happy ending to the meal; so, too, can an assortment of cheese and crackers.

Baked Custard

1 quart milk *or* 2 cups	½ teaspoon salt
evaporated milk and	¼ cup sugar
2 cups water	1 teaspoon vanilla extract
4 eggs	Cinnamon or nutmeg

1. Scald the milk in top of double boiler over boiling water.
2. Lightly grease a 1½-quart baking dish with butter.
3. Set oven for slow heat (325°F.).
4. Break eggs into a bowl; beat until foamy.
5. Add salt, sugar and vanilla; slowly stir in hot milk.
6. Strain mixture into baking dish; sprinkle with cinnamon or nutmeg.
7. Place baking dish in a baking pan; pour warm water into pan to within 1 inch of top of baking dish.
8. Bake 1 to 1¼ hours or until a knife inserted in center comes out clean.
9. Remove baking dish from oven and pan; place on cooling rack.

Makes 8 servings.

Variations of Baked Custard

Baked Cup Custards: Follow basic recipe for Baked Custard, straining custard mixture into 8 custard cups. Bake as directed, with cups set in a pan of hot water, for 45 minutes.

Chocolate Custard: Melt 2 squares (2 ozs.) unsweetened chocolate and stir into scalded milk in basic recipe for Baked Custard.

Caramel Cup Custards: Heat 6 tablespoons sugar in heavy skillet, stirring constantly, until sugar becomes a brown syrup. Pour at once into 8 custard cups. Then follow basic recipe, straining custard mixture over caramel syrup. Bake as directed for Cup Custards. If desired, unmold chilled custards into serving dishes, letting caramel run down over custards.

Fruited Custard: Make ½ recipe Baked Custard, straining custard mixture over 2 cups finely chopped dried fruits—dates, raisins, figs, soaked prunes or apricots—in buttered 1½-quart cas-serole. Bake as directed for Baked Custard.

Custard Rice Pudding: Combine 1½ cups drained, cooked rice (½ cup raw rice makes 1½ cups cooked) and ½ cup raisins in buttered 1½-quart baking dish. Make ½ recipe Baked Custard, straining custard mixture over rice and raisins. Bake as directed for Baked Custard, stirring once after baking ½ hour.

Soft Custard

2 cups milk	⅛ teaspoon salt
2 eggs *or* 4 egg yolks	1 teaspoon vanilla
¼ cup sugar	extract

Scald milk in top of double boiler over boiling water. Beat eggs slightly; add sugar and salt. Stir in hot milk gradually. Pour mix-ture back into top of double boiler and cook over hot, not boil-ing, water, stirring constantly, until mixture thickens and coats the spoon. Place top of double boiler over cold water and con-tinue stirring until custard is slightly cooled. (If custard curdles, remove at once from heat. Place over cold water and beat until smooth.) Add vanilla. Pour custard into serving dish or dishes. Makes 6 servings.

For a crispy meringue topping on cup custards, drop a marshmallow into each cup before pouring in the custard mixture.

Orange Floating Island

1 cup milk
1 cup orange juice
½ cup sugar
3 tablespoons cornstarch
¼ teaspoon salt

2 eggs, separated
1 tablespoon grated
orange peel
1½ cups orange sections

Scald milk and ¾ cup of the orange juice in top of double boiler over boiling water. Mix together sugar, cornstarch and salt; stir in remaining ¼ cup orange juice, blending well, then stir into hot liquid in double boiler. Cook over boiling water, stirring, until thick and smooth. Cover and cook 15 minutes longer, stirring occasionally. Beat egg yolks. Blend a little of the hot mixture into egg yolks; stir gradually into remaining hot mixture. Cook 3 minutes longer, stirring. Remove from heat; stir in orange peel. Cool. Serve chilled pudding over orange sections and top with islands of meringue made with the egg whites, using Two-egg-white Meringue recipe, page 209. Makes 6 servings.

Basic Dessert Soufflé

¼ cup butter
¼ cup flour
1 cup milk

1½ cups sugar
4 eggs, separated
1 teaspoon vanilla extract

1. Make a white sauce of the butter, flour and milk. Add sugar, stir until well blended and remove from heat.
2. Beat egg yolks until light and stir into white sauce mixture along with vanilla.
3. Beat egg whites until stiff and fold into white sauce mixture.
4. Turn into a buttered and lightly sugared 1-quart baking dish with straight sides and bake in moderate oven (350°F.) 45 minutes. Sprinkle with confectioners' sugar and serve at once.
Makes 6 servings.

Variation of Basic Dessert Soufflé

Chocolate Soufflé: Melt and add 3 squares (3 ozs.) unsweetened chocolate to white sauce in recipe for Basic Soufflé. Omit vanilla.

Basic Bread Pudding

3 cups milk *or* 1½ cups
   evaporated milk and
   1½ cups water
2 tablespoons butter or
   margarine
3 slices bread

2 eggs
½ cup sugar
¼ teaspoon salt
¼ teaspoon nutmeg
1 teaspoon vanilla extract
½ cup raisins (if desired)

1. Scald milk and butter in top of double boiler over boiling water.
2. Cut bread into ½-inch cubes; add to milk. Cover and remove from heat.
3. Beat eggs until frothy; add sugar and salt.
4. Stir hot milk and bread into egg mixture; add nutmeg, vanilla and raisins, mixing well.
5. Pour into buttered 1½-quart casserole or baking dish, placed in pan of hot water.
6. Bake in moderate oven (350°F.) about 1 hour or until a knife inserted in the center comes out clean.

Makes 6 servings.

Variations of Basic Bread Pudding

Meringue-topped Bread Pudding: Follow basic recipe for Bread Pudding, substituting 1 whole egg and 2 egg yolks for eggs. Bake as directed 45 minutes. Using 2 leftover egg whites and 4 tablespoons sugar, make meringue, page 209, and spread over top of pudding. Return pudding to oven in pan of hot water and continue baking 12 to 15 minutes or until meringue is golden.

Jam Meringue Bread Pudding: Make Meringue-topped Bread Pudding, spreading pudding with 6 tablespoons tart jam or jelly before topping with meringue.

Basic Tapioca Cream

1 egg, separated
5 tablespoons sugar
2 cups milk *or* 1 cup
   evaporated milk and
   1 cup water

3 tablespoons quick-
   cooking tapioca
⅛ teaspoon salt
½ teaspoon vanilla
   extract

1. Beat egg white until foamy.
2. Add 2 tablespoons sugar, 1 tablespoon at a time, and continue beating until mixture stands in soft peaks.
3. Mix egg yolk with a small amount of the milk in a saucepan; add tapioca, remaining 3 tablespoons sugar, salt and remaining milk.
4. Cook over medium heat until mixture comes to a full boil, stirring constantly. Remove from heat. Mixture will be thin.
5. Pour a small amount of the hot mixture on egg white; blend.
6. Quickly stir in remaining hot mixture; add vanilla.
7. Cool, stirring once after 15 to 20 minutes. Then chill.

Makes 4 to 5 servings.

Variations of Basic Tapioca Cream

Chocolate Tapioca Cream: Follow basic recipe for Tapioca Cream, adding 1 square (1 oz.) unsweetened chocolate, cut in pieces, in Step 3. Thoroughly blend melted chocolate into mixture before pouring over egg white in Step 5.

Orange-apricot Tapioca: Make Tapioca Cream. Cool slightly, then fold in 1 orange, peeled and sectioned, and ½ cup sliced fresh, canned, or soaked dried apricots.

 Use seasonal fresh fruits often for dessert when they are plentiful and low in cost. Fresh fruits are ideal between-meal snacks for children.

Blanc Mange or Cornstarch Pudding

3 cups milk   ¼ teaspoon salt
½ cup sugar   1½ teaspoons vanilla
5 tablespoons cornstarch   extract

1. Scald 2½ cups milk in top of double boiler over boiling water.
2. Mix together sugar, cornstarch and salt, and slowly stir in remaining ½ cup cold milk.
3. Stir cornstarch mixture into scalded milk.
4. Cook over boiling water, stirring, until thick and smooth.
5. Cover and cook 15 minutes longer, stirring occasionally.
6. Remove from heat; stir in vanilla.
7. Pour into bowl or individual serving dishes; chill.

Makes 6 servings.

Variation of Blanc Mange

Chocolate Blanc Mange: Follow basic recipe for Blanc Mange, melting 2 or 3 squares (2 or 3 ozs.) unsweetened chocolate in milk in Step 1 and increasing sugar to ⅔ cup.

Baked Rice Pudding

½ cup uncooked rice   ½ teaspoon salt
1 quart milk *or* 2 cups   ⅓ cup sugar
    evaporated milk and   ½ teaspoon nutmeg
    2 cups water   ½ cup raisins

Combine all ingredients; pour into a greased 1½-quart casserole or baking dish. Bake uncovered in moderate oven (325°F.) 2 to 2½ hours or until rice is tender. Stir several times during first hour of baking. Makes 4 to 6 servings.

 To keep sliced peaches, bananas, pears and apples from darkening, sprinkle at once with a little lemon or orange juice and turn to coat all sides.

Half-hour Indian Pudding

2 cups milk
3 tablespoons yellow
    corn meal
¼ cup sugar
½ cup molasses

½ teaspoon salt
1 teaspoon cinnamon
2 tablespoons butter or
    margarine
2 eggs, slightly beaten

Scald 1½ cups milk. Mix corn meal, sugar, molasses, salt and cinnamon with remaining cold milk and add to scalded milk. Cook over low heat until slightly thickened, stirring constantly. Add butter and eggs. Pour into greased 1-quart casserole and bake in moderate oven (375°F.) 30 minutes. Makes 6 servings.

Lemon Cake-top Pudding

2 tablespoons flour
¾ cup sugar
1 tablespoon butter

2 eggs, separated
¼ cup lemon juice
1 cup milk

Cream together flour, sugar and butter. Add beaten egg yolks, lemon juice and milk. Fold in stiffly beaten egg whites. Pour into an ungreased 8 x 8 x 2-inch dish, set in a pan of water and bake in moderate oven (375°F.) 35 minutes. This pudding separates into a cake and a custard layer. Makes 4 servings.

 Prepare the children's favorite vanilla, chocolate, tapioca or rice pudding and fold in some drained canned fruit cocktail. Top with a sprinkle of toasted coconut.

Steamed Plum Pudding

2 cups sifted flour
¼ cup sugar
1 teaspoon salt
1 teaspoon baking soda
1½ teaspoons cinnamon
½ teaspoon ground cloves
2 eggs, beaten

⅔ cup molasses
¼ cup shortening, melted
2 cups raisins, cut in half
2 cups seeded dates or
   figs, chopped
1 cup citron, chopped
¼ cup milk

Sift together the first six ingredients. Stir eggs and molasses into flour mixture. Add shortening, then fruit and milk. Fill well-greased molds three-fourths full. (1-pound coffee cans, 1-quart heatproof mixing bowls or 12-ounce baking powder cans can be used as molds.) Cover pudding molds that do not have tight-fitting lids with 2 layers of wax paper and heavy brown paper tied over the top. Steam 1-pound coffee cans or 1-quart heatproof bowls 3 hours; steam 12-ounce baking powder cans for 1½ hours; steam individual molds 1 hour. Makes 12 to 14 servings.

Chocolate Mousse

½ package (6 ozs.) semi-
   sweet chocolate pieces

1 tablespoon water
3 eggs, separated

Combine chocolate pieces and water in top of double boiler, over hot, not boiling, water. Stir until smooth; remove from heat and add egg yolks, one at a time, beating well after each addition. Beat the egg whites until stiff, and fold gently into chocolate mixture. Spoon into sherbet glasses and chill. Garnish with whipped cream and chocolate pieces, if desired. Makes 4 to 6 servings.

Applesauce

6 to 8 apples
⅓ cup water
⅓ to ½ cup white or
   brown sugar

¼ teaspoon nutmeg or cin-
   namon *or* 1 teaspoon
   grated lemon or
   orange peel

Wash and pare apples, cut in eighths and remove core. Place in saucepan with the water, cover and cook slowly 15 to 20 minutes or until apples are soft. Mash with potato masher or force through coarse strainer. Stir in sugar and nutmeg while hot. Serve warm or cold with or without cream. Makes 6 servings.

Baked Apples

6 baking apples
6 tablespoons brown sugar

¾ cup water

Wash apples, core and pare ⅓ way down from stem end. Place in casserole or deep baking dish. Put 1 tablespoon of the sugar into core hole of each apple, pour water around apples and bake in moderate oven (350°F.) 45 minutes or until tender. (If baked uncovered, baste occasionally.) Serve warm or cold with cream.

Baked Pears

Pare 6 ripe pears, halve lengthwise and remove cores. Sprinkle with ⅓ cup sugar, dot with butter or margarine and pour on ½ cup water plus 2 tablespoons lemon juice. Cover and bake in moderate oven (350°F.) 50 minutes or until tender.

 When baking apples for children, fill the centers with surprises such as chopped, dried prunes or figs, raisins or chopped nutmeats, orange marmalade, marshmallows or cranberry sauce.

Stewed Rhubarb

2 pounds rhubarb   ½ cup water
1 cup sugar

Discard leaves and root ends of rhubarb. Scrub stalks and remove discolored portions, but do not peel. Cut into 1 to 1½-inch pieces. Combine sugar and water in saucepan, bring to boiling. Reduce heat, add rhubarb. Cover and simmer 10 minutes or until tender but not mushy. Serve warm or cold. Makes 6 servings.

Broiled Grapefruit

3 grapefruit   Brown sugar, honey,
   Melted butter or   molasses or maple
     margarine   syrup

Halve grapefruit, remove seeds and cut around each section to free it from surrounding skin and membrane. Brush each half with butter and sweeten as desired. Place on broiler rack and broil 10 minutes or until nicely browned. Serve warm.

Coconut Banana Rolls

6 ripe bananas   Freshly grated coconut
   Juice of 1 lemon

Peel bananas and cut in half lengthwise. Brush with lemon juice, then sprinkle with coconut. Place in shallow buttered baking pan and bake in hot oven (400°F.) 15 minutes or until bananas are tender. Serve with Lemon Nutmeg Sauce, page 239.

 To flute banana slices, peel banana and scrape lengthwise with tines of a fork before slicing. Slice small bananas on a slant to get larger slices.

Orange Ambrosia

6 seedless oranges   ½ cup coconut
¼ cup confectioners' sugar

Peel and slice oranges. (Cut into bite-size pieces for little folk.)
Sprinkle with sugar and coconut. For special occasions add sliced
maraschino cherries. Makes 4 to 6 servings.

Strawberry Pilau

2 cups sliced, fresh or   ½ pound marshmallows
   frozen strawberries   1 cup heavy cream,
½ cup sugar   whipped
2 cups cooked rice   Whole strawberries

Combine strawberries and sugar. Add rice and marshmallows.
Chill for 1 hour. Fold in whipped cream. Serve in sherbet glasses,
garnished with whole strawberries. Makes 6 to 8 servings.
NOTE: If frozen strawberries are used, reduce sugar to ¼ cup.

Apple Snow

2 egg whites   1 teaspoon lemon juice
¼ teaspoon salt   Dash of cinnamon or
¼ cup sugar   nutmeg
1¾ cups unsweetened   1 teaspoon vanilla
   applesauce or grated   extract
   raw apple

1. Beat egg whites and salt until soft peaks form.
2. Add sugar, 2 tablespoons at a time, beating after each addition. Continue beating until stiff peaks form.
3. Fold in applesauce or grated apple, lemon juice, spice and
   vanilla extract.
4. Serve chilled. (This dessert should be served within an hour
   after it is made.)
Makes 4 to 6 servings.

Variations of Apple Snow

Banana Snow: Follow basic recipe for Apple Snow, substituting 1½ cups mashed banana (4 to 5 bananas) for applesauce and increasing lemon juice to 1 tablespoon.

Pineapple Snow: Follow basic recipe, substituting 1½ cups well-drained, canned, crushed pineapple for applesauce and decreasing sugar to 3 tablespoons.

Prune Snow: Follow basic recipe, substituting 1½ cups pitted prunes, finely cut, for applesauce.

Apple Betty

¼ cup butter or margarine	½ teaspoon cinnamon
2 cups soft bread crumbs	1 tablespoon lemon juice
5 medium-size apples	2 teaspoons grated lemon
½ cup brown sugar	peel
½ teaspoon nutmeg	¼ cup hot water

1. Melt butter in skillet or frying pan; add bread crumbs and stir over medium heat until crumbs are golden.
2. Pare and core apples; slice into a mixing bowl.
3. Sprinkle apples with brown sugar, spices, lemon juice and peel; mix thoroughly.
4. Place ⅓ bread crumbs in greased baking dish; arrange half of apples on top of crumbs.
5. Cover apples with another ⅓ crumbs, add remaining apples, and top with remaining crumbs.
6. Pour on hot water.
7. Bake in moderate oven (375°F.) 40 minutes or until apples are tender. Makes 6 servings.

Variation of Apple Betty

Peach Betty: Follow basic recipe for Apple Betty, substituting 6 medium-size peaches, peeled and sliced, for apples.

Apple Spice Pandowdy

4 medium-size apples
2 tablespoons butter or
   margarine

½ cup brown sugar
½ box spice cake mix
⅓ cup water

Pare, core and slice apples; arrange in buttered 8-inch square baking dish. Dot with butter or margarine and sprinkle with sugar. Follow directions on spice cake package, using ⅓ cup of water to half the package, so that batter will be a trifle thicker than for cake. Drop by spoonfuls on top of apples, leaving spaces between for steam to escape. Bake in moderate oven (350°F.) 35 minutes or until apples are soft and cake springs back to the touch. Serve warm with whipped cream. Makes 6 servings.

Fruit Cobbler

¾ cup sugar
1 tablespoon cornstarch
½ cup water
3 cups fresh fruit
2 tablespoons butter
   Nutmeg or cinnamon
1 cup sifted flour

1 tablespoon sugar
1½ teaspoons baking
   powder
½ teaspoon salt
3 tablespoons shortening
½ cup milk

Combine ¾ cup sugar and cornstarch in a saucepan. Gradually stir in the water. Bring to a boil and boil 1 minute, stirring constantly. Stir in fruit, any juice from the fruit, and butter. Pour into 1½-quart baking dish and sprinkle with spice. Sift together flour, 1 tablespoon sugar, baking powder and salt. Cut in shortening. Stir in milk. Drop by spoonfuls onto hot fruit. Bake in hot oven (400°F.) 30 to 35 minutes or until lightly browned. Serve warm with cream. Makes 6 to 8 servings.

NOTE: If using canned fruit, substitute 1 can (1 lb. 13 ozs.) fruit, well drained, for the fresh fruit. Cut sugar from ¾ cup to 6 tablespoons and use ⅓ cup of the fruit syrup in place of water.

Basic Fruit Shortcake

2 cups flour	1 teaspoon salt
2 tablespoons sugar	½ cup shortening
3 teaspoons baking	1 egg
powder	⅓ cup milk

1. Sift first four ingredients together into mixing bowl.
2. With pastry blender or two knives, cut shortening into dry ingredients until mixture resembles coarse crumbs.
3. Beat egg with milk. Add to flour mixture, stirring only until all ingredients are moistened.
4. Turn dough onto lightly floured board; divide in half and pat out each half to fit an 8-inch layer-cake pan.
5. Place dough rounds in two 8-inch round pans and bake in very hot oven (450°F.) 15 to 20 minutes.
6. Cool. Then put layers together with desired fruit filling.

Makes 6 servings.

Variations of Basic Fruit Shortcake

Individual Shortcakes: Follow basic recipe for Shortcake. Pat out dough to ½-inch thickness on floured board; cut with floured 3-inch biscuit cutter. Place rounds on greased cookie sheet and bake in very hot oven (450°F.) 12 to 15 minutes. Split each shortcake into two layers while hot. Cool; then put layers together with desired fruit filling. Makes 6 individual shortcakes.

Strawberry Shortcake: Wash and hull 1 quart strawberries. Slice and combine with ¾ cup to 1 cup sugar, depending upon sweetness desired. Spread sugared berries between layers and over top of shortcake. Serve with cream or top with whipped cream.

Raspberry Shortcake: Follow recipe for Strawberry Shortcake substituting 1 quart red or black raspberries, crushed and sweetened, for strawberries.

Peach Shortcake: Follow recipe for Strawberry Shortcake, substituting 1 quart sliced, sweetened peaches (7 or 8 peaches) for strawberries.

Fruit Gelatin Whip

1 envelope unflavored
    gelatin
	1¼ cups hot apricot
	    nectar

½ cup cold orange or pineapple juice	⅓ cup sugar ⅛ teaspoon salt

Soften gelatin in cold juice for 5 minutes. Then add hot apricot nectar, sugar and salt, and stir mixture until gelatin is dissolved. Refrigerate until mixture becomes thick but not firm. Beat the gelatin mixture until it is light and fluffy, and the amount has about doubled. Pour into a fancy mold or individual molds, and place in the refrigerator to chill until firm. Unmold and garnish with whipped cream or fresh fruit. Makes 4 to 6 servings.

Strawberry Chiffon Dessert

1 envelope unflavored gelatin	3 tablespoons lemon juice 1 teaspoon lemon peel
½ cup cold water	1 tall can (1⅔ cups)
⅔ cup sugar	evaporated mik,
¼ teaspoon salt	thoroughly chilled
1 pint strawberries, crushed	6 whole strawberries

Soften gelatin in cold water in top of double boiler. Place over boiling water and stir until gelatin is dissolved. Remove from heat and add sugar and salt, stirring until dissolved. Mix in strawberries, lemon juice and peel; chill until slightly set. Whip chilled evaporated milk until stiff; beat in gelatin mixture. Turn into 1½-quart mold and chill until firm. Unmold and serve garnished with whole or sliced strawberries. Makes 6 to 8 servings.

Variation of Strawberry Chiffon Dessert

Pineapple Chiffon Dessert: Substitute one can (1 lb. 4 ozs.) crushed pineapple for strawberries. Drain pineapple and soften gelatin in ½ cup pineapple juice. Reduce sugar to ¼ cup.

Strawberry Bavarian Cream

1 envelope unflavored
  gelatin
¼ cup cold water
2 tablespoons lemon juice
½ cup sugar
  Dash of salt

½ cup boiling water
1 cup crushed, ripe
  strawberries
1 cup heavy cream,
  whipped
6 whole strawberries

Soften gelatin in cold water. Add lemon juice, sugar, salt and boiling water. Stir until gelatin is dissolved. Chill until slightly thickened, then stir in crushed strawberries. Fold in whipped cream and chill until set. Serve in sherbet glasses, each garnished with a whole strawberry. Makes 6 servings.
NOTE: Add more sugar if berries seem sour.

Spanish Cream

1 envelope unflavored
  gelatin
3 cups milk
3 eggs, separated

¾ cup light corn syrup
  or ½ cup sugar
¼ teaspoon salt
1 teaspoon vanilla extract

Soften gelatin in ½ cup of the cold milk. Beat egg yolks and add remaining milk, syrup or sugar and salt. Cook in top of double boiler over hot water until of custard consistency, stirring constantly. Add softened gelatin and stir until dissolved. Remove from heat. Cool and add vanilla. Chill in refrigerator until mixture begins to thicken, then fold in stiffly beaten egg whites. Pour into a serving bowl or 6 individual molds. Chill until set. Makes 6 servings.

Frozen Desserts

For most children there is no dessert quite like ice cream. It's a special food that has a party air—and no matter what the occasion, ice cream is always a treat.

Basic Refrigerator Vanilla Ice Cream

3 egg whites	¼ cup milk
6 tablespoons sugar	1 teaspoon vanilla extract
3 egg yolks	1 cup heavy cream

1. Turn temperature control of refrigerator to coldest point.
2. Beat egg whites until stiff peaks form.
3. Add sugar, 2 tablespoons at a time, beating after each addition to form soft meringue.
4. Beat egg yolks until creamy; add milk and vanilla, and fold gently into meringue.
5. Beat cream until it barely holds its shape; fold into meringue.
6. Pour mixture into freezing tray and freeze in automatic refrigerator until ice cream is firm.
7. Turn temperature control to a little colder than normal setting to keep ice cream until serving time.

Makes about 1¼ quarts.

Variations of Basic Refrigerator Vanilla Ice Cream

Chocolate Ice Cream: Melt 1 square (1 oz.) unsweetened chocolate in ¼ cup milk in top of double boiler over boiling water; blend well. Then make Vanilla Ice Cream, increasing sugar to ½ cup and folding chocolate mixture into meringue in Step 4.

Coffee Ice Cream: Make Vanilla Ice Cream, dissolving 2 teaspoons instant coffee in the milk (warmed) and cooling before adding in Step 4.

Strawberry Ice Cream: Combine 1½ cups crushed strawberries (1 pint) with ¼ cup sugar. Then make Vanilla Ice Cream, omitting milk and vanilla and adding crushed strawberries in Step 4.

Banana Ice Cream: Make Vanilla Ice Cream, omitting milk and vanilla and adding 1½ cups mashed bananas (4 to 5 bananas) and 2 teaspoons lemon juice in Step 4.

Peach Ice Cream: Combine 1½ cups crushed peaches with 3 tablespoons sugar and 1 teaspoon almond extract. Then make Vanilla Ice Cream, omitting milk and vanilla and adding crushed peaches in Step 4.

Lemon Ice Cream: Make Vanilla Ice Cream, omitting milk and vanilla and adding ¼ cup lemon juice, ¼ cup sugar and 4 teaspoons grated lemon peel in Step 4.

Basic Orange Sherbet

2 cups orange juice	½ cup sugar
½ envelope unflavored gelatin	1 egg white
	Dash of salt
2 tablespoons cold water	2 tablespoons sugar

1. Turn temperature control of refrigerator to coldest point.
2. Heat 1 cup orange juice in top of double boiler.
3. Soften gelatin in cold water.
4. Add softened gelatin and ½ cup sugar to hot orange juice, stirring until well blended.
5. Remove from heat; add remaining 1 cup orange juice. Cool.
6. Pour into freezing tray and freeze until firm but not hard.
7. Beat egg white and salt until stiff peaks form.
8. Add 2 tablespoons sugar and continue beating until soft meringue forms.
9. Break up frozen mixture; add to meringue and beat until just blended.
10. Return to tray and freeze 3 or 4 hours or until firm.
11. Set refrigerator control at colder than normal setting to keep sherbet until serving time.

Makes about ¾ quart.

Variations of Basic Orange Sherbet

Apricot Sherbet: Cook 1 cup dried apricots in 1 cup water until tender; put through coarse sieve and add water, if necessary, to make 2 cups. Then follow basic recipe for Orange Sherbet, dissolving gelatin and sugar in hot apricot pulp in Step 4 and decreasing orange juice to 1 cup, which is added in Step 5.

Three-fruit Sherbet: Combine ½ cup mashed banana (1 banana) and ½ cup canned crushed pineapple. Then follow basic recipe, decreasing sugar in Step 4 to 6 tablespoons and substituting banana-pineapple mixture for 1 cup of the orange juice, added in Step 5.

Lemon Sherbet: Follow basic recipe for Orange Sherbet, adding softened gelatin and 1 cup sugar to 1 cup boiling water in Step 4 and adding ½ cup lemon juice, ½ cup cold water and 1 teaspoon grated lemon peel in Step 5.

Baked Alaska

1 strip fine sponge cake	⅛ teaspoon salt
1 quart brick ice cream	6 tablespoons sugar
4 egg whites	

Cut cake so that it will extend approximately ¼ of an inch beyond edge of ice cream brick. Arrange sponge cake on heavy paper on a cookie sheet or on a wooden plank. To make meringue, beat egg whites and salt until soft peaks form. Add sugar, 1 tablespoon at a time, beating well after each addition. Continue to beat until peaks formed are stiff but not dry. Remove ice cream from carton, place on top of cake strip and frost quickly with meringue, completely covering top and sides of ice cream and cake. Bake in very hot oven (450°F.) 4 to 5 minutes or until lightly browned. Remove from baking sheet to chilled platter or tray and serve at once. Makes 8 servings.

Eggs and Cheese

Ounce for ounce, eggs and cheese are our richest food source of protein and therefore well equipped to play the main role on any menu. Fortunately there are so many ways to serve these valuable foods that it's no trick to include them often in family meals.

To many people, breakfast isn't complete without eggs—soft-cooked, scrambled, poached or fried. But eggs are right at home on dinner and luncheon menus, too. Omelets, baked eggs, creamed eggs and soufflés provide a welcome change and help stretch the family food budget.

American Cheddar cheese is the most popular and versatile of the many cheeses available today. Whether natural or process, sharp or mild, it adds nourishment and taste appeal to bland foods such as macaroni, rice and potatoes. Teamed with eggs in omelets and soufflés, cheese boosts both flavor and food value.

125

Anyone can learn to cook eggs so they are tender and appetizing. The secret is watchful cooking at low to moderate temperature. A high temperature toughens.

For soft-cooked eggs, cover eggs with cold water, bring rapidly to boiling point, remove from heat, cover and let stand 2 to 4 minutes as desired. Run cold water over eggs briefly to prevent further cooking and to make eggs easy to handle. If cooking more than 4 eggs, do not remove from heat but reduce it so water barely simmers.

To hard-cook eggs, follow directions for soft-cooked eggs but let stand 15 minutes. Cool promptly in cold water. This makes the shells easier to remove and helps prevent a dark ring forming around yolk.

Eggs may also be soft or hard cooked by first placing in warm water (to avoid cracked shells) and then lowering into rapidly boiling water. Turn off heat (or reduce heat so water barely simmers) and let stand 6 to 8 minutes to desired doneness.

For tender fried eggs, heat 1 to 2 tablespoons butter or margarine in a skillet until just hot enough to sizzle a drop of water. Break eggs into the skillet, reduce heat and cook slowly 3 to 4 minutes. To cook tops, baste with the butter during cooking, cover skillet or turn eggs over. Another method is to cook eggs as above about 1 minute, then add ½ teaspoon water for each egg and cover tightly. The resulting steam cooks top of eggs.

To poach eggs, bring about two inches of water, broth or milk to the boiling point in a shallow pan, then reduce heat so liquid simmers. Break one egg at a time into a saucer and slip quickly into the liquid. Cook 3 to 5 minutes depending on degree of doneness desired. Remove eggs with slotted spoon to drain.

 For glorified eggs, fold golden cream-style corn and diced cooked ham into slightly beaten eggs and scramble.

Scrambled Eggs

6 eggs   ⅛ teaspoon pepper
½ cup milk or light cream   2 tablespoons butter or
½ teaspoon salt   margarine

Beat eggs slightly; add milk, salt and pepper. Blend thoroughly
and cook in skillet or double boiler as directed below.
Makes 4 servings.

Skillet Method

1. Melt butter in skillet or frying pan, tilting pan to distribute
   butter over bottom and sides.
2. Add egg mixture and cook over low heat, scraping mixture
   from bottom and sides of pan with a spoon as it becomes firm
   and allowing uncooked mixture to flow underneath.
3. Continue cooking until all egg mixture is set but not dry.
4. Remove from heat and serve at once.

Double-boiler Method

1. Melt butter in top of double boiler over boiling water; tilt to
   cover bottom and sides with butter.
2. Add egg mixture to melted butter and cook over boiling water
   until of creamy consistency. Frequently stir mixture and
   scrape sides and bottom.
3. Remove from boiling water and serve at once.
NOTE: If scrambling one or two eggs allow approximately 1 tablespoon milk for each egg.

Variations of Scrambled Eggs

Scrambled Eggs with Ham: Follow basic recipe for Scrambled
Eggs, adding ⅓ cup chopped, cooked ham before cooking.
Scrambled Eggs with Tuna: Follow basic recipe, cooking by
skillet method. When eggs are partially cooked, push them to
one side of skillet and add contents of 1 can (6½ ozs.) tuna,

drained. Continue cooking over low heat until eggs are set. Serve eggs and tuna on toast as brunch or luncheon dish.

Scrambled Eggs with Cheese: Follow basic recipe, adding ½ cup shredded American cheese before cooking.

Luncheon Scrambled Eggs: Cook ⅓ cup chopped green pepper and 2 tablespoons chopped onion in 3 tablespoons butter in skillet until tender, about 10 minutes. Then make Scrambled Eggs with Cheese, and cook in skillet with the vegetables without additional fat. Makes 4 or 5 servings.

Plain Omelet

8 eggs	⅛ teaspoon pepper
½ cup milk or water	2 tablespoons butter,
1 teaspoon salt	margarine or bacon fat

1. Beat eggs slightly with milk or water and seasonings.
2. Melt butter in skillet or frying pan, tilting pan to distribute butter evenly over bottom and sides.
3. Pour egg mixture into pan and cook over low heat. As omelet cooks, lift edges with a spatula and tilt pan to allow uncooked portion to flow underneath.
4. Continue cooking until whole omelet is set. Then loosen edges with spatula, crease omelet across the center and fold in half. Serve at once.

Makes 4 to 6 servings.

Variations of Plain Omelet

Parsley Omelet: Follow basic recipe for Plain Omelet, folding 3 to 4 tablespoons chopped parsley into uncooked egg mixture.

Cheese Omelet: Follow basic recipe, sprinkling ⅓ cup shredded Cheddar cheese over omelet during last half of cooking.

Jelly Omelet: Follow basic recipe, spreading omelet with 3 tablespoons tart jelly just before folding.

Spanish Omelet: Make ½ recipe Spanish Sauce, page 234, and pour over Plain Omelet just before serving.

Puffy Omelet

8 eggs
½ cup water
1 teaspoon salt

⅛ teaspoon pepper
2 tablespoons butter,
   margarine or bacon fat

1. Separate eggs, putting whites into a large bowl, yolks into a smaller one.
2. Add water, salt and pepper to egg whites and beat until stiff peaks form.
3. Beat egg yolks until thick; fold gently but thoroughly into egg whites.
4. Set oven for slow heat (325°F.).
5. Heat butter in skillet or frying pan with heat-resistant handle, tilting pan to distribute butter evenly over bottom and sides.
6. Add egg mixture and cook over low heat without stirring until omelet puffs up, about 5 minutes.
7. Place omelet pan in slow oven (325°F.) and bake 12 to 15 minutes, or until top of omlet springs back when lightly touched with the finger.
8. Remove pan from oven. Loosen edges of omelet with spatula, crease across the center and fold in half. Serve at once.

Makes 4 to 6 servings.

 Keep one or two hard-cooked eggs in the refrigerator —ready at a moment's notice for sandwiches, salads or garnishing.

 To keep whole leftover egg yolks from drying out, cover with 1 or 2 tablespoons cold water and store, covered, in refrigerator.

Creamed Eggs

6 hard-cooked eggs   1½ cups Medium White
                                      Sauce, page 231

Cut eggs in fourths and add to white sauce, stirring carefully.
Serve on toast. Garnish with paprika or chopped parsley. Makes
4 to 6 servings.

NOTE: For variety add any of the following to creamed eggs:
½ cup shredded Cheddar cheese, ½ cup diced cooked ham, ½
cup cooked peas, ½ cup chopped or sliced, cooked mushrooms.

Eggs Goldenrod

6 hard-cooked eggs   1 tablespoon minced parsley
1½ cups Medium White   1 teaspoon Worcestershire
   Sauce, page 231   sauce

Cut eggs in halves lengthwise. Remove yolks and press through
a sieve. Dice egg whites and set aside. To white sauce add parsley and Worcestershire sauce. Fold in diced egg whites. Pour
egg sauce over hot fluffy rice or crisp buttered toast. Sprinkle
with sieved egg yolks. Garnish with paprika or sprigs of parsley.
Makes 4 to 6 servings.

Toad-in-the-hole

1 slice bread   1 egg
1 tablespoon butter or   Salt and pepper
   margarine

Remove center from bread with biscuit cutter. Melt butter in
saucepan and brown rest of slice on one side. Turn slice and slip
egg into center whole. Cook egg to desired firmness. Season to
taste. Makes 1 serving.

Tomato Egg Delight

1 can condensed tomato
   soup
4 eggs

¼ cup shredded American
   cheese
4 slices toast

Pour tomato soup into greased, glass pie plate. Break eggs into soup, then sprinkle with shredded cheese. Bake in hot oven (400°F.) until eggs are set. Place a slice of toast on each plate, top with an egg carefully lifted out with a pancake turner and pour the tomato soup over all. Makes 4 servings.

Deviled Eggs

6 hard-cooked eggs
5 tablespoons mayonnaise
1 teaspoon vinegar
½ teaspoon Worcestershire
   sauce
¼ teaspoon dry mustard

¼ teaspoon salt
Dash of pepper
2 teaspoons minced onion
2 teaspoons minced
   pimiento
Paprika

Cut hard-cooked eggs in halves lengthwise. Remove yolks from the whites and mash yolks until fine. Add mayonnaise, vinegar, Worcestershire sauce, mustard, salt and pepper, and beat until smooth and creamy. Fold in minced onion and pimiento. Pile yolk mixture into the whites and garnish with paprika. Makes 6 servings.

 Remember that eggs are easier to separate when very cold, but egg whites beat to greater volume if allowed to warm to room temperature.

 If, when separating eggs, a bit of yolk gets into the egg white, lift out with a piece of eggshell.

Eggs à la King

½ green pepper, chopped
1 cup sliced mushrooms
¼ cup butter
1 tablespoon flour
2 cups milk

½ teaspoon salt
⅛ teaspoon pepper
1 pimiento, cut in strips
6 hard-cooked eggs, sliced

Sauté green pepper and mushrooms in the butter about 10 minutes, then add flour and blend well. Add milk and seasonings. Stir and cook until smooth and thick. Add pimiento and sliced eggs, and heat thoroughly. Serve on toasted English muffins. Makes 6 servings.

Eggs Baked in Spinach

2½ cups cooked spinach,
    chopped
5 eggs
3 tablespoons butter or
    margarine
3 tablespoons flour

¾ teaspoon salt
1½ cups milk
½ teaspoon prepared
    mustard
1 cup shredded
    American cheese

Divide spinach into five individual baking dishes. Make a depression in the center of each and break an egg into each depression. Melt butter in saucepan over low heat; blend in flour and salt. Remove from heat and gradually add milk. Stir until smooth and continue to stir over low heat until mixture thickens and boils. Add mustard; remove from heat and stir in cheese until melted. Pour sauce over eggs and spinach. Bake in moderate oven (375°F.) 15 minutes or until egg whites are quite firm. Makes 5 servings.

Variation: Place two deviled-egg halves in center of the spinach nest; cover with sauce. Heat under broiler until sauce is lightly flecked with brown.

Egg and Cheese Casserole

¼ cup butter or margarine
⅓ cup flour
1 teaspoon salt
¼ teaspoon pepper
2 cups milk

2 cups shredded
    American cheese
2 tablespoons diced
    pimiento
5 hard-cooked eggs, diced
Round, scalloped crackers

Melt butter over low heat; stir in flour, salt and pepper. Remove
from heat and gradually stir in milk. Return to heat and cook,
stirring constantly, until thick and smooth. Add cheese and stir
until melted. Add pimiento and eggs. Turn into a greased 1½-
quart casserole and top with round, scalloped crackers. Bake in
moderate oven (350°F.) 20 to 25 minutes. Makes 6 servings.

Baked Eggs with Cheese

4 eggs
1 tablespoon butter
Salt and pepper

Milk
¼ cup shredded cheese
Dry bread crumbs

Break eggs into a buttered shallow baking dish. Dot with butter
and sprinkle with salt and pepper. Cover with milk. Sprinkle
with cheese and bread crumbs. Bake in moderate oven (350°F.)
until eggs are set and crumbs lightly browned.

*Cook cheese slowly at low heat because high heat
tends to make cheese tough and stringy. Shred cheese
or cut into small pieces before cooking because it
melts or blends with other foods more quickly.*

Cheese Soufflé

¼ cup butter or
  margarine
¼ cup flour
1 cup milk
½ teaspoon salt

Dash of cayenne, if
  desired
2 cups shredded American
  cheese
4 eggs, separated

Melt butter and gradually add flour, stirring until smooth. Remove from heat, and slowly add milk and seasonings. Return to heat, add cheese and continue stirring until cheese is melted and sauce is smooth and thick. Remove from heat. Add beaten egg yolks to cheese sauce, stirring constantly. Beat the egg whites until stiff but not dry. Fold whites into cheese sauce. Pour into an ungreased 2-quart soufflé dish. Set in pan of hot water. Bake in slow oven (325°F.) about 1¼ hours. Serve immediately. Makes 4 servings.

Easy Cheese Soup-flé

1 can condensed cream of
  mushroom soup

1 cup shredded American
  process cheese
6 eggs, separated

Heat soup slowly; add cheese and cook, stirring constantly until cheese is melted. Add slightly beaten egg yolks; cool. Fold stiffly beaten egg whites into soup mixture. Pour into an ungreased 2-quart casserole. Bake in slow oven (300°F.) 1 to 1¼ hours or until soup-flé is golden brown. Serve immediately. Makes 4 to 6 servings.

 Make a protein-rich main dish in minutes by stirring pasteurized process cheese spread into freshly cooked rice or macaroni.

Cheese Fondue

1 cup milk	1 tablespoon butter or
1 cup bread crumbs	margarine
1 cup shredded American	½ teaspoon salt
cheese	3 eggs, separated

Scald milk in double boiler; add bread crumbs and cheese. When cheese is melted add butter and salt. Add cheese mixture to beaten egg yolks; fold in stiffly beaten whites. Pour into greased 1-quart baking dish, set in pan of hot water and bake in moderate oven (350°F.) 30 to 40 minutes. Makes 6 servings.

Cheese Noodles

2 slices process cheese	1 tablespoon butter
(about 2 ounces)	1½ cups cooked, drained
3 tablespoons milk	noodles

Cut cheese in pieces and put in saucepan with milk. Stir over medium heat until smooth. Stir butter into hot noodles and then mix with the cheese sauce. Makes 2 to 3 servings.

Tomato Cheese Rice

½ cup tomato sauce	3 cups cooked rice
4 ounces Cheddar cheese	Salt and pepper

Heat tomato sauce. Add cheese, cut in pieces, and stir over medium heat until smooth. Add cooked rice and season to taste. Mix lightly with a fork. Makes 4 servings.

Welsh Rabbit

1 teaspoon dry mustard
¾ cup evaporated milk
1 pound shredded
   Cheddar cheese

2 teaspoons Worcestershire
   sauce
1 teaspoon salt
1 teaspoon caraway seed

Blend mustard with milk in top of double boiler. Add remaining ingredients. Cook over boiling water until cheese is melted and ingredients well blended. Serve on toast. Makes 6 servings.

Family Rabbit

1 medium onion, diced
1 tablespoon butter or
   margarine
2 cups stewed tomatoes *or*
   1½ cups tomato juice

2 cups shredded, mild
   Cheddar cheese
1 egg, well beaten
Salt and pepper

Sauté onion in butter until tender. Add tomatoes or juice and heat. Add cheese and stir over low heat until melted. Add egg and blend. Season to taste, and serve over crackers. Makes 4 to 6 servings.

Meals-in-a-Dish, Casseroles

The one-dish meal was undoubtedly created by an imaginative cave woman who tossed a few edible roots into the pot of meat she was cooking over an open fire. From that day to this, it has meant good eating at its simple best.

A meal-in-a-dish has two principal ingredients: a protein food such as meat, fish, cheese, poultry or eggs and a vegetable or a carbohydrate food such as rice or macaroni. But it is capable of great variation, not only in the basic ingredients, but in the vegetables, sauces, spices and seasonings added.

Because it needs no last-minute preparation, the one-dish meal is a boon to mothers. Safe in the oven or simmering on the back of the stove, it leaves her free to feed the baby and put him to bed, to help an older child with homework, or to rest and freshen up before dinner. Casseroles are also an aid to impromptu entertaining because they can be prepared and frozen ahead, ready to bake and serve when needed.

Of course, the term "meal-in-a-dish" is a slight exaggeration. A beverage, breadstuff and dessert are needed to round out the meal, and a salad makes a welcome addition.

137

Rice

Spanish Rice

1 cup uncooked rice	2 cans (8 ozs. each)
1 cup chopped onion	tomato sauce
½ cup chopped green	1½ cups boiling water
pepper	½ teaspoon salt
2 tablespoons salad oil	Dash of pepper
½ pound ground beef	

Sauté rice, onion, green pepper and beef in salad oil over low heat until rice begins to brown. Add remaining ingredients and bring to a boil. Turn heat low, cover and simmer for 20 minutes or until rice is tender and sauce absorbed. Makes 6 servings.

Rice and Cheese Loaf

1 tablespoon chopped onion	½ teaspoon Worcestershire sauce
3 tablespoons butter or margarine	1¼ teaspoons salt
¼ cup flour	Dash of pepper
½ teaspoon dry mustard	3 eggs, slightly beaten
1¼ cups milk	3 cups cooked rice
1½ cups shredded cheese	Parsley
	Pimiento strips

Sauté onion in butter over low heat. Place over hot water in double boiler, add flour and mustard, and mix well. Add milk gradually and cook, stirring constantly, until thickened. Add cheese, Worcestershire sauce, salt and pepper, and stir until the cheese is melted. Gradually add to the eggs. Add cooked rice, mix well and pour into a greased loaf pan. Bake in moderate oven (350°F.) 1 hour or until firm. Turn out of pan and garnish with parsley and strips of pimiento. Makes 6 servings.

Rice Savory

6 slices bacon, diced
¼ cup coarsely grated
onion
1 tablespoon flour
2½ cups stewed tomatoes

3 cups cooked rice
¾ teaspoon salt
¼ teaspoon dried savory
½ cup shredded Cheddar
cheese

Cook bacon and onion until onion is slightly soft. Blend in flour, add tomatoes and bring to a boil. Add the rice and seasonings, and turn into a greased 2-quart casserole. Sprinkle cheese over top. Bake in moderate oven (350°F.) about 1 hour. Makes 6 servings.

Rice and Sausage Casserole

1 pound country sausage
meat
3 cups cooked rice
1 onion, finely chopped

1 can condensed cream
of tomato soup
2 tablespoons shredded
Cheddar cheese

Brown sausage in skillet and drain the fat. Arrange rice and sausage meat in alternate layers in a greased casserole. Sprinkle each layer with onion. Pour on undiluted tomato soup. Top with shredded cheese. Cover and bake in moderate oven (350°F.) 30 minutes. Makes 4 to 6 servings.

Use a canned soup such as cream of celery, mushroom or chicken for a quick and flavorful casserole sauce.

Chicken and Rice Ring

2 cups cooked chicken, cut
    in small pieces
1 cup soft bread crumbs
¾ cup cooked rice
½ teaspoon salt
⅛ teaspoon white pepper
¼ cup chopped pimiento

2 eggs, beaten
¼ cup butter, margarine
    or chicken fat, melted
1¼ cups milk (a little more
    if needed to moisten
    mixture)

Combine the ingredients in the order given and pack into a well-greased 7 or 8-inch ring mold. Bake in moderate oven (350°F.) 45 minutes. Allow the mold to set for 10 minutes when finished before unmolding on serving platter. Fill center with a cooked green vegetable. Makes 4 to 6 servings.

Macaroni, Spaghetti, Noodles

Macaroni in Cheese Sauce

8 ounces elbow macaroni
    (about 2 cups)
1½ cups Medium White
    Sauce, page 231
2 cups shredded
    American cheese

1 teaspoon Worcester-
    shire sauce
2 tablespoons butter or
    margarine
¾ cup fine dry bread
    crumbs

1. Cook macaroni in a large quantity of boiling, salted water until tender, about 15 minutes.
2. Meanwhile make 1½ cups Medium White Sauce.
3. Add cheese and Worcestershire sauce to white sauce, and continue to cook, stirring, until cheese melts. Remove from heat.
4. Melt butter in skillet; add crumbs and stir over low heat until crumbs are golden and evenly coated.

5. Drain macaroni and turn into heated serving dish.
6. Pour hot cheese sauce over macaroni, sprinkle with crumbs, and serve at once.

Makes 6 servings.

Baked Macaroni and Cheese: Follow basic recipe for Macaroni in Cheese Sauce, adding ½ cup additional milk with cheese in Step 3. Place drained, cooked macaroni in a greased 1½-quart casserole; pour on cheese sauce and top with buttered crumbs. Bake uncovered in slow oven (325°F.) 30 minutes.

Macaroni Tomato Pie

2 cups cooked macaroni
2 cups stewed tomatoes, canned or fresh
1 teaspoon salt
⅛ teaspoon pepper
Dash of oregano
¼ cup shredded Cheddar cheese
¼ cup buttered bread crumbs

Grease a 9-inch pie plate and line bottom and sides with macaroni. Pour tomatoes into macaroni shell. Season with salt, pepper and oregano. Sprinkle top with shredded cheese. Cover all with buttered bread crumbs. Bake in moderate oven (350°F.) 20 minutes or until crumbs are browned. Makes 4 servings.

One-half pound natural or process cheese makes two cups when shredded. A main dish containing ½ pound Cheddar cheese supplies the recommended protein for one meal for a family of four.

Macaroni Tuna Casserole

2 cups shell or elbow
    macaroni
1¼ cups milk
1 can condensed cream
    of mushroom soup
1 cup cooked peas
1 teaspoon salt

½ teaspoon onion salt
Dash of pepper
1 can (6½ ozs.) chunk-
    style tuna, flaked
½ cup buttered bread
    crumbs

Cook macaroni according to package directions. Drain and rinse with boiling water. Drain again. Add milk to mushroom soup and heat, stirring constantly until well blended. Add peas, seasonings and tuna. Combine with macaroni. Mix lightly with a fork and put into a greased 1½-quart casserole. Cover with bread crumbs. Bake in moderate oven (350°F.) 20 to 25 minutes, until bubbling hot and golden brown. Makes 4 to 6 servings.

Noodle Cheese Ring

1 package (8 ozs.)
    noodles
1 cup shredded American
    cheese
½ cup soft bread crumbs
1½ cups milk, scalded
2 eggs, beaten

1 teaspoon salt
⅛ teaspoon pepper
1 tablespoon chopped
    parsley
2 tablespoons chopped
    pimiento

Cook noodles according to package directions. Drain. Add all other ingredients to noodles. Mix well and pour into well-greased 8-inch ring mold. Set in pan of hot water and bake in moderate oven (350°F.) 40 minutes. Unmold ring and fill center with creamed sea food. Makes 6 to 8 servings.

Noodle Beef Casserole

3 cups cooked noodles
¼ cup bacon drippings
or fat
½ cup diced celery
¼ cup chopped green
pepper
¼ cup finely chopped onion
1 pound ground beef

1 beef bouillon cube
1¼ cups boiling water
1 can condensed tomato
soup
1½ teaspoons salt
¼ teaspoon pepper
½ cup buttered bread
crumbs

Heat bacon drippings and add celery, green pepper and onion. Sauté until tender. Add beef and brown lightly. Dissolve bouillon cube in boiling water, add tomato soup and seasonings, and heat, stirring constantly until smooth. Combine meat-vegetable mixture, noodles and soup mixture in greased 2-quart casserole, and top with crumbs. Bake in moderate oven (350°F.) 25 to 30 minutes, or until crumbs are golden brown and casserole is thoroughly heated. Makes 6 servings.

NOTE: If this casserole is to be made ahead of time and stored in the refrigerator before baking, use 1½ cups of boiling water instead of 1¼ cups as given in recipe.

Chili Noodle Pie

3 cups cooked noodles
2 tablespoons butter
½ onion, chopped
½ pound ground beef
1 teaspoon chili powder

½ teaspoon salt
⅛ teaspoon pepper
2 firm tomatoes, sliced
¼ cup buttered bread
crumbs

Grease a 9-inch pie plate and line bottom and sides with noodles. Melt butter and in it sauté onion until transparent. Remove and add combined meat, chili powder and seasonings. Cook until meat browns. Pile meat mixture and onions into noodle shell.

Top with tomato slices and cover with bread crumbs. Bake in moderate oven (350°F.) 20 minutes or until heated through. Makes 4 servings.

Chicken Casserole De Luxe

1 stewing chicken, 4 to 5 lbs. ready-to-cook weight
2 teaspoons salt
1 quart water
1 package (8 ozs.) fine noodles, broken into 2-inch pieces
½ pound fresh mushrooms
6 tablespoons butter or margarine
6 tablespoons flour
1 cup light cream or evaporated milk
⅛ teaspoon pepper
1 cup buttered soft bread crumbs
¼ cup grated Parmesan cheese
Paprika

Place chicken in kettle with 1¼ teaspoons of the salt. Add water. Cover and simmer 1½ hours or until tender. Cool. Remove skin and bones from chicken; dice the meat. Bring stock to a boil, add noodles and cook 5 minutes. Drain, but reserve broth. Add bones and skin to the broth, boil to reduce to 2 cups and strain. Wash, dry and slice mushrooms, then add to butter and cook slowly until mushrooms are tender, about 10 minutes. Stir in flour, then chicken stock and light cream. Cook, stirring constantly, until thickened. Add diced chicken, remaining ¾ teaspoon salt and pepper. Add cooked noodles. Turn into 2-quart casserole. To heat for serving, place in moderate oven (350°F.) until mixture is thoroughly heated, about 30 minutes. Remove from oven and put bread crumbs around edges of casserole, making a band about 2 inches wide. Sprinkle cheese in center of casserole. Dust with paprika. Return to oven, increase temperature to 450°F. and bake until flecked with brown. Makes 8 servings.

Garden Casserole

1 cup sliced onions
1 pound ground beef
3 tablespoons fat
1 green pepper, chopped
1 cup chopped celery
1 cup diced carrots
4 large, firm tomatoes,
    quartered

¾ teaspoon salt
⅛ teaspoon pepper
1 tablespoon brown sugar
3 cups seasoned, mashed
    potatoes
2 tablespoons melted
    butter or margarine
Parsley sprigs

Lightly brown onions and beef in fat, stirring to prevent burning. Add green pepper, celery, carrots, tomatoes, seasonings and sugar. Simmer 20 minutes. Pour into 2-quart casserole and top with mounds of fluffy, mashed potatoes. Brush lightly with butter. Place in moderate oven (350°F.) until potato topping is golden brown. Garnish with sprigs of parsley. Makes 6 servings.

Hearty Lentil Casserole

2 cups dried lentils
1 large onion
2 tablespoons olive oil
1 can (8 ozs.) tomato sauce
1 cup milk or light cream
1 tablespoon sugar

1 tablespoon chopped
    green pepper
½ teaspoon salt
¼ teaspoon pepper
1 cup shredded sharp
    Cheddar cheese

Wash lentils under cold running water. Place in a large kettle with enough water to cover the lentils. Cover with a tight-fitting lid and cook over medium heat 45 minutes. Remove cover and simmer lentils until all the liquid evaporates. Meanwhile, chop the onion and sauté in hot olive oil until lightly browned. Add tomato sauce and heat thoroughly, stirring occasionally. Remove from heat and add the milk or cream, sugar, green pepper, salt and pepper (sour milk or sour cream gives added zest). Add cooked lentils to the sauce and blend well. Place in a lightly greased 1½-quart casserole and top with the shredded sharp cheese. Bake in hot oven (400°F.) 15 minutes or until cheese is golden brown. Serve with piping hot corn meal muffins made from your favorite recipe or, as a time saver, from a prepared corn meal muffin mix. Makes 4 to 6 servings.

Savory Meat Pie

1 cup sliced onions	½ teaspoon paprika
¼ cup fat or bacon drippings	Dash of ginger
	Dash of allspice
1 pound round steak, cut in 1-inch cubes	2½ cups boiling water
	2 cups raw, diced potatoes
¼ cup flour	½ Pastry recipe, page
1 teaspoon salt	196
⅛ teaspoon pepper	

Sauté onions in fat until yellow. Roll steak in combined flour and seasonings. Remove onions and brown meat in hot fat. Add boiling water, cover and simmer about 50 minutes or until steak is tender. Add potatoes and cook 10 minutes longer. Pour into a greased 2-quart casserole, place onions on top and cover with pastry. Slash pastry to allow steam to escape. Bake 20 to 25 minutes in very hot oven (450°F.). Makes 4 to 6 servings.

Meat and Onion Pie

5 large onions, sliced
2 tablespoons butter or
   margarine
1 teaspoon sugar
½ pound ground beef
¼ pound chopped bacon
½ cup bread crumbs

1¼ cups milk
1 teaspoon salt
¼ teaspoon pepper
3 tablespoons chopped
   parsley
1 Baking Powder Biscuit
   recipe, page 45

Brown onions in the butter and sprinkle with sugar. Combine the beef, bacon, bread crumbs, milk, seasonings and parsley. Lightly grease a 1½-quart casserole. Place half the onions on the bottom, then add the meat mixture and the remaining onions. Prepare biscuit dough, roll out to ½-inch thickness on lightly floured board. Cut small biscuits (about 1½ inches in diameter). Place in circle around edge of casserole, leaving about ½ inch between biscuit rounds. Bake in hot oven (400°F.) 30 minutes or until biscuits are golden. Makes 4 to 6 servings.

Shepherd's Pie

2 tablespoons minced
   onion
2 tablespoons butter
1¼ cups diced, cooked
   meat
½ cup diced, cooked
   carrots

1 cup condensed tomato
   soup
½ teaspoon Worcestershire
   sauce
½ teaspoon salt
Dash of pepper
1 cup hot, mashed potatoes

Sauté onion in the butter until golden brown. Add meat, carrots, tomato soup and seasonings. Mix well and transfer to a greased 9-inch pie plate. Cover with a thin layer of mashed potatoes. Swirl potatoes with back of spoon to make an attractive design. Dust with paprika and bake in hot oven (400°F.) 20 minutes or until potatoes are golden brown. Makes 4 servings.

Chicken Broccoli Pie

1 can condensed cream of
  chicken soup
¼ cup milk
2 cups cooked rice, well
  seasoned
1 cup diced, cooked
  broccoli

1 cup diced, cooked
  chicken
Salt and pepper
¼ cup shredded cheese
¼ cup cracker crumbs
¼ cup chopped nuts
Dash of paprika

Blend soup and milk. Cover bottom and sides of a greased 9-inch pie plate with the rice. Add a layer of broccoli and a layer of chicken. Sprinkle with salt and pepper. Pour soup mixture over all. Combine cheese, cracker crumbs and nuts, and sprinkle over top. Dust lightly with paprika. Bake in hot oven (400°F.) 20 minutes until heated through and top is a golden brown. Makes 4 servings.

Beef Stew

1½ pounds beef, cut in
   1-inch cubes
 ½ cup flour
 2 teaspoons salt
 ¼ teaspoon pepper
 1 teaspoon paprika

2 tablespoons fat
2 cups boiling water
4 potatoes, diced
4 medium onions, diced
4 carrots, diced
1 cup turnips, cubed

Dredge beef with a mixture of the flour, salt, pepper and paprika. Melt fat in a heavy skillet. Add beef and brown evenly on all sides. Add boiling water and simmer 1½ hours. Add potatoes, onions, carrots and turnips, and continue to cook slowly for 30 minutes, adding more water if necessary. To thicken gravy, add 3 tablespoons flour, blended with ½ cup cold water, and cook until smooth and thickened, stirring constantly. Makes 6 servings.

Browned Chili Stew

2 pounds stew meat
   (beef, lamb or veal)
   cut in 1-inch cubes
½ cup flour
½ teaspoon salt
⅛ teaspoon pepper
1 teaspoon chili powder

⅛ teaspoon garlic salt
¼ cup fat or bacon
   drippings
1 cup tomato juice
5 small onions
5 carrots, quartered
5 potatoes, halved

Roll meat in the mixture of flour, salt, pepper, chili powder and garlic salt. Brown in hot fat and add tomato juice and enough water to cover. Cook in a tightly covered kettle for about 1½ hours, or until meat is tender. Add vegetables and cook, covered, until they are tender. If thicker gravy is desired, remove vegetables and meat to heated platter, and to gravy add 3 tablespoons flour blended with 3 tablespoons water. Makes 6 servings.

El Burgos

5 large potatoes, thinly
   sliced
2 green peppers, chopped
2 bunches scallions,
   chopped (tops and all)
1 pound ground beef
1 tablespoon fat

2 cups shredded Cheddar
1 teaspoon salt
1 teaspoon monosodium
   glutamate
1 tablespoon brown sugar
2 cans (8 ozs. each) tomato
   sauce

Parboil separately for 10 minutes the potatoes, green peppers and scallions. Sauté the beef in fat until redness disappears. While beef is cooking, add cheese, salt, monosodium glutamate and sugar to tomato sauce. Place a layer of meat in a greased 2-quart casserole, cover with peppers, then scallions, then potatoes. Repeat layers until all ingredients are used. Pour cheese-tomato sauce mixture over all. Bake in moderate oven (350°F.) about 30 minutes until heated through. Makes 8 servings.

Veal-stuffed Cabbage Rolls

12 medium cabbage leaves   1 teaspoon salt
1½ cups cooked veal,   Dash of thyme
      ground   1 tablespoon melted
1 onion, grated   butter or margarine
1 cup cooked rice   ½ cup tomato juice

Cook cabbage leaves 3 minutes in boiling, salted water; drain
and dry. Combine veal, onion, rice and seasonings. Put about ¼
cup on each cabbage leaf. Roll and fasten each cabbage leaf with
wooden picks. Place rolls close together in greased baking dish.
Brush rolls with the melted butter and pour tomato juice over
them. Bake in moderate oven (375°F.) until cabbage leaves are
tender, about 15 minutes. Remove wooden picks before serving.
Makes 6 servings.

Frankfurter Cabbage Pie

6 cups coarsely shredded   3 tablespoons lemon juice
      cabbage   2 tablespoons butter or
½ pound frankfurters (4)   margarine
3 tablespoons brown sugar

Cook cabbage 7 minutes in boiling, salted water. Drain and
reserve liquid for soup another day. Place cabbage in a greased
9-inch pie plate. Slit frankfurters lengthwise, cut in halves crosswise and arrange attractively on bed of cabbage, cut side down.
Sprinkle with combined sugar and lemon juice. Dot with butter.
Bake in hot oven (400°F.) about 10 minutes or until frankfurters are browned and crusty. Makes 4 servings.

Sweet Potato and Sausage Casserole

2 cups mashed sweet potatoes (about 4)	½ teaspoon salt
1 tablespoon brown sugar	1 pound link sausages
2 tablespoons butter	2 tablespoons water
	¼ cup orange juice

Combine sweet potatoes, sugar, butter and salt in a 1½-quart casserole. Place sausage links in skillet with water. Cover and simmer 5 minutes; drain. Cook slowly, turning often until well browned. Arrange sausages on sweet potatoes. Pour on juice; bake in moderate oven (350°F.) 30 minutes. Makes 4 servings.

Ham Supper Casserole

6 medium potatoes, pared and sliced	2 cups diced cooked ham
3 medium onions, sliced	3 cups Thin White Sauce, page 231

Arrange potatoes, onions and ham in layers in a greased 3-quart casserole. Pour on Thin White Sauce. Cover and bake in moderate oven (375°F.) 45 minutes. Uncover and bake 15 minutes longer, or until top forms brown crust. Makes 6 servings.

Ham Curry with Limas

3 tablespoons fat	½ teaspoon bottled brown bouquet sauce
1 teaspoon minced onion	½ cup shredded Cheddar cheese
3 tablespoons flour	2 cups diced, cooked ham
½ teaspoon curry powder	2½ cups cooked lima beans
1½ cups milk	
½ teaspoon salt	

Melt fat in a large skillet and add onion. Brown onion slightly, 'hen stir in flour and curry. Add milk, salt and bottled bouquet sauce. Cook over moderate heat, stirring until sauce thickens. Add cheese and stir until melted. Add ham and lima beans; cook until thoroughly heated. Makes 4 to 6 servings.

Corn and Liver Sausage Pie

½ pound liver sausage,   ¼ cup pimiento
    sliced   ½ teaspoon salt
2 tablespoons bacon fat   ½ cup crumbled corn chips
½ cup minced onion   Butter or margarine,
2 cups cream-style corn   melted

Brown liver sausage slices in bacon fat in a skillet. Remove and line a 9-inch pie plate with the sausage. Sauté onions lightly in remaining fat. Add corn, pimiento and salt, and pour into liver shell. Top with corn chips. Brush with butter. Bake in hot oven (400°F.) 20 minutes until lightly browned. Makes 4 servings.

Fish Dinner Casserole

½ cup butter   1 small onion, thinly
1½ tablespoons flour   sliced
1½ cups milk   1 pound fish fillets
1 teaspoon chopped   1 cup cooked or canned
    parsley   shrimp
¼ cup sliced mushrooms   3 raw potatoes, sliced

Melt ¼ cup of the butter in saucepan, stir in flour and then milk. Cook over low heat, stirring constantly, until smooth and thickened. Add parsley and set aside. Sauté mushrooms and onion in remaining fat. Add fish fillets, cut in 1-inch pieces, and add shrimp. Mix with 1 cup of the white sauce and pour into greased 2½-quart casserole. Top with layer of sliced potatoes; pour remaining white sauce over all. Bake in moderate oven (375°F.) 40 minutes or until potatoes are done. Makes 6 servings.

Tuna Mushroom Pie

1 can condensed cream of
  mushroom soup
¼ cup milk
2 cups cooked lima beans
1 can (6½ ozs.) tuna,
  flaked

2 tablespoons lemon
  juice
⅛ teaspoon pepper
1 cup crushed potato
  chips
2 tablespoons butter

Blend soup and milk. Spread lima beans on bottom of a greased
9-inch pie plate and in a ring around the edge. Then add layer
of tuna. Sprinkle with lemon juice and pepper. Cover with soup
mixture and top with potato chips. Dot with butter. Bake in
hot oven (400°F.) 20 minutes until heated through and lightly
browned on top. Makes 4 servings.

Chili Con Carne

1 cup chopped onion
½ cup chopped green
  pepper
2 tablespoons fat or
  bacon drippings
1 pound ground beef
1 can (1 lb.) kidney beans
½ cup hot water

1 can condensed tomato
  soup
1½ teaspoons salt
⅛ teaspoon cayenne
  pepper
1 to 2 teaspoons chili
  powder
1 tablespoon vinegar

Sauté onion and green pepper in fat. Add beef and cook until
browned, breaking it apart with a fork. Place cooked mixture in
greased 3-quart casserole; add kidney beans. Combine remaining
ingredients, stirring until smooth, and pour into casserole. Cover
and bake in moderate oven (350°F.) 45 minutes. Garnish with
corn chips or crisp cereal. Makes 6 servings.

Monterey Beans and Cheese

1 can (1 lb.) kidney beans
2 slices bacon
½ medium onion, sliced
½ green pepper, diced
2 cups shredded
   Cheddar cheese

2 ripe tomatoes, diced
¼ cup beef bouillon or
   tomato juice
1 teaspoon chili powder
½ teaspoon salt
Dash of pepper

Drain beans, if necessary, and set aside. Fry bacon, drain and break into pieces. Sauté onion and green pepper in the bacon fat until tender. Add cheese and stir until it is melted. Add beans, bacon bits and remaining ingredients. Cook slowly, stirring constantly, until ingredients are blended and cheese is smooth and creamy, about 5 minutes. Makes 6 servings.

Chicken Chow Mein

2 tablespoons butter or
   margarine
1 cup sliced onions
1½ cups diced celery
1 teaspoon salt
⅛ teaspoon pepper
1 can (1 lb.) bean sprouts
2 teaspoons sugar

1 can (3 or 4 ozs.) sliced
   mushrooms, drained
2 cups chicken stock
2 tablespoons cornstarch
3 tablespoons soy sauce
2 cups thinly sliced or
   diced, cooked chicken
½ cup almonds

Melt butter. Add onion, celery and seasonings, and sauté 2 minutes. Add bean sprouts, sugar, mushrooms and stock; cover and cook 10 minutes. Blend cornstarch and soy sauce, and stir into vegetable mixture. Add chicken and simmer 3 minutes or until mixture thickens. Garnish with almonds. Serve with canned fried noodles and soy sauce. Makes 6 servings.

American Chop Suey

2 tablespoons fat
1 teaspoon salt
Dash of pepper
2 cups leftover roast pork,
cut in narrow strips
½ cup sliced onions
1 can (1 lb.) chop suey
vegetables

½ cup vegetable liquid
1 medium green pepper,
cut in strips
2 tablespoons cornstarch
2 teaspoons soy sauce
¼ cup cold water

Melt fat in preheated skillet, stir in salt and pepper. Add roast pork and onions, and cook until both are lightly browned. Drain liquid from chop suey vegetables, measure ½ cup of this liquid and add, with green pepper strips, to pork and onions. Cover and simmer 5 minutes. Add chop suey vegetables and stir until heated through. Blend cornstarch, soy sauce and cold water. Gradually stir into mixture and cook until thick and clear, stirring constantly. Serve immediately with hot, boiled rice and Chinese noodles. Makes 4 or 5 servings.

Pork Pancake Special

4 eggs
⅔ cup diced cooked pork
⅓ cup finely chopped
onion
½ large green pepper,
diced

1½ cups cooked green
beans, drained
1 tablespoon soy sauce
¾ teaspoon salt
⅛ teaspoon pepper
4 teaspoons bacon fat

Beat eggs until light. Add pork, onion, green pepper, green beans, soy sauce and seasonings. Mix lightly. Melt fat on a griddle or large skillet and drop the pancake mixture onto it using a large spoon. As soon as the pancakes are firm on the bottom, turn them over. Turn only once. Makes 4 servings.

Lasagne

Sauce

2 cloves garlic, minced   ½ can (6 ozs.) tomato
¼ cup olive oil   paste
1 can (1 lb. 13 ozs.) Italian   ½ cup hot water
   peeled tomatoes   Salt and pepper

Sauté garlic in hot olive oil about 3 minutes. Add tomatoes and tomato paste blended with hot water. Bring to boiling, then reduce heat, cover and simmer 1 hour. Season to taste. (The flavor of this sauce improves if allowed to mellow overnight in covered jar in refrigerator.)

Filling

½ pound Italian sausage   1 cup Mozzarella, cut
1 pound lasagne   in pieces
¾ cup grated Romano   1 pound ricotta cheese
   cheese

Fry sausage until brown on both sides, about 20 minutes, and cut into small pieces. Cook lasagne as package directs until tender but not too soft, drain and rinse. Pour a little sauce into an 8 x 12-inch baking dish, cover with a layer of noodles, then add a layer of Romano, more sauce, a layer of Mozzarella and half the sausage. Dot all over with tablespoons of ricotta. Repeat these layers once more, and end with a layer of noodles, sauce and Romano. Bake in moderate oven (350°F.) 15 to 20 minutes. Makes 6 to 8 servings. (This dish may be prepared early in the day and stored in the refrigerator until baking time.)

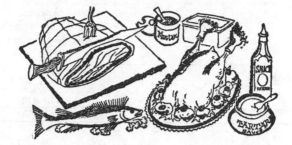

Meat, Poultry and Fish

How do you go about planning a meal? Chances are you start
with the meat, poultry or fish and then decide on the vegetables,
salad and dessert to go with it.

Although meat, poultry and fish are all high protein foods, they
vary greatly in cost and in flavor. This section tells how to prepare choice cuts of beef, lamb, pork and veal, and how to make
the less expensive cuts taste just as good as steak or chops. Included are recipes for cooking liver, kidney and heart, which
deserve special mention because they contain all the nutrients in
meat plus a vitamin and mineral bonus.

There are recipes for preparing chicken, from the tenderest
broiler to the hardiest fowl, step-by-step directions for stuffing
and roasting a festive turkey, and recipes for fresh, frozen and
canned fish dishes.

There are also suggestions for making the most of leftovers.
With such a wide choice, it's easy to find main dishes that fit the
food budget and rate cheers from the family as well.

CHART FOR ROASTING MEAT

Type of Roast	Weight in Pounds	Approximate Time in Minutes at 325° F.	Internal Temperature in degrees Fahrenheit
BEEF			
Standing ribs	6-8	120-150	140 (rare)
		150-180	160 (medium)
		200-270	170 (well done)
Rolled rib	4-6	120-180	140 (rare)
		150-195	160 (medium)
		180-240	170 (well done)
Rolled rump (high quality)	5	180-195	160-170
PORK—FRESH			
Loin—Center	3-5	90-175	170
Picnic shoulder	5	150	170
boned and rolled	4	180	170
cushion	5	200	170
Boston butt	4	180	170
Fresh ham, whole	10-14	250-420	170
PORK—CURED			
Ham—whole	12-16	210-255	160
half	6	150	160
Ham (fully cooked)			
half	5-7	90-180	130
LAMB			
Leg	6-7	195-240	180
Shoulder	3-6	135-195	180
boned and rolled	3-5	150-180	180
cushion	5	180	180
VEAL			
Leg roast	5-8	150-210	170-180
Loin	5	180	170-180
Shoulder	6	210	170
boned and rolled	3-5	180-210	170-180

Pork

Baked Pork Chops and Vegetables

4 pork chops
2 tablespoons fat
1 tablespoon chopped
   onion
1 tablespoon chopped
   green pepper

2 cups tomatoes, fresh
   or canned
1 teaspoon salt
Dash of pepper
½ cup uncooked rice

Brown chops in fat in heavy skillet. Remove chops and place in
a greased 1½-quart casserole. Sauté onion and green pepper
slowly about 5 minutes in remaining fat in skillet. Add tomatoes,
salt and pepper, and simmer until sauce is thick. Stir in rice,
pour mixture over chops, and cook in moderate oven (350°F.) 40
minutes or until meat is thoroughly cooked. Makes 4 servings.

Baked Spareribs

Place 3 to 4 pounds spareribs in shallow baking pan; season
with salt and pepper. Bake in moderate oven (350°F.) 1½ hours
or until meat is tender. Makes 6 servings.

Baked Spareribs and Sauerkraut

Place 3 to 4 pounds spareribs in roasting pan with cover. Bake,
uncovered, in hot oven (400°F.) 30 minutes. Remove ribs. Put 1
quart sauerkraut in pan, arrange ribs on top, and season with salt
and pepper. Pour on ½ cup hot water, cover and bake in moderate oven (350°F.) 1 hour. Makes 6 servings.

Orange-glazed Baked Ham

Bake ham according to directions on chart on page 158. Forty-five minutes before end of baking time, take ham from oven and remove rind. Cut diagonal gashes ¼-inch deep across the fat side of the ham and insert a whole clove in each diamond. Then mix together 1 cup brown sugar, 1 tablespoon powdered mustard and enough cider vinegar or lemon juice (1 to 2 tablespoons) to make a thick paste. Spread evenly over top of ham. Bake in slow oven (325°F.); during last ½ hour baste with this glaze:

Orange Glaze

3 tablespoons sugar	1½ cups orange juice
1 tablespoon cornstarch	

Combine sugar, cornstarch and orange juice in a saucepan. Cook, stirring constantly, until slightly thickened. Baste ham with one-third of the sauce during baking. Serve remaining sauce with the ham. For extra eye appeal, top the bowl of sauce with a clove-studded orange slice.

Ham and Sweet Potatoes Hawaiian

4 large sweet potatoes	¼ teaspoon ground cloves
1½ pounds ham, sliced	2 tablespoons brown sugar
1 inch thick	1 can (1 lb. 13 ozs.) sliced
¼ teaspoon powdered	pineapple
mustard	¼ cup melted butter

Boil unpeeled sweet potatoes 15 minutes. Cool. Remove skins and cut in halves lengthwise. Place ham in 8 x 12-inch baking pan. Sprinkle with mustard, cloves and sugar, and cover with pineapple slices. Dip potatoes in butter and place around ham. Pour pineapple syrup over all to depth of ½ inch. Bake, uncovered, in moderate oven (350°F.) 45 to 60 minutes. Makes 6 servings.

Beef

Swiss Steak

½ cup flour
2 teaspoons salt
¼ teaspoon pepper
2 pounds beef round,
   chuck or rump

3 tablespoons fat
3 medium onions, sliced
2 stalks celery, diced
1 can (1 lb.) tomatoes

Combine flour, salt and pepper; sprinkle over meat, pounding in thoroughly with wooden mallet or edge of a plate. Heat fat in Dutch oven or heavy skillet with a cover. Brown meat on both sides. Add remaining ingredients; cover and simmer gently 1½ to 2 hours or until meat is tender. Makes 6 servings.

Baked Flank Steak

2 pounds flank steak,
   thinly sliced
½ cup flour
2 teaspoons salt

¼ teaspoon pepper
¼ cup chopped onion
2 tablespoons fat
½ cup hot water

Score steak; dip into combined flour, salt and pepper. Brown steak and onion in hot fat. Add water, cover and bake in moderate oven (350°F.) 1½ hours or until tender. Makes 6 servings.

Stuffed Flank Steak

Spread Bread and Onion Stuffing, page 185, on a 2-pound flank steak. Roll up steak with stuffing inside and fasten with string or skewers. Brown on all sides in 3 tablespoons hot fat. Add ¾ cup tomato juice, cover and simmer gently 1½ to 2 hours or until meat is tender. Makes 6 servings.

Family Meat Loaf

1½ pounds ground beef
½ pound ground pork
½ cup nonfat dry milk
1 teaspoon salt
¼ teaspoon pepper
½ teaspoon powdered
  mustard

1 egg, slightly beaten
¾ cup condensed tomato
  soup or catsup
1½ cups coarse bread
  crumbs
1 onion, minced

Sprinkle meat with dry milk and mix thoroughly. Add remaining ingredients and mix well. (Mixture will be sticky.) Place in a lightly greased 9 x 5 x 3-inch loaf pan. Bake uncovered in moderate oven (350°F.) 1½ hours. Makes 6 to 8 servings.

Pot Roast with Vegetables

3 tablespoons fat
3 to 4 pounds rolled, boned
  beef chuck or round
2 teaspoons salt
¼ teaspoon pepper
½ cup water

6 carrots, scraped and
  halved
2 pounds white onions,
  peeled
6 medium potatoes, pared
  and halved

Heat fat in Dutch oven or heavy kettle with a cover. Add meat and brown well on all sides. Sprinkle with salt and pepper; add water. Cover and simmer gently 2 hours, turning roast several times for even cooking. Add vegetables and more water, if needed; cover and cook 45 minutes to 1 hour longer, or until meat is tender. Remove meat and vegetables to heated platter and keep warm while making Brown Gravy, page 232. Makes 6 servings with meat left over for second meal.

Roast Beef Hash

2 cups chopped leftover
   roast beef
3 cups diced cooked
   potatoes
1 medium onion, chopped
½ teaspoon salt

⅛ teaspoon pepper
1 teaspoon Worcestershire
   sauce
⅓ cup dairy half and half
3 tablespoons fat

1. Combine all ingredients except fat, mixing lightly.
2. Melt fat in skillet, tilting pan to distribute fat over bottom and sides.
3. Spread hash mixture evenly over bottom of skillet and cook over low heat without stirring 35 to 40 minutes, or until underside is well browned.
4. Loosen hash from pan by slipping spatula or pancake turner under the edges; then crease through center and fold over, omelet fashion.
5. Serve hash plain or with Quick Tomato Sauce, page 233, or Creamy Mustard Sauce, page 233. Or top each serving with a poached egg.

Makes 4 to 6 servings.

Variation of Roast Beef Hash

Corned Beef Hash: Follow basic recipe for Roast Beef Hash, omitting salt and substituting 2 cups chopped, cooked corned beef or one 12-ounce can corned beef, chopped, for roast beef.

Fill orange shells with mashed sweet potatoes, cranberry sauce or diced fresh fruit to use as an accompaniment to roasts, broiled meats or poultry.

New England Boiled Dinner

3 to 4 pounds corned beef
   brisket
1 bay leaf
3 peppercorns
6 medium potatoes, pared
   and halved

6 white turnips, pared
   and quartered
6 carrots, scraped and
   quartered
1 medium cabbage, cut
   in sixths

Place meat in a deep kettle with a cover. Add bay leaf, peppercorns and enough cold water to cover meat. Cover kettle, bring to a boil and simmer gently 3 to 3½ hours. Skim fat. Add potatoes, turnips and carrots, and continue to cook, covered, 25 minutes. Add cabbage and cook 15 minutes longer or until both meat and vegetables are tender. Makes 6 servings with meat left over for second meal.

Braised Short Ribs

2 tablespoons fat
3 pounds short ribs of
   beef, cut into 3-inch
   pieces
1 tablespoon salt
½ teaspoon pepper

½ bay leaf
1 onion, chopped
2 cups hot water
2 tablespoons flour
¼ cup cold water

Heat fat in Dutch oven or heavy skillet with a cover. Add short ribs and brown on all sides. Add seasonings, onion and hot water; cover and simmer gently about 2 hours, or until meat is tender.* Remove ribs to heated platter. Blend together flour and cold water; stir into liquid in pan and continue to cook, stirring, until gravy boils and thickens. Season gravy to taste, pour over short ribs and serve at once. Makes 6 servings.

* If fatty, cook covered ½ hour and drain before adding seasonings.

Cereal-flake Hamburgers

½ cup slightly crushed
   cereal flakes
1½ pounds ground beef
2 tablespoons finely
   diced onion

1 egg
1½ teaspoons salt
⅛ teaspoon pepper
¼ teaspoon powdered
   mustard

Lightly combine all ingredients and shape into 6 patties. Sauté in a little hot fat for about 4 minutes on each side. Or broil at high heat for 2 to 4 minutes on each side. Makes 6 servings.

Company Meat Roll

1 pound ground lamb
1 pound ground pork
   or beef
1 teaspoon salt
¼ teaspoon pepper
2 eggs, beaten
6 cups toasted bread cubes

½ cup finely chopped onion
½ cup ripe olives, pitted
3 tablespoons minced
   parsley
¼ teaspoon sage
1 cup soup stock or water
2 tablespoons melted fat

Combine ground meats. Season and blend with eggs. Pat into an 8 x 10-inch oblong on wax paper. Combine bread cubes, onions, half of olives (chopped), parsley, sage and stock, and season to taste. Spread this dressing over meat and roll as for jelly roll. Place meat roll in greased pan and brush top with fat. Press remaining whole olives into rolled loaf in an attractive design. Bake in moderate oven (350°F.) 1¾ hours. Slice to serve. Makes 6 to 8 servings.

Meat Balls with Spaghetti

1 pound lean beef,
   ground twice
⅓ cup fine dry bread
   crumbs
1 egg, slightly beaten
1 medium onion, grated
1 tablespoon chopped
   parsley
1½ teaspoons salt
⅛ teaspoon pepper
2 tablespoons salad oil
2 cloves garlic

1 can (1 lb.) tomatoes
1 can (6 ozs.) tomato
   paste
1 tomato paste can cold
   water
1½ teaspoons crumbled
   dried basil
1 package (8 ozs.) thin
   spaghetti
½ cup grated Parmesan
   cheese

Combine ground beef, crumbs, egg, onion, parsley, 1 teaspoon salt and dash of pepper. Form into 16 small balls about 1 inch in diameter. Heat oil in large skillet until very hot. Then reduce heat and brown meat balls slowly. Remove meat balls. Sauté garlic in skillet until light brown, then remove and discard. Pour tomatoes into skillet and cook about 10 minutes. Add tomato paste diluted with cold water. Season with remaining ½ teaspoon salt, pepper and basil, and cook slowly 1 hour, stirring occasionally to prevent sticking. Add meat balls and cook for another half hour. Cook spaghetti according to package directions. Add sauce and meat balls to spaghetti and serve with grated Parmesan cheese. Makes 4 to 6 servings.

 To flour meat or chicken, shake pieces in a paper bag with seasoned flour.

Pepper Steak

¼ cup salad oil	6 green peppers
⅛ teaspoon pepper	1½ cups diced celery
1½ pounds round steak	1 cup beef bouillon
⅓ cup finely chopped	3 tablespoons cornstarch
onion	¼ cup water
1 garlic clove, minced	1 tablespoon soy sauce

Heat salad oil and add pepper. Cut meat into 1-inch strips, ⅛-inch thick; add to fat. Cook over high heat, stirring until brown. Add onion and garlic. Cut green peppers into 1-inch pieces and add, with celery and bouillon, to steak. Cover pan and cook over moderate heat until meat and vegetables are tender, about 10 minutes. Blend cornstarch, water and soy sauce, add to steak and cook, stirring constantly, until sauce thickens. Add salt, if necessary. Serve over rice. Makes 6 servings.

Beef Stroganoff

2 pounds round steak	1 bay leaf
½ cup flour	½ teaspoon thyme
1 teaspoon salt	½ teaspoon oregano
1 teaspoon paprika	1 can (3 or 4 ozs.) mush-
¼ cup salad oil	room caps, drained
½ cup chopped onion	2 tablespoons sherry,
1 can consommé	if desired
½ can water	1 cup dairy sour cream

Cut meat into strips ½-inch wide and 3-inches long. Shake in sack with flour, salt and paprika, then brown in hot salad oil. Add onion and cook until just tender. Add consommé, water and herbs. Cover and simmer 45 minutes to 1 hour, or until meat is tender, adding a little more water if necessary. Just before serving, stir in mushrooms, sherry and sour cream. Heat and serve over hot rice. Makes 6 to 8 servings.

Veal

Breaded Veal Cutlet

2 pounds veal cutlet,
   ½-inch thick
1 egg
3 tablespoons milk
½ teaspoon salt

⅛ teaspoon pepper
1 cup fine dry bread
   crumbs
¼ cup fat

Cut veal into 6 serving-size pieces, discarding bone and skin. Beat egg slightly; stir in milk and seasonings. Dip veal pieces in bread crumbs, then into egg mixture, and again into crumbs. Heat fat in skillet; add veal and cook over low heat 30 minutes, or until well browned, turning only once. Makes 6 servings.

Braised Veal with Vegetables

2 pounds veal shoulder
3 tablespoons fat
½ cup hot water
6 to 8 small onions
1 pound green beans, cut
   in 1-inch lengths
3 stalks celery, cut up

1 green pepper, cut in
   strips
1 can (1 lb.) tomatoes
1 teaspoon salt
⅛ teaspoon pepper
2 tablespoon flour
½ cup cold water

Cut veal in small pieces and brown in hot fat. Add hot water, cover and simmer ½ hour. Then add vegetables and seasonings. Cover and cook slowly for 1 to 1½ hours or until meat is tender. Thicken gravy by adding flour blended with cold water. Cook until smooth and thickened, stirring constantly. Makes 6 servings.

Curry-stuffed Veal Birds

1½ pounds veal cutlet
2 cups day-old bread
   crumbs
¼ cup minced onion
1 teaspoon salt
⅛ teaspoon pepper
½ to 1 teaspoon curry
   powder, to taste

¼ cup bacon fat
Flour
2 tablespoons shortening
   or salad oil
1 can condensed cream of
   mushroom soup
1 can hot water

Ask butcher to cut veal into individual portions and flatten. Combine crumbs, onion, salt, pepper, curry powder and bacon fat in a bowl and mix thoroughly. Place stuffing on "birds," dividing it evenly among pieces. Roll up and fasten with a wooden pick in center and at each end so stuffing cannot escape. Roll each "bird" in a little flour and brown on all sides in hot fat in a big skillet. Add combined soup and water and simmer, covered, 1 hour or until tender, turning once. Makes 4 to 6 servings.

Lamb

Stuffed Lamb Shoulder

1 medium onion, minced
1 medium apple, diced
1 stalk celery, diced
¾ cup soft bread crumbs
2 teaspoons salt

½ teaspoon pepper
4 pounds lamb shoulder,
   boned and cut with
   pocket for stuffing
½ cup vinegar

Mix onion, apple, celery and crumbs with 1 teaspoon of the salt and half the pepper. Stuff and sew up pocket of lamb. Place in shallow baking dish; sprinkle with vinegar and remaining salt and pepper. Bake in slow oven (325°F.) about 3 hours, basting once or twice. Makes 6 servings.

Lamb Patty and Peach Grill

1½ pounds ground lamb   6 strips bacon
   shoulder or breast   6 canned peach halves
Salt and pepper   1 tablespoon brown sugar

Season ground lamb with salt and pepper. Divide into six portions and shape into patties 1-inch thick. Wrap a slice of bacon around each patty and fasten with a wooden pick. Place patties on broiler rack with top 2 inches below source of heat. Broil 8 to 10 minutes. Sprinkle hollow side of each peach half with brown sugar. Turn lamb patties; place fruit on broiler rack hollow side up. Broil 8 to 10 minutes to finish cooking patties and brown the peaches. Makes 6 servings.

Lamb Kebabs

2 pounds lamb shoulder   ½ teaspoon salt
½ cup salad oil   ⅛ teaspoon pepper
2 tablespoons vinegar   1 medium onion,
2 tablespoons lemon juice   chopped
1 teaspoon powdered   4 tomatoes
  mustard   3 medium onions
¼ teaspoon thyme   2 green peppers

Have lamb shoulder cut in 1½-inch cubes. Blend salad oil, vinegar, lemon juice, seasonings and chopped onion in a bowl. Add lamb cubes and refrigerate 2 to 3 hours. Drain. Cut tomatoes in halves, onions in ¼-inch slices, and green peppers in 1-inch squares. Arrange lamb, tomatoes, onion slices and peppers alternately on metal skewers. Repeat, ending with lamb cube. Cook in moderate oven (350°F.) about 20 minutes, turning skewers occasionally. Slide meat and vegetables off skewers onto individual plates. Makes 6 to 8 servings.

Curry of Lamb

1½ pounds boneless lamb shoulder
5 tablespoons salad oil
1 large onion, sliced
1 clove garlic
2 teaspoons curry powder
1 teaspoon salt
⅛ teaspoon pepper
1 cup chopped celery
1 tart apple, peeled and chopped
Boiling water

Cut lamb into 1-inch pieces. Heat oil in large skillet, add onion and garlic, and cook until onion is lightly browned. Remove and discard garlic. Add curry powder, salt and pepper; cook 5 minutes. Add lamb, celery, apple and enough boiling water to cover. Mix well. Cover and simmer 30 minutes or until lamb is tender. Serve with rice and assorted condiments such as chutney, raisins, coconut and peanuts. Makes 6 servings.

Variety Meats

Pan-fried Calf Liver

1 pound calf liver, sliced ½-inch thick
½ cup flour
1 teaspoon salt
⅛ teaspoon pepper
2 tablespoons fat or bacon drippings

Roll each slice of liver in flour, seasoned with salt and pepper. Melt fat in skillet. Turn heat to moderate, and brown liver on each side, about 2 minutes. Makes 4 servings.

NOTE: Pan broil lamb or pork liver for one minute before pan frying as directed above. Liver combines well with crisp, fried bacon or fried onion rings.

Broiled Liver

1½ pounds calf or   ¼ teaspoon salt
   lamb liver   ¼ teaspoon celery salt
2 tablespoons salad oil   ½ teaspoon grated onion
1 tablespoon vinegar

Cut liver into slices ½ to ¾-inch thick. Mix remaining ingredients. Add liver slices, turning until thoroughly coated. Cover and refrigerate 30 minutes. Drain excess liquid, place liver on greased broiler and broil 4 inches from heat about 5 minutes, turning to brown both sides. Makes 4 to 6 servings.

Liver Western Style

1 small onion, sliced   ¾ teaspoon salt
1 pound beef liver, sliced ¼ teaspoon pepper
2 slices bacon   ½ cup tomato juice

Line oblong baking dish with large sheet of aluminum foil. Arrange a layer of onion slices on foil and over them place the liver. Top with bacon strips, season with salt and pepper, and pour tomato juice over all. Fold over the aluminum foil to cover the dish and bake in moderate oven (350°F.) 40 minutes. Open aluminum foil during last 10 minutes of baking to brown the liver and crisp the bacon. Makes 4 servings.

Liver Patties

1 pound liver   1 egg, beaten
1 cup salted water   1 teaspoon salt
1 small onion, chopped   ⅛ teaspoon pepper
1 cup dry bread crumbs   ¼ teaspoon paprika
½ cup milk   3 tablespoons fat

Simmer liver in salted water until tender. Put through food chopper, and combine with remaining ingredients except fat. Form into patties and cook in fat until brown on both sides and cooked through. Serve with Quick Tomato Sauce, page 233. Makes 4 servings.

Liver Loaf

1½ pounds liver, sliced	1 teaspoon Worcester-
2 tablespoons bacon fat	shire sauce
1 small onion	¾ teaspoon salt
¾ cup milk	⅛ teaspoon pepper
2 cups soft bread crumbs	¼ cup chopped parsley
2 eggs, beaten	

Cook liver in fat about 5 minutes. Cool. Remove skin and any tough membranes, and put liver and onion through a food chopper. Add remaining ingredients and drippings in which the liver was cooked. Mix well and press into a greased loaf pan lined with wax paper. Bake in moderate oven (350°F.) about 1 hour. Turn out of pan, remove wax paper and serve hot or cold. Makes 6 servings.

Beef Kidney with Brown Rice

1 beef kidney	2 tablespoons bacon fat
¼ cup flour	1½ cups boiling water
¾ teaspoon salt	3 cups cooked brown
⅛ teaspoon pepper	rice

Cut kidney into small cubes, discarding fat and connective tissue. Coat with flour, seasoned with salt and pepper. Melt fat in skillet, add floured kidney cubes and sauté over medium heat, stirring constantly until well browned, about 10 minutes. Add the water and continue stirring until gravy thickens and bubbles. Simmer 5 minutes. Serve on rice. Makes 4 servings.

Baked Beef Heart

1 beef heart	1 onion, diced
Salt	2 tablespoons diced
2 tablespoons fat or	celery
salad oil	1 cup canned tomatoes,
2 cups soft bread crumbs	strained
½ teaspoon salt	Flour
⅛ teaspoon pepper	1½ cups tomato juice

Wash heart and remove any tough membranes. Sprinkle the inside with salt. Add melted fat or salad oil to bread crumbs. Add seasonings, onion, celery and tomatoes. Mix well and fill heart. Sew opening. Roll in flour and brown in heavy kettle or Dutch oven in a small amount of fat. Add tomato juice. Cover and cook slowly for 3 to 3½ hours. Makes 4 servings.

English Steak and Kidney Pie

1½ pounds beef steak,	1 teaspoon salt
chuck or round	⅛ teaspoon pepper
1 beef kidney	2 cups boiling water
¼ cup flour	½ recipe Pastry, page 196

Cut steak and kidney into 1-inch cubes, discarding fat and connective tissue. Combine flour, salt and pepper. Toss meat in the seasoned flour to coat each piece as evenly as possible. Put the floured meat in a saucepan, barely cover with boiling water and simmer for 45 minutes. Pour into 2-quart casserole and allow to cool. Roll out the pastry ¼-inch thick (about twice as thick as for ordinary crust). Place an inverted egg cup in the center to support the crust, or, if the pastry is to rest directly on the meat, pour off a little gravy to reheat and serve separately. Dampen the edges of the casserole and press the pastry down. Make rose and leaf trimmings from pastry scraps. Moisten lightly

and arrange on the top. Brush with beaten egg, if desired. Bake
in hot oven (425°F.) 45 minutes. Makes 6 servings.

Baked Tongue with Raisin Sauce

3½ pounds smoked tongue	¼ teaspoon salt
½ cup water	¼ teaspoon cinnamon
½ cup sugar	⅛ teaspoon ground
½ cup raisins	cloves
2 tablespoons butter	½ cup tart jelly
1 tablespoon vinegar	1 teaspoon cornstarch

Cover tongue with boiling water; simmer 3 hours or until tender.
Remove from heat; let cool in liquid in kettle. Remove skin and
fat from tongue; place in greased baking dish. Cook water and
sugar together 5 minutes. Add raisins, butter, vinegar, salt,
spices and jelly. Mix well; bring to a boil. Dissolve cornstarch in
a little of the hot sauce and add. Stir until sauce thickens slightly.
Pour sauce over tongue. Cover and bake in moderate oven
(350°F.) 30 minutes. Makes 6 to 8 servings.

Broiled Sweetbreads

Wash 3 pairs of sweetbreads in cold water. Cover with 1 quart
boiling water, and add 1 tablespoon vinegar and 1 teaspoon salt.
Bring to a boil, cover and simmer 15 minutes. Drain, plunge in
cold water, drain, and remove fat, membrane and tubes. Dry and
split in halves lengthwise. Brush with melted butter, sprinkle
with salt and pepper, and broil about 10 minutes, until golden
brown, turning occasionally. Serve on toast. Makes 6 servings.

Sautéed Brains

Wash 1½ pounds veal, lamb or pork brains in cold water. Soak
½ hour in cold water to which 1 tablespoon of salt has been

added. Drain and remove membranes. Cover with boiling water and add 1 teaspoon salt and 1 tablespoon lemon juice or vinegar. Let come to a boil, cover and simmer 15 to 20 minutes, until tender. Drain, drop in cold water and drain again. Dry brains and dredge with seasoned flour. Sauté in butter or margarine until golden brown on both sides. Makes 6 servings.

Scrambled Brains and Eggs

Prepare brains as in recipe above up to dredging with seasoned flour. Chop fine; sauté in butter or margarine. Combine 4 well-beaten eggs with ¾ teaspoon salt and ⅛ teaspoon pepper, and pour over brain mixture. Cook slowly, stirring only to scramble. Serve on hot buttered toast. Makes 6 servings.

Poultry

ROAST POULTRY TIMETABLE

ROASTS	WEIGHT	APPROX. TOTAL TIME FOR STUFFED BIRD AT 325°F.
Chicken, Roaster	2½ to 4½ lbs.	2 to 3½ hrs.
Capon	4 to 8 lbs.	2½ to 3½ hrs.
Turkey	6 to 8 lbs.	3 to 3½ hrs.
Turkey	8 to 12 lbs.	3½ to 4½ hrs.
Turkey	12 to 16 lbs.	4½ to 5½ hrs.
Duckling	4 to 5 lbs.	2 to 3 hrs.
Goose	6 to 8 lbs.	3 to 3½ hrs.
Goose	10 to 12 lbs.	3¾ to 4¼ hrs.

Stuffed Roast Chicken

1 roasting chicken, up to 5 pounds	¼ cup chopped green pepper
½ teaspoon salt	½ cup chopped celery
1 quart soft bread crumbs	1 teaspoon salt
¼ cup finely chopped onion	⅛ teaspoon pepper
⅓ cup melted butter	½ tablespoon poultry seasoning

Wash, clean and dry chicken. Rub inside with ½ teaspoon salt. Combine remaining ingredients to make stuffing. Stuff neck region and cavity. Fasten neck skin to back with skewer or poultry pins. Bring tips of wings onto the back. Tie legs together and fasten securely to the tail. Place breast-side up on rack in open roasting pan. Brush bird thoroughly with melted butter and sprinkle with salt, pepper and paprika. Cover with a cloth dipped in melted butter, or place foil, tent fashion, over the chicken, allowing it to remain loose so heat can circulate around it. Roast in slow oven (325°F.) 2½ to 3 hours. To test for doneness, grasp the end of the leg bone. If bird is done the drumstick thigh joint will break or move easily and drumstick meat will be very soft when pressed between fingers. Do not pierce meat with a fork. Serve with gravy made from juice in pan.

Fried Chicken

1 cup flour	2 broiler-fryers, 2½ to 3 pounds each, cut into serving pieces
1½ teaspoons salt	
1 teaspoon pepper	
1½ teaspoons paprika	Fat for frying

Combine flour, salt, pepper and paprika in a paper bag. Wash and dry chicken pieces. Drop into paper bag and shake until chicken is coated with flour mixture. Heat fat in heavy frying pan, using enough so it is ½ to ¾ inch in depth when melted. Brown chicken pieces well at moderate heat, turning frequently until golden brown. Cover and cook over low heat until chicken is tender, about 35 to 50 minutes. For crisp-coated chicken, place uncovered in moderate oven (350°F.) for last 15 minutes of cooking. Remove chicken and keep it warm while making gravy from the drippings. Makes 6 servings.

Oven-baked Chicken Maryland

1 broiler-fryer, 3 pounds, cut into serving pieces
½ cup fine dry bread crumbs
1 teaspoon salt
⅛ teaspoon pepper
1 egg

1 tablespoon water
½ cup butter or margarine
¼ cup fat from baking pan
¼ cup flour
2 cups hot milk
½ cup chopped parsley

Dip each piece of chicken into bread crumbs that have been combined with salt and pepper. Shake off loose crumbs. Then dip into egg beaten with water. Drain chicken and redip in bread crumbs. Place pieces of chicken in well-greased casserole or baking pan. Bake, uncovered, in moderate oven (350°F.) 45 to 60 minutes or until tender. Baste frequently with butter. Remove chicken, and make a gravy of the fat left in baking pan, flour and hot milk. Season to taste and add parsley. Serve over chicken. Makes 4 servings.

 Take the work out of blending flour and water or milk for gravy by putting liquid in small jar, adding flour and shaking until smooth.

Broiled Chicken with Barbecue Sauce

¼ cup salad oil, melted
   butter or margarine
1 clove garlic
1 teaspoon salt
⅛ teaspoon pepper
2 tablespoons vinegar
2 tablespoons Worcester-
   shire sauce

1 medium onion,
   grated
1 bay leaf
¾ cup catsup
¾ cup water
1 broiler-fryer, 3½ to
   4 pounds, cut into
   pieces

Mix all ingredients except chicken in saucepan; bring to a boil and simmer 5 minutes. Remove garlic and bay leaf. Arrange chicken on ovenproof platter or baking pan without a rack, skin side down. Pour sauce over chicken. Broil under low to medium heat 45 minutes to 1 hour, basting frequently with sauce and turning pieces of chicken as they brown. Makes 4 to 6 servings.

Braised Chicken in Giblet Gravy

1 broiler-fryer, 3½ to 4
   pounds, cut into
   serving pieces
½ cup seasoned flour
3 tablespoons fat
½ cup chopped onion
2 cups boiling water
1 teaspoon salt

¾ teaspoon monosodium
   glutamate
Chicken giblets
3 carrots, diced
Milk
¼ cup flour
6 tablespoons cold water
Salt and pepper

Roll chicken pieces in seasoned flour; brown on all sides in hot fat. Add onion and brown lightly. Place chicken in baking pan; add onion, water, salt and ½ teaspoon monosodium glutamate. Cover and bake in moderate oven (350°F.) 1½ hours. Meanwhile, cook giblets and carrots; drain and reserve broth; chop giblets. When chicken is done, remove to platter and keep warm. Measure liquid in baking pan; add giblet broth and enough milk to make 3 cups. Blend flour and cold water to a smooth paste. Add to liquid with remaining ¼ teaspoon monosodium glutamate. Stir over low heat until thickened. Add giblets and carrots. Season to taste. Serve with chicken. Makes 6 servings.

Chicken in the Pot

1 stewing chicken, 4 to 5 pounds, cut into serving pieces	⅛ teaspoon pepper
½ cup diced celery	1½ quarts hot water
1 bay leaf	12 small white onions
1 tablespoon salt	6 young whole carrots
	6 medium whole potatoes

Place chicken pieces in covered kettle or Dutch oven with celery, bay leaf, salt, pepper and hot water. Simmer, covered, 3 to 4 hours or until tender, adding more water if necessary. One hour before fowl is done, add onions and potatoes. Half an hour later, add carrots. When chicken is tender, drop Dumplings, below, by teaspoonfuls on top of chicken and vegetables. Cook dumplings as directed. Serve immediately. Makes 6 servings.

Dumplings

2 cups sifted flour	3 tablespoons shortening
3 teaspoons baking powder	1 cup milk
1 teaspoon salt	

Sift together first three ingredients, blend in shortening, add milk, and mix quickly and lightly. Drop by teaspoonfuls onto boiling stew, soup, etc., and cook 12 to 15 minutes, covered. Makes 6 servings.

NOTE: If the spoon used for add'ng dumplings is dipped into

the hot liquid each time a dumpling is dropped, the batter will not stick to it.

Water Cress Dumplings

Follow basic recipe for Dumplings, folding in 1 cup chopped, fresh water cress after adding milk.

Chicken à la King

2 tablespoons butter or margarine

½ pound fresh mushrooms, washed and sliced

¼ cup chopped green pepper

2 cups Medium White Sauce, page 231

2 cups diced, cooked chicken

3 tablespoons chopped pimiento

½ cup light cream or dairy half-and-half

1. Heat butter in skillet; add mushrooms and green pepper, and sauté over medium heat 10 minutes, stirring occasionally.
2. Make 2 cups Medium White Sauce in a large saucepan, using 1 cup chicken broth or 1 chicken bouillon cube dissolved in 1 cup boiling water for half the liquid.
3. Add chicken, pimiento, cream, mushrooms and green pepper to sauce; reheat, stirring constantly.
4. Serve in pastry shells or on crisp toast, boiled noodles or rice, hot biscuits or waffles.

Makes 6 servings.

Sautéed Poultry Livers

Sauté chicken livers in butter 10 minutes or until pink color inside disappears, turning to brown evenly. Or fry bacon in a skillet, then remove and sauté livers in bacon drippings.

Baked Chicken Croquettes

1 cup cold Thick White
  Sauce, page 231
2 cups ground, leftover,
  cooked chicken
2 teaspoons minced onion
1 teaspoon minced parsley

½ teaspoon salt
⅛ teaspoon pepper
1 egg, well beaten with
  1 tablespoon water
1 cup fine dry bread
  crumbs

Place sauce in a mixing bowl and add chicken, onion, parsley, salt and pepper. Shape the mixture into flat patties. Dip into the egg-water mixture and coat with bread crumbs. Refrigerate for about 1 hour to dry the coating. Bake in a greased pan in hot oven (400°F.) until browned on the bottom, about 10 minutes; then turn to brown on other side. Makes 4 to 6 servings.

Roast Turkey

Most turkeys today, large or small, are sold either of two convenient ways: ready-to-cook, fresh, or ready-to-cook, fresh frozen. When buying birds of 12 pounds or more, allow ½ to ¾ pounds (ready-to-cook weight) per serving. When buying turkeys under 12 pounds, allow ¾ to 1 pound per serving.

Find out drawn weight of bird for figuring roasting time and amount of stuffing required.

Thawing and Storage

Fresh chilled turkey can be held 5 to 6 days in the coldest part of the refrigerator. Make sure wrappings are loose enough to allow circulation. Remove giblets, cook promptly; chill.

Turkeys frozen with neck and giblets inside the body and neck cavities need to be thawed before cooking. Then remove neck and giblets, cook them promptly; refrigerate.

a) *Thawing in refrigerator*—place turkey, in its original wrap on tray or drip pan in refrigerator. b) *Thawing in water*—place turkey, in its original wrap, in sink covered with cool or cold water. Change water often to hasten thawing. *c*) *Thawing at room temperature*—leave in original wrap and place frozen turkey in brown paper bag, or wrap in 2 or 3 layers of newspapers. Place on tray or in baking pan and allow to thaw until turkey is pliable and giblets can be removed easily. Roast turkey immediately.

TIMETABLES FOR THAWING

Pounds	Refrigerator	Cool Water	Room Temp.
4 to 8	1 to 1½ days	3 to 4 hours	6 to 8 hours
8 to 12	1½ to 2 days	4 to 6 hours	8 to 12 hours
12 to 16	2 to 2½ days	6 to 7 hours	12 to 14 hours
16 to 20	2½ to 3 days	7 to 8 hours	14 to 16 hours
20 to 24	3 to 3½ days	8 to 10 hours	16 to 18 hours

Stuffing and Trussing

1. Make stuffing (pages 184 to 186), allowing 1 cup stuffing per pound, ready-to-cook weight.
2. Rinse and dry body cavity; stuff loosely stuffing expands during roasting. Skewer body opening; lace with string. Or sew together.
3. Stuff neck loosely. Pull neck skin to back and secure with skewer, or sew with strong thread.
4. Slip wing tips behind upper part of wing, so they're against bird. Tie ends of legs together with string. Then, drawing legs down toward tail, tie them to tail firmly.

Roasting

1. Place bird, breast side up, on rack in uncovered shallow roasting pan. Or use broiler pan.
2. Rub bird all over with melted fat or salad oil. If a roast meat thermometer is to be used, insert so that bulb is in center of the inside thigh muscle or thickest part of the breast meat. Be sure bulb does not touch bone.
3. Cover top and sides of bird with a piece of clean cloth, well moistened with melted fat, or a loose cap of aluminum foil.
4. Roast at 325°F., without adding water, until thermometer reaches 185°F. See Timetable, page 176.

5. If cloth becomes dry during roasting, moisten with drippings from bottom of pan.

6. About ½ hour before end of roasting time, test turkey for doneness. Turkey is done if thigh joint gives readily when end of leg is moved up and down, and if drumstick meat is very soft when pressed between protected fingers.

7. When turkey is done, remove skewers and string. Place bird on a hot platter and keep warm until serving time.

8. Make gravy, using drippings from roasting pan.

NOTE: Plan to have the turkey done 40 minutes before dinner is scheduled—to allow extra roasting time in case turkey is not quite done and to free oven for other foods that require baking. Also, turkey slices better on standing.

Roast Long Island Duckling with Rice and Mushroom Stuffing

1 ready-to-cook duckling   ¼ cup honey
   4 to 5 pounds, thawed   2 teaspoons bottled brown
   if bought frozen   bouquet sauce
1 quart Stuffing (page 185)

Remove giblets and neck from frozen duckling. Wash thoroughly in cold water, drain and pat dry. Cook giblets and neck in 3 cups boiling salted water until tender, about 45 minutes. Drain broth and reserve for gravy. Prepare stuffing and add chopped giblets. Stuff duckling. Fasten vent opening by lacing string around poultry pins. Place duck breast side up on rack in open roasting pan not more than 3 inches deep. Roast in slow oven (325°F.) 2½ to 3 hours or until drumstick meat is soft when pressed between fingers. To glaze duckling, drain or spoon drippings down to the brown meat juices. Increase oven temperature to 400°F. Brush duckling all over with a mixture of the honey and bottled brown bouquet sauce. Continue roasting until nicely glazed, 15 to 30 minutes. Remove from oven, remove vent lacings and place duckling on preheated serving platter. Makes 4 to 5 servings.

Rice and Mushroom Stuffing

¼ cup finely chopped onion	1 teaspoon poultry
1 cup sliced mushrooms	seasoning
6 tablespoons butter	1 teaspoon salt
3 cups cooked rice (brown, white or wild)	⅛ teaspoon pepper

Sauté onion and mushrooms in butter in skillet until onion is tender. Add rice and seasonings. Makes 1 quart stuffing.

Bread and Onion Stuffing

1½ cups butter	3 quarts cubed, day-old
1 cup finely chopped onion	bread
2 teaspoons salt	1½ cups hot water or bouillon
¼ teaspoon pepper	¼ cup buttered bread
2 teaspoons poultry seasoning	crumbs or slivered almonds

1. Melt ¼ cup butter in a large skillet.
2. Add onion and sauté until yellow but not brown.
3. Add remaining butter and stir in seasonings.
4. Add half of bread (cut in ½-inch cubes) and cook about 4 minutes, stirring constantly.
5. Combine with rest of bread cubes in a large mixing bowl.
6. Sprinkle hot water or bouillon over mixture, tossing until well blended. Pile lightly into poultry.
7. Shape the remaining dressing into small balls, adding more liquid if necessary to hold together. Roll in crumbs or almonds and bake along with the poultry for the last 20 minutes.

Makes enough stuffing to fill a 12-pound turkey with enough left over to make 10 dressing balls to adorn the turkey platter.

Variations of Bread and Onion Stuffing

Celery: Add 2 cups chopped celery, parboiled or uncooked.
Chestnut: Add 1 pound chestnuts, cooked and chopped.
Mushroom: Add ¼ to ½ pound mushrooms that have been sautéed in butter. Or add a small can of sliced mushrooms.
Oyster: Add 1 pint chopped oysters heated in a little butter.
Sausage: Add a few cooked and cubed pork sausages.
Prune: Add 2 cups unsweetened prunes, pitted and chopped.
Raisin and Apple: Soak 1 cup raisins and drain. Combine with 1 cup diced, unpeeled apple and add to stuffing.

 Ready-seasoned prepared stuffing mixes make quick work of preparing the bird for the oven. Just moisten and mix as directed.

Fish

A dash of color, a contrasting flavor, can turn a plain fish dish into an attractive and appetizing one. Choose from among these colorful garnishes: Carrot curls, sliced cucumbers, green pepper rings, hard-cooked eggs, lemon wedges, paprika, pickle fans, pimiento, radish roses and water cress.

Sautéed Fish

2 pounds fish fillets, steaks
   or small whole fish
1 egg
2 tablespoons water

½ cup bread or cracker
   crumbs or corn meal
1 teaspoon salt
¼ cup hot fat or salad oil

Cut fillets into individual portions. Dip into egg beaten with water, then into crumbs or corn meal combined with salt. Brown in fat 2 to 3 minutes or until golden brown. Turn and sauté 2 to 3 minutes more. Drain on absorbent paper and serve immediately. Makes 6 servings.

Baked Stuffed Fish

1 fish, 3 to 4 pounds,
   dressed
1½ teaspoons salt

½ recipe for Rice and
   Mushroom Stuffing
¼ cup melted butter

Clean, wash and dry fish. Sprinkle inside and out with salt. Stuff fish loosely with Rice Stuffing, and sew opening with needle and string or close with skewers. Place fish in greased baking dish. Brush with butter. Bake in moderate oven (350°F.) 40 to 60 minutes or until fish flakes easily from the bone when tested with a fork. Baste occasionally with drippings or melted butter. Remove string or skewers and serve immediately on a hot platter, plain or with a sauce. Makes 6 servings.

Baked Fish Fillets with Dressing

1 pound fish fillets
Salt and pepper
¼ cup butter or
   margarine

1 small onion, sliced
2 cups dry bread crumbs
½ teaspoon mixed poultry
   seasoning

Place fillets in a greased baking dish lined with foil, and sprinkle with salt and pepper. Melt butter and in it sauté onion until slightly yellow. Remove from heat and add bread crumbs and poultry seasoning. Blend well. Spread dressing over the fillets. Cover with foil and bake in moderate oven (350°F.) 20 to 30 minutes. Remove foil cover for last 10 minutes of baking to brown dressing. Serve fish from dish in which it is baked. Makes 4 servings.

Fish Fillets Baked in Mushroom Cheese Sauce

1½ pounds fish fillets
  1 can condensed cream
     of mushroom soup
 ½ onion, grated

½ cup shredded Cheddar
   cheese
2 tablespoons crushed
   corn flakes

Arrange fillets in greased baking dish. Heat soup. Remove from heat, add onion and blend in cheese. Pour sauce over fillets and sprinkle with corn flakes. Bake in moderate oven (350°F.) until tender, 15 to 30 minutes. Makes 5 to 6 servings.

 Give fish fillets a piquant flavor by brushing with French dressing before broiling. Use mayonnaise to brush swordfish.

Fillets of Sole Amandine

2 pounds fillets of sole
½ cup flour
½ teaspoon salt
⅛ teaspoon paprika

Butter or margarine
¼ cup slivered blanched
    almonds
Lemon and parsley

Dip fish in flour seasoned with the salt and paprika. Melt enough butter in skillet to cover bottom well; sauté fish until a delicate brown, turning once. Remove fish to hot platter. Melt additional butter in skillet, brown almonds lightly and pour over fish. Garnish with lemon and parsley. Makes 6 servings.

NOTE: Other fish fillets may be prepared the same way.

Flaked Fish Ring

2 pounds cooked fish
2 eggs, beaten
½ cup tomato juice
1½ cups soft bread
    crumbs
1 teaspoon salt

½ teaspoon pepper
2 tablespoons lemon
    juice
¼ cup parsley, minced
3 tablespoons chopped
    celery

Flake fish. Mix in remaining ingredients. Place mixture in buttered 8 or 9-inch ring mold and bake in hot oven (400°F.) 30 minutes. Run a knife around edge and turn out on platter. Fill center with cooked broccoli or other green vegetable. Top with hard-cooked egg slices or with a sprinkling of grated egg yolk. Circle ring with greens. Makes 6 servings.

 Flake leftover cooked fish to mix with cooked rice, and chopped celery and onion, to stuff tomatoes. Serve cold or baked.

Tuna or Salmon Loaf

2 cups tuna or salmon,   ½ cup chopped green
   flaked   pepper
2 teaspoons lemon juice   1 tomato, finely chopped
1 cup bread crumbs   ½ teaspoon salt
1 egg, beaten   ⅛ teaspoon pepper
¼ cup butter or margarine   ¼ teaspoon tarragon
½ onion, minced

Mix tuna or salmon with lemon juice; add bread crumbs and egg, and mix. Melt butter in saucepan over low heat; sauté onion, pepper and tomato until lightly browned. Add with seasonings to fish mixture; mix well. Bake in greased 9 x 5 x 3-inch loaf pan in moderate oven (375°F.) about 40 minutes. Makes 6 servings.

Salmon Rice Patties

1 can (7¾ ozs.) salmon   2 tablespoons chopped
2 cups cooked rice   parsley
1 egg   2 tablespoons flour
1 tablespoon lemon juice   ½ teaspoon salt
2 tablespoons finely   Dash of pepper
   chopped scallions   Bread crumbs

Remove skin and bones from salmon; flake salmon. Combine salmon with rice. Beat egg slightly, and add lemon juice, scallions, parsley, flour, salt and pepper. Mix well. Combine with salmon-rice mixture. Form into 8 patties, coat with crumbs and place in a greased baking pan. Bake in moderate oven (350°F.) 30 minutes or until golden brown. Makes 4 to 6 servings.

Shellfish

Fried Oysters

1 egg, beaten	1½ pints oysters, drained
⅛ teaspoon salt	¾ cup fine bread crumbs
Dash of pepper	or cracker crumbs
1 tablespoon cold water	Fat for frying

Combine egg, seasonings and cold water. Dip oysters in egg mixture and roll in crumbs. Sauté in skillet in about ¼ inch hot fat, turning to brown on both sides. Serve with Tartare Sauce, page 234. Makes 4 servings.

Oysters in Patty Shells

1 Single-crust Pie Pastry	1½ pints oysters, drained
page 196	½ cup chopped, raw
2 cups Thick White	celery
Sauce, page 231	6 patty shells

Prepare pie crust and roll lightly to ⅛-inch thickness. Cut out six 5-inch rounds. Fit each round over the back of a muffin tin and prick all over with a fork. Bake in very hot oven (450°F.) 10 minutes or until lightly browned. Cool slightly before removing from tins and allow to cool further while preparing creamed oyster filling. Make 2 cups White Sauce, using liquid drained from oysters as part of liquid. When sauce thickens and boils, add oysters and celery. Cook slowly until edges of the oysters curl, about 4 minutes. Pour into patty shells and garnish with a sprig of parsley or stuffed olive slices. Makes 6 servings.

Scalloped Oysters

2 cups coarse cracker
   crumbs
¼ cup melted butter or
   margarine
1 pint oysters, drained
¼ cup oyster liquid

½ teaspoon salt
Dash of pepper
½ cup milk
1 teaspoon Worcester-
   shire sauce

Combine crumbs and butter. Put a layer of crumbs in the bottom of a greased baking dish. Arrange alternate layers of oysters and crumb mixture, reserving 2 tablespoons crumbs for topping. Combine oyster liquid with remaining ingredients and pour over all. Top with reserved crumbs. Bake in hot oven (425°F.) 30 minutes. Makes 4 servings.

Panned Scallops

1½ pounds scallops
½ cup fine, dry bread
   crumbs
¼ teaspoon salt
⅛ teaspoon white pepper
   Dash of paprika

½ cup butter
3 tablespoons lemon juice
2 teaspoons minced parsley
3 slices buttered toast,
   cut diagonally into 6
   pieces

Roll scallops in bread crumbs seasoned with the salt, pepper and paprika. Melt ¼ cup of the butter in a large skillet and sauté scallops about 10 minutes, turning often until golden brown. Remove scallops to hot serving platter. Add remaining ¼ cup butter to skillet and, when melted, stir in lemon juice and parsley; pour over scallops. Arrange toast triangles around scallops and garnish with parsley sprigs. Makes 4 to 6 servings.

Steamed Clams

6 dozen clams   1 cup boiling water

Scrub clams thoroughly to remove sand from shells. Place in a large kettle and add water. Cover tightly and simmer 10 minutes or until shells open. Remove clams to a hot platter and serve with individual dishes of melted butter to which lemon juice has been added. Makes 6 servings.

Shrimp Creole

3 strips bacon
2 medium onions, sliced
1 green pepper, cut in
   rings
½ cup diced celery
1 can (1 lb. 13 ozs.)
   tomatoes

1 teaspoon salt
1 cup cooked green peas
2 cans (4½ to 5 ozs. each)
   cleaned and deveined
   shrimp
1 teaspoon chili powder
3 cups hot boiled rice

Cook bacon until crisp. Remove from skillet and break into ¼-inch pieces. Sauté onions in bacon fat until tender. Add green pepper, celery, tomatoes and salt. Cook until vegetables are tender and sauce thickens, about 15 minutes. Add peas, shrimp and chili powder, and cook 5 minutes longer. Add the cooked bacon. Pack rice into a greased 9-inch tube pan. Carefully turn rice out on a serving platter. Pour sauce in center and around the ring. Makes 6 servings.

 Saltwater fish and shellfish are good sources of iodine as well as protein and therefore should be served at least once a week.

Shrimp Wiggle

¼ cup butter or
   margarine
2 tablespoons flour
1¼ cups milk

1 cup cooked shrimp
1 cup cooked peas
⅛ teaspoon paprika
⅛ teaspoon celery salt

Melt butter. Stir in flour until blended. Add milk gradually; bring to boil, stirring constantly. Add shrimp, peas and seasonings. Serve hot on crackers or toast. Makes 4 to 6 servings.

Lobster Newburg

2 cups Thin White Sauce
2 egg yolks, slightly beaten
2 cans (6½ ozs. each)
   lobster meat or 2½
   cups cooked fresh
   lobster meat

¼ cup cooking sherry,
   optional
2 teaspoons lemon juice
¼ teaspoon salt

1. Make the white sauce in top of double boiler over direct heat.
2. Add a little of the sauce to egg yolks, then stir into hot sauce; place over boiling water and cook 5 minutes, stirring.
3. Add lobster, cut into pieces, sherry, lemon juice and salt, and reheat over boiling water.
4. Serve on crisp toast or boiled rice, or in patty shells.
Makes 6 servings.

NOTE: A true Newburg uses sherry. If sherry is omitted, add a little milk to thin sauce to desired consistency.

Variation of Lobster Newburg

Shrimp Newburg: Follow basic recipe for Lobster Newburg using 2 cans (4½ to 5 ozs. each) shrimp or 2½ cups cleaned, cooked fresh shrimp.

Pastry and Pies

Every cook dreams of being able to turn out tender, flaky pie crusts every time. And so she tries very hard, too hard probably, for the secret of good pastry lies in a light, swift touch. Easy does it.

While pies are generally considered too rich for young children, there's no reason why dad and the older children should be deprived of pie, be it delectable cherry or coconut cream. Some of the filling can always be reserved for the toddler's dessert; a few graham cracker or cereal crumbs sprinkled on top will make it seem like grown-up pie.

Oven temperatures are very important in pie baking. Follow instructions to the degree and the minute for best results.

 Use leftover scraps of pastry to make jelly tarts for the children. Better yet, let them make their own.

195

Pastry

2¼ cups sifted flour	5 to 6 tablespoons cold
1 teaspoon salt	water
¾ cup shortening	

1. Sift together flour and salt into a mixing bowl; add shortening.
2. With pastry blender or two knives, cut shortening into flour until all particles are the size of rice grains.
3. Sprinkle cold water over the mixture, a little at a time, pressing dampened particles together with a fork.
4. Continue until all flour is dampened, using just enough water to form a dough which leaves the sides of the bowl clean.
5. Turn dough out onto wax paper and form into a ball; divide into two equal portions (for upper and lower crusts).
6. Wrap in wax paper and chill in refrigerator at least ½ hour before rolling as directed below.

Makes enough pastry for 1 double-crust 8 or 9-inch pie or 2 single-crust pies.

Double-crust Pie

1. Roll out half the pastry into a round, ⅛-inch thick, on lightly floured board or pastry cloth. Roll outward from the center, using short, light strokes of the rolling pin.
2. Loosen pastry from board with spatula; fold in half. Lift onto pie pan, placing fold across center of pan.
3. Unfold pastry and ease it snugly into bottom and around sides of pan. Do not stretch pastry. Trim off edges under outer rim of pan with sharp knife or kitchen shears.
4. Fill with desired filling.
5. Roll out other half of pastry into a round, ⅛-inch thick; gash in several places (to let steam escape during baking).
6. Moisten rim of lower crust with water; transfer upper crust to filled pie, pressing to lower crust all around rim.

7. Trim off upper crust ½ inch beyond edge of pie pan; turn edges under and press together firmly with tines of a fork or crimp into a high-standing edge between thumb and finger of one hand and forefinger of the other.
8. Bake as directed in pie recipe.

Single-crust Pie

1. Make half the pastry recipe on page 196 and follow Steps 1, 2, and 3 for Double-crust Pie.
2. Trim off pastry 1 *inch beyond* edge of pie pan all around.
3. Turn overhanging pastry under and crimp into a high-standing edge between thumb and finger of one hand and forefinger of the other.
4. Fill and bake as directed in pie recipe.

Baked Pie Shell

1. Make half the pastry recipe on page 196 and follow Steps 1, 2 and 3 for Double-crust Pie, taking special care not to stretch pastry.
2. Trim off pastry 1 *inch beyond* edge of pie pan all around.
3. Turn overhanging pastry under and crimp into a high-standing edge between thumb and finger of one hand and forefinger of the other.
4. Prick surface of pastry with a fork to remove air bubbles.
5. Bake in very hot oven (450°F.) 12 to 15 minutes or until lightly browned.
6. Cool; then fill as directed in pie recipe.

Lattice-top Pie

1. Roll out half of pastry following Steps 1, 2 and 3 for Double-crust Pie.
2. Trim off pastry 1 *inch beyond* edge of pie pan all around.
3. Fill with desired filling.
4. Roll out other half of pastry into a rectangle about 9 x 6 inches;

cut lengthwise strips about ½-inch wide with a sharp knife.
5. Moisten rim of lower crust with water. Place 4 or 5 pastry strips parallel to each other and about 1 inch apart across top of pie; arrange remaining strips at right angles to the first.
6. Trim strips even with edge of lower crust; press strips to rim of lower crust firmly. Turn edges under all around and crimp into a high-standing edge.
7. Bake as directed in pie recipe.

Tart Shells

1. Roll out full recipe Pastry ⅛-inch thick on floured board or pastry cloth.
2. Cut into rounds with floured 4-inch cutter, or cut around a 4-inch circle of cardboard with a sharp, pointed knife.
3. Lift rounds from board with spatula and shape snugly over backs of 3-inch muffin tins, trimming to fit.
4. Prick entire surface of pastry with a fork to remove air bubbles.
5. Bake, pastry side up, on the muffin tins in very hot oven (450°F.) 12 to 15 minutes or until lightly browned.
6. Cool; then fill with desired filling.

Makes 12 tart shells.

Pastry Snacks

Roll pastry trimmings ⅛-inch thick. Sprinkle with sugar and cinnamon; fold in half with sugar mixture inside, and roll again to ⅛-inch thickness. Cut as desired; bake in very hot oven (450°F.) 12 to 15 minutes.

Stir and Roll Pastry

2 cups sifted flour   ½ cup salad oil
1½ teaspoons salt   ¼ cup cold milk

1. Sift together flour and salt.
2. Pour salad oil and milk into measuring cup, but do not stir.
3. Pour oil and milk all at once into flour mixture.
4. Stir lightly until mixed and form dough into a ball; divide into two equal portions (for upper and lower crusts).
5. Wrap in wax paper and chill in refrigerator at least ½ hour before rolling.
6. Roll out pastry between two 12-inch squares of wax paper. Peel off top paper. Gently ease and fit pastry (with paper side up) into 8 or 9-inch pie pan. Carefully peel off paper.
7. Bake as directed in pie recipe.

Makes enough pastry for one double-crust 8 or 9-inch pie.

Graham Cracker Crumb Pie Crust

1⅔ cups fine graham   ¼ cup softened butter or
    cracker crumbs   margarine
    (about 20 crackers)   ½ teaspoon cinnamon
¼ cup sugar   (optional)

1. Combine all ingredients.
2. Put crumb mixture into a 9-inch pie plate.
3. Set an 8-inch pie plate on top of crumbs and press them firmly into an even layer on bottom and sides of plate.
4. Bake in moderate oven (375°F.) about 8 minutes.

Variations of Graham Cracker Crumb Pie Crust

Vanilla Wafer Crumb Pie Crust: Follow basic recipe for Graham Cracker Crumb Pie Crust substituting 1⅓ cups fine vanilla wafer crumbs for 1⅔ cups graham cracker crumbs.

Cereal Crumb Pie Crust: Follow basic recipe, substituting 1¼ cups finely crushed cereal flakes for graham cracker crumbs and increasing shortening to ⅓ cup.

Apple Pie

½ cup sugar
¼ cup brown sugar
½ teaspoon cinnamon
¼ teaspoon nutmeg
⅛ teaspoon salt
3 tablespoons flour

6 cups sliced apples
1 to 3 teaspoons lemon juice
1 Double-crust Pie Pastry, page 196
1 tablespoon butter or margarine

1. Combine sugars, spices, salt and flour in a mixing bowl.
2. Add apples and lemon juice (amount depending upon tartness of apples); mix lightly.
3. Line a 9-inch pie pan with pastry as directed for Double-crust Pie.
4. Add apple mixture; dot with butter.
5. Cover with pastry as directed for Double-crust Pie.
6. Bake in very hot oven (450°F.) 10 minutes; lower heat and bake in moderate oven (350°F.) 35 to 40 minutes longer.

Variation of Apple Pie

Deep-dish Apple Pie: Follow steps 1 and 2 for Apple Pie. Turn apple mixture into greased 6 x 10-inch baking dish; dot with butter. Roll out 1 recipe Pastry into a rectangle about 8 x 12 inches; cut gashes to allow steam to escape during baking. Lay pastry over apples; trim off to ½ inch beyond rim of baking dish all around. Turn edges under rim of dish, pressing to rim firmly with tines of a fork. Bake as for Apple Pie.

Cherry Pie

1¼ cups sugar	1 quart pitted sour red
¼ cup flour	cherries, fresh, frozen
⅛ teaspoon salt	or canned *
¼ teaspoon nutmeg	1 Double-crust Pie Pastry
½ teaspoon cinnamon	2 tablespoons butter

1. Combine sugar, flour, salt and spices in mixing bowl; add cherries and mix well.
2. Line a 9-inch pie pan with pastry as directed for Double-crust Pie, page 196.
3. Fill with cherry mixture; dot with butter.
4. Cover with pastry as directed for Double-crust Pie.
5. Bake in very hot oven (450°F.) 10 minutes; reduce heat and bake in moderate oven (350°F.) 35 to 40 minutes longer.

* Do not drain canned cherries; measure 1 quart combined cherries and juice. If frozen cherries are used, thaw cherries thoroughly before measuring; reduce sugar to 1 cup.

Variations of Cherry Pie

Lattice-top Cherry Pie: Make Cherry Pie, handling pastry according to directions for Lattice-top Pie, page 197.

Blackberry Pie: Follow basic recipe for Cherry Pie, substituting 1 quart fresh blackberries for cherries. Bake in hot oven (425°F.) 10 minutes; reduce heat and bake in moderate oven (350°F.) 40 minutes longer.

Blueberry Pie: Follow basic recipe, substituting 1 quart fresh blueberries for cherries and adding 1 tablespoon lemon juice to fruit mixture in Step 1.

Glazed Strawberry Pie

1 quart fresh strawberries	1 tablespoon butter or
¾ cup water	margarine
3 tablespoons cornstarch	1 9-inch Baked Pie
1 cup sugar	Shell, page 197

Wash, hull and slice strawberries. Combine 1 cup strawberries with water in a saucepan and simmer 4 to 5 minutes. Blend together cornstarch and sugar; stir into cooked berries and continue to cook, stirring constantly, until syrup thickens and becomes clear. Remove from heat; stir in butter. Turn remaining uncooked berries into pie shell; pour on cooked syrup. Chill thoroughly. Serve topped with whipped cream, if desired.

Sunny Peach Pie

2½ cups cooked, unsweetened, dried peaches	¼ teaspoon nutmeg
	2 tablespoons lemon
⅓ cup cooking liquid	juice
from peaches	1 tablespoon butter or
2 teaspoons cornstarch	margarine
½ cup sugar	1 Lattice-top Pie Pastry,
Dash of salt	page 197
¼ teaspoon cinnamon	

Drain peaches. Heat cooking liquid, add cornstarch, sugar, salt and spices. Cook and stir until clear and thickened. Remove from heat, and blend in lemon juice and butter. Pour over peaches arranged in pastry-lined pan. Top with pastry strips as directed. Bake in hot oven (400°F.) 25 to 35 minutes.

Rhubarb Raisin Pie

3 cups fresh, canned or
    quick-frozen rhubarb
    (cut into 1-inch pieces)
½ cup raisins
½ cup sugar
¾ cup light corn syrup

1 teaspoon cinnamon
¼ cup flour
1 Lattice-top Pie Pastry,
    page 197
1 egg

Drain rhubarb, if canned; thaw, if frozen. Combine raisins, sugar, corn syrup, cinnamon and flour; add to rhubarb. Pour into pastry-lined pie plate and cover with lattice of pastry strips. Beat egg until frothy. Spread over top with pastry brush, allowing it to run through lattice crust onto filling. Bake in very hot oven (475°F.) 10 minutes. Reduce heat to moderate (350°F.) and bake about 30 minutes longer, or until pastry is brown and rhubarb tender.

Prune Apricot Pie

2 cups prunes
1 cup dried apricots
¼ cup brown sugar
3 tablespoons lemon juice
1 egg, beaten

½ teaspoon cornstarch
⅛ teaspoon salt
1 Lattice-top Pie Pastry,
    page 197

Soak prunes and apricots overnight. Pit prunes; then for 45 minutes simmer prunes and apricots in enough fresh water to cover, adding sugar and lemon juice during the last 5 minutes of cooking time. There should be about ¼ cup of juice left after cooking fruit. Remove from heat and while fruit is cooling, stir egg into cornstarch and salt, and add to fruit. Pour slightly cooled fruit mixture into pastry-lined pie pan and top with lattice strips. Bake in hot oven (425°F.) 25 to 30 minutes.

Pecan Pie

4 eggs, slightly beaten
1 cup brown sugar
1 cup light corn syrup

1 cup pecans
1 Single-crust Pie Pastry,
    page 197

Combine first four ingredients and pour into pastry-lined pie plate. Bake in hot oven (425°F.) 5 minutes. Reduce heat to slow (300°F.) and bake about one hour.

Pumpkin Pie

2 cups cooked or canned
    pumpkin
½ teaspoon salt
1 cup sugar
½ teaspoon cinnamon
¼ teaspoon ground cloves
½ teaspoon mace

½ teaspoon ginger
2 eggs
1 cup milk
½ cup cream or
    evaporated milk
1 Single-crust Pie Pastry,
    page 197

Mix together pumpkin, salt, sugar and spices. Beat eggs with milk and cream; add to pumpkin mixture, stirring well. Pour into pastry-lined, 9-inch pie plate. Bake in very hot oven (450°F.) 10 minutes. Reduce heat to slow (325°F.) and bake 40 minutes longer or until knife blade inserted in center comes out clean.

Custard Pie

1 Single-Crust Pie Pastry,
    page 197
4 eggs, well beaten
½ cup sugar

¼ teaspoon salt
2½ cups milk
¾ teaspoon vanilla extract
¼ teaspoon nutmeg

1. Line a 9-inch pie pan with pastry.
2. Combine eggs, sugar and salt.

3. Stir in milk and vanilla, and mix well.
4. Pour into pastry-lined pie pan and sprinkle with nutmeg.
5. Bake in hot oven (425°F.) 25 to 35 minutes or until knife inserted in center comes out clean.

Variation of Custard Pie

Coconut Custard Pie: Add 1 cup shredded or flaked coconut to custard mixture before pouring into pastry shell. Sprinkle top with ¼ cup coconut in place of nutmeg.

Basic Cream Pie

2 cups milk or 1 cup evaporated milk plus 1 cup water	3 egg yolks
	2 tablespoons butter or margarine
½ cup sugar	1 teaspoon vanilla extract
⅛ teaspoon salt	1 9-inch Baked Pie Shell,
⅓ cup flour	page 197

1. Scald milk in top of double boiler.
2. Combine sugar, salt and flour, blending well; stir gradually into scalded milk.
3. Cook over boiling water, stirring constantly, until mixture thickens. Then cover and cook 10 minutes longer, stirring occasionally.
4. Beat egg yolks. Blend a few tablespoons of hot milk mixture into egg yolks, then stir egg yolks into hot milk mixture in double boiler.
5. Cook over boiling water 2 minutes, stirring constantly.
6. Remove from heat; add butter and vanilla. Cool.
7. Pour into pie shell. Chill.
8. Serve topped with whipped cream, if desired.

Variations of Cream Pie

Coconut Cream Pie: Follow basic recipe for Cream Pie, folding ½ cup grated fresh coconut or a ready-to-use coconut into cooled filling just before pouring into pie shell. Sprinkle filled pie with ½ cup additional coconut.

Banana Cream Pie: Follow basic recipe, slicing 3 peeled bananas into cooled pie shell just before pouring in filling.

Chocolate Cream Pie: Follow basic recipe, adding 2 squares (2 ozs.) unsweetened chocolate to the scalded milk in Step 2.

Butterscotch Cream Pie: Follow basic recipe, substituting ¾ cup brown sugar for the ½ cup sugar and increasing butter or margarine to 3 tablespoons.

NOTE: If desired, Cream Pies may be made with Cereal or Vanilla Wafer Crumb Crusts, pages 199 and 200.

Chocolate Chiffon Pie

2 squares (2 ozs.) unsweetened chocolate	3 eggs, separated
1 cup milk	¼ teaspoon salt
1 envelope unflavored gelatin	1 teaspoon vanilla extract
¾ cup sugar	1 9-inch Baked Pie Shell, page 197

Melt chocolate in milk in top of double boiler over boiling water; stir until well blended. Mix gelatin thoroughly with ½ cup of the sugar; add to hot mixture, stirring until dissolved. Beat egg yolks with remaining ¼ cup sugar; slowly add hot mixture, stirring to blend. Chill until slightly thickened. Beat egg whites with salt and vanilla until stiff peaks form; fold into chocolate mixture. Pour into pie shell and chill until firm, about 4 hours. Serve plain or topped with whipped cream.

Lemon Chiffon Pie

1 envelope unflavored
  gelatin
¼ cup cold water
4 eggs, separated
½ cup lemon juice
⅔ cup sugar

⅛ teaspoon salt
1 teaspoon grated lemon
  peel
1 9-inch Graham Cracker
  Crumb Pie Crust,
  page 199

Sprinkle gelatin on cold water and set aside. Beat egg yolks until creamy; stir in lemon juice, ½ cup sugar and salt. Cook in top of double boiler over boiling water, stirring constantly for 5 minutes or until thickened. Remove from heat and add lemon peel. Add softened gelatin to hot custard mixture and stir until dissolved. Beat egg whites until stiff; add remaining sugar gradually and continue to beat until all sugar has been added. Fold custard into beaten egg whites. Pour filling gently into crust and chill until firm.

Berry Chiffon Pie

1 package berry flavored
  gelatin
1 cup hot water
⅓ cup sugar
1 pint strawberries or
  raspberries

2 egg whites, stiffly
  beaten
⅛ teaspoon salt
1 9-inch Baked Pie
  Shell, page 197

Dissolve gelatin in hot water. Mix sugar with washed and hulled berries. Crush and let stand 15 minutes. Drain juice from berries and add to gelatin mixture. Chill until mixture begins to thicken. Beat until fluffy, then fold in berries and egg whites to which salt has been added. Pour mixture into pastry shell. Chill until set.

Quick Nesselrode Pie

1 package lemon flavored   ½ cup chopped mara-
  gelatin   schino cherries
1 cup heavy cream,   1 teaspoon rum flavoring
  whipped   1 9-inch Baked Pie
½ cup broken pecans   Shell, page 197

Prepare gelatin as directed on package and chill until syrupy.
Beat until light and fluffy. Fold in whipped cream, pecans, cherries and rum flavoring. Spoon into crust. Chill until set.

Lemon Meringue Pie

5 tablespoons cornstarch   Grated peel of 1 lemon
1½ cups sugar   1 9-inch Baked Pie Shell,
3 cups hot milk   page 197
3 egg yolks, beaten   Meringue Topping,
5 tablespoons lemon juice   page 209

Mix cornstarch and sugar in top of double boiler. Add hot milk
and cook over boiling water until thick and smooth, stirring constantly. When thick, cover and cook 15 minutes. Pour some of
the cornstarch mixture over beaten egg yolks, add to double
boiler and cook another minute. Add lemon juice and peel; mix
well. Pour into pastry shell. Cover with Meringue Topping and
brown in moderate oven (350°F.) about 20 minutes.

Variation of Lemon Meringue Pie

Chocolate Meringue Pie: Make Chocolate Cream Pie, page 206,
and top with meringue (made with the three leftover egg whites)
instead of whipped cream. Follow directions for Meringue Topping, page 209.

Meringue Topping

Two-egg-white Meringue	Three-egg-white Meringue
2 egg whites	3 egg whites
¼ teaspoon salt	¼ teaspoon salt
½ teaspoon vanilla	¾ teaspoon vanilla
extract, if desired	extract, if desired
¼ cup sugar	6 tablespoons sugar

1. Beat egg whites, salt and vanilla until soft peaks form.
2. Add sugar, 1 tablespoon at a time, beating well after each addition.
3. Continue beating until peaks formed are stiff but not dry.

Meringue Pies

Make two-egg-white meringue for 8-inch pie; three-egg-white meringue for 9-inch pie. Spoon onto thoroughly cooled pie filling, spreading so that meringue touches edge of pie shell all around. Bake in moderate oven (350°F.) 12 to 15 minutes or until meringue is lightly browned.

Meringue Pie Shell

3 egg whites	¾ cup sugar, sifted
⅛ teaspoon cream of	¾ cup finely chopped
tartar	walnuts
Dash of salt	1 teaspoon vanilla extract

Beat egg whites until foamy, add cream of tartar and salt. Continue beating until mixture stands in soft peaks. Gradually add sugar and beat until very stiff. Fold in walnuts and vanilla. Turn meringue into buttered 9-inch pie pan, building up the sides so there's room for a filling. Bake in hot oven (400°F.) 50 to 55 minutes. Cool.

Mocha Angel Pie

4 ounces sweet cooking   1 cup heavy cream,
   chocolate   whipped
3 tablespoons strong black   1 9-inch Meringue Pie Shell,
   coffee   page 209
1 teaspoon vanilla extract

Combine chocolate and coffee, and cook over low heat until
chocolate melts and is smooth. Cool and add vanilla. Fold
chocolate mixture into whipped cream and turn into Meringue
Pie Shell. Chill at least 2 hours before serving.

North Carolina Cracker Pie

3 egg whites   20 round buttery crackers,
1 cup sugar   rolled very fine
1 teaspoon baking powder   ¾ cup chopped walnuts
   Dash of salt

Beat egg whites until stiff. Fold in sugar, baking powder and
salt. Combine cracker crumbs and chopped walnuts. Fold very
lightly into egg white mixture. Pour into buttered 8-inch pie
plate and bake in moderate oven (350°F.) 25 to 30 minutes.
Cool and top with whipped cream or dairy sour cream.

Salads and Salad Dressings

Salads are a delightful challenge to the ingenious cook. They can be served as first course, main course, accompaniment to the main course or as dessert—and they are open to endless variation in the ingredients used and the dressings selected.

A green, leafy vegetable is the base or background of most salads. Your ingenuity comes into play, however, when you leave the inevitable lettuce leaf and parsley, and explore the possibilities of kale, spinach, water cress, swiss chard, escarole, endive and beet greens, to name a few of those readily available at the greengrocer's. If you live in the country, grape leaves, dandelion greens, sweet flag and nasturtium leaves should start you out on a really creative search. Remember, in selecting any green, that the darker, outer leaves are the most nutritious. If they are not presentable whole, they can be shredded for tossed salads or sandwich fillings.

Salad dressings are almost as variable as the salads they accompany. In general, hearty salads such as meat, fish and egg should be served with a light dressing while vegetable and fruit salads are enhanced by a dressing containing cream, eggs, cheese or nuts. A good opportunity, there, to slip in extra food value.

Basic Coleslaw

1 quart shredded cabbage
1 teaspoon salt
   Dash of pepper
1 tablespoon sugar
1 tablespoon cider vinegar

1 teaspoon celery seed
½ cup Cooked Salad
   Dressing or Mayon-
   naise, page 223

1. Combine all ingredients and mix thoroughly.
2. Served chilled. Makes 6 servings.

Variations: Make coleslaw and add shredded raw carrots, chopped green pepper, diced red-skinned apples, canned pineapple chunks.

Mixed Green Salad

1 clove garlic (optional)
½ head lettuce
½ bunch water cress
½ head romaine lettuce

1 cucumber
2 tomatoes
½ cup well-seasoned
   French Dressing

Rub salad bowl with cut clove of garlic; discard garlic. Break greens into bite-size pieces. Run tines of a fork lengthwise through green peel of the cucumber; cut crosswise into thin slices. Cut tomatoes into wedges. Combine greens, cucumber slices and tomato wedges. Just before serving add French Dressing; toss lightly. Makes 6 to 8 servings.

Variations: Make Mixed Green Salad using endive, escarole, chicory or celery cabbage instead of romaine. Add minced onion, chives or scallions. Use other vegetables—onion rings, green pepper rings, diced celery, slivered carrots, thin slices of unpeeled radish, crisp cauliflowerets, avocado slices—with or instead of tomato and cucumber. For variations of French Dressing, see page 222.

Chef's Salad Bowl

1 clove garlic (optional)
6 cups broken greens—
    lettuce, water cress,
    romaine, chicory
¾ cup cooked tongue
¾ cup cooked ham

¾ cup cooked chicken
¾ cup Swiss cheese
1 hard-cooked egg,
    chopped
½ to ¾ cup French
    Dressing, page 222

Cut several gashes in clove of garlic and rub salad bowl. Discard garlic. Shred or tear greens and place in salad bowl. Over greens, arrange the tongue, ham, chicken and cheese, all cut in match-like strips. Place egg in center of bowl. When ready to serve, pour on French Dressing and toss lightly. Other meat combinations such as beef, lamb, pork, salami, boiled ham, pressed or canned meat loaf may be used. Makes 6 servings.

Potato Salad

4 cups diced cooked
    potatoes
1 teaspoon salt
¼ teaspoon ground pepper
1 medium onion, diced
½ cup celery, chopped
½ cup chopped sweet
    pickles

4 hard-cooked eggs, diced
¼ cup pickle juice *or*
    2 tablespoons vinegar
1 tablespoon prepared
    mustard
1 cup mayonnaise
Herb salad blend, if
    desired

Combine potatoes, salt, pepper, onion, celery, pickles and diced eggs. Blend pickle juice and mustard with mayonnaise; add to potatoes and mix until all ingredients are well coated with dressing. Add herb salad blend to taste. Cover salad and refrigerate overnight so flavors will mingle. Before serving, heap salad in large bowl, tuck crisp lettuce leaves around edge of salad and garnish with sliced radishes or tomatoes. Makes 8 servings.

Hot Potato Salad

5 to 6 medium potatoes
¼ pound bacon
1 tablespoon finely
  chopped onion
½ cup diced celery
2 teaspoons salt
2 tablespoons flour

¼ teaspoon powdered
  mustard
3 tablespoons sugar
½ cup vinegar
¼ cup water
1 tablespoon finely
  chopped parsley

Cook potatoes in skins until tender. While potatoes are still hot, peel and slice into ¼-inch pieces. In a skillet, cook bacon slowly over low heat until crisp; remove from pan, crumble and add to potatoes. Sauté the onion and celery in the bacon fat and add to the potatoes. Combine remaining ingredients, except parsley, and heat to boiling point. After mixture thickens and boils, pour over potatoes. Mix lightly with a fork being careful not to break potatoes. Place in casserole and reheat in moderate oven (375°F.) 10 minutes. Sprinkle with parsley and serve. Makes 6 servings.

Macaroni Salad

4 cups cooked elbow or sea
  shell macaroni
½ cup finely chopped
  celery
¼ cup finely chopped
  green pepper

2 tablespoons minced
  onion
¼ cup mayonnaise
2 tablespoons French
  dressing
1 teaspoon salt
⅛ teaspoon pepper

Combine macaroni, celery, green pepper and onion. Mix mayonnaise, French dressing and seasonings; pour over salad and mix lightly but well. Chill thoroughly. Garnish with sliced stuffed olives and parsley before serving. Makes 6 to 8 servings.

Golden Porcupine

2 cups cottage cheese
Chicory

2 medium carrots, cut in
2-inch sticks

Place a mound of cottage cheese on a bed of chicory. Insert the carrot sticks at close intervals in the cheese, and lo! a porcupine ready to be served the children. Makes 6 servings.

Carrot Raisin Salad

6 carrots
½ cup raisins
½ teaspoon salt

¼ cup Mayonnaise or
Cooked Salad Dress-
ing, page 223

Peel or scrape carrots; grate or put through food chopper. Combine with raisins, salt and dressing; chill. Serve on lettuce or water cress. Makes 6 servings.

Tomato-petal Salad

Wash fresh tomatoes; cut out hard portion at stem end and any blemishes. Make six cuts in each tomato, forming six wedges left joined at the blossom end. Pull wedges open, petal fashion. Place each tomato on lettuce; sprinkle with salt and pepper, and fill with desired stuffing, such as cottage cheese, coleslaw, or chicken, sea food or egg salad.

To separate leaves of head lettuce without breaking, remove core with sharp, pointed knife and run cold water into cavity.

Basic Fish Salad

2 cups cooked fish, flaked	¼ teaspoon salt
1 cup diced celery	⅛ teaspoon pepper
1 tablespoon minced onion	1 tablespoon vinegar
	½ cup salad dressing

1. Combine all ingredients and mix lightly.
2. Chill.
3. Serve on crisp salad greens.

Makes 6 servings.

Variations of Basic Fish Salad

Tuna Salad: Substitute 2 cans (6½ ozs. each) tuna, flaked, for the fish.

Salmon Salad: Substitute 1 can (1 lb.) salmon for the fish.

Shrimp Salad: Substitute 2 cups drained, canned shrimp or fresh cooked shrimp for the fish.

Lobster Salad: Substitute 2 cans (6½ ozs. each) lobster or 2 cups fresh, flaked lobster meat for the fish.

Crab Meat Salad: Substitute 2 cans (6½ ozs. each) crab meat or 2 cups fresh or frozen cooked crab meat for the fish.

Chicken Salad

3 cups chopped, cooked chicken *or* 2 cans (12 ozs. each) boned chicken	1 cup mayonnaise or salad dressing
1½ cups chopped celery	1½ teaspoons salt
½ cup sliced ripe olives	2 hard-cooked eggs, diced

Combine all ingredients and mix thoroughly. Chill at least one hour before serving. Makes 6 servings.

Egg Salad

4 hard-cooked eggs,
   chopped
¾ cup chopped celery
½ teaspoon powdered
   mustard

¼ teaspoon salt
¼ teaspoon Worcestershire
   sauce
½ cup mayonnaise or
   salad dressing

Combine eggs and celery. Add mustard, salt and Worcestershire to mayonnaise; blend into egg mixture. Makes 4 servings.

Waldorf Salad

½ cup mayonnaise
1½ cups diced, unpeeled
   apples

1 cup diced celery
¼ cup chopped walnuts

Add mayonnaise to apples and mix together immediately to prevent discoloration of apples. Fold in celery and nuts. Serve on chilled, crisp lettuce. Makes 6 servings.

Citrus Avocado Salad

2 grapefruits
3 oranges

1 large avocado
Lettuce

Peel and section grapefruits and oranges. Chill, covered, until serving time. Just before serving, halve avocado lengthwise; remove seed and peel. Cut in crosswise slices. For each serving, arrange grapefruit, orange and avocado alternately, like flower petals, on crisp lettuce. Serve with Pink Lemonade Dressing, page 224. Makes 6 servings.

Basic Gelatin Salads

Molded Vegetable Salad

1 envelope unflavored
  gelatin
½ cup cold water
1 cup boiling water
3 tablespoons vinegar
1 tablespoon lemon juice

1 tablespoon sugar
1 teaspoon salt
2 cups sliced or shredded
  vegetables (see com-
  binations below)

1. Soften gelatin in cold water; dissolve in boiling water.
2. Add vinegar, lemon juice, sugar and salt, stirring until sugar is dissolved.
3. Chill until syrupy; then fold in vegetables.
4. Pour into one large or six individual molds. Chill until firm.
5. Unmold on salad greens and serve with any desired dressing.
Makes 6 servings.

Variations of Molded Vegetable Salad

Molded Cabbage Salad: Make Vegetable Salad using 1 cup shredded red or white cabbage, ¼ cup chopped green pepper and ½ cup diced celery.

Molded Cabbage Carrot Salad: Make Molded Vegetable Salad using 1 cup shredded cabbage, ½ cup shredded carrot and ½ cup sliced unpeeled radishes.

Molded Celery Cucumber Salad: Make Molded Vegetable Salad using 1 cup diced celery, ½ cup diced cucumber, ½ cup chopped green pepper and 2 tablespoons minced onion.

Molded Beet Salad: Make Molded Vegetable Salad using beet juice for part of water, increasing lemon juice to 2 tablespoons, and using 1½ cups diced cooked or canned beets, ½ cup diced celery and 3 tablespoons horseradish for vegetables.

Basic Tomato Aspic

1 envelope unflavored gelatin	1 tablespoon lemon juice
	1 teaspoon grated onion
½ cup cold tomato juice	¼ teaspoon salt
1¼ cups hot tomato juice	Salad greens

1. Soften gelatin in cold tomato juice.
2. Add hot tomato juice and stir until gelatin is dissolved.
3. Stir in lemon juice, onion and salt.
4. Pour into 1-pint ring mold, or 4 individual molds.
5. Chill until firm.
6. Unmold on salad greens and fill center with any of the following fillings: shrimp salad, cottage cheese, egg salad, tuna salad, chicken salad, mixed greens, coleslaw, sliced cucumbers, diced avocado.

Makes 4 servings.

NOTE: Canned cocktail vegetable juices may be substituted for tomato juice.

Variations of Basic Tomato Aspic

Sea Food Aspic: Prepare Tomato Aspic. Chill until mixture is the consistency of unbeaten egg whites. Fold in 1 cup diced or shredded shrimp, crab meat or lobster and ½ cup diced celery before pouring into mold in step 4.

Olive Cucumber Aspic: Prepare Tomato Aspic. Chill until mixture is the consistency of unbeaten egg whites. Fold in ¼ cup sliced, stuffed olives and 1 cup diced cucumber before step 4.

Vegetable Tomato Aspic: Prepare Tomato Aspic. Chill until mixture is consistency of unbeaten egg whites. Fold in 1 cup finely shredded cabbage, 1½ cups diced celery and 2 tablespoons chopped green pepper before step 4.

Chicken, Meat or Fish Mousse

1 envelope unflavored
  gelatin
½ cup cold water
¾ cup cooked salad dress-
  ing or mayonnaise
1 cup cooked minced
  chicken, minced meat
  or flaked fish

½ cup chopped celery
2 tablespoons minced
  green pepper
¼ cup chopped olives
½ teaspoon salt
¼ teaspoon paprika
1 tablespoon lemon juice
  Dash of cayenne

Soften gelatin in cold water in top of double boiler. Place over boiling water and stir until gelatin is dissolved. Cool slightly, add salad dressing or mayonnaise and mix well. Add remaining ingredients and blend well. Pour into 1-quart mold and chill until set. Garnish with olives and sliced hard-cooked eggs. Makes 6 servings.

Sunshine Salad

1 package lemon flavored
  gelatin
1 cup boiling water
1 cup canned pineapple
  syrup (drained from
  fruit)
1 tablespoon vinegar

½ teaspoon salt
1 cup drained, crushed
  or cubed canned
  pineapple
1 cup grated raw
  carrot
  Salad greens

Dissolve gelatin in boiling water. Add pineapple syrup, vinegar and salt. Chill until mixture begins to thicken. Add pineapple and carrot, and turn into individual molds. Chill, unmold and serve on a bed of crisp salad greens. Makes 6 servings.

Fruit Ginger Ale Mold

1 package orange flavored
   gelatin
¾ cup hot orange juice
2 tablespoons lemon juice
1 cup chilled ginger ale

½ cup diced pears
½ cup halved, seedless
   grapes
½ cup halved, pitted
   cherries

Dissolve gelatin in hot orange juice. Stir in lemon juice, ginger ale and fruit. Turn into a ring mold and chill until firm. To serve, unmold on a bed of salad greens and fill center with seasoned cottage cheese. Garnish with orange slices and other fresh fruit, if desired. Makes 4 to 6 servings.

NOTE: 1½ cups drained, canned fruit cocktail may be substituted for the pears, grapes and cherries.

 To unmold a gelatin salad quickly and easily, dip mold in hot water to the depth of the gelatin. Loosen edge with knife or spatula. Place serving dish on top of mold and turn upside down. Shake lightly and carefully lift off mold.

Salad Dressings

Basic French Dressing

½ teaspoon salt	Dash of black pepper
½ teaspoon sugar	¼ cup vinegar or
¼ teaspoon paprika	lemon juice
½ teaspoon powdered	½ cup salad oil
mustard	

1. Combine first five ingredients in a jar and mix well.
2. Add vinegar; cover jar and shake.
3. Add oil and shake again, vigorously.
4. Shake each time before using.

Makes ¾ cup.

Variations of Basic French Dressing

Bacon Dressing: To basic recipe add ⅓ cup crumbled, cooked, crisp bacon.

Blue Cheese Dressing: To basic recipe add ⅓ cup crumbled Blue or Roquefort cheese. Blend thoroughly.

Chiffonade Dressing: To basic recipe add 2 tablespoons chopped, hard-cooked egg, 1 tablespoon chopped green pepper, 1 tablespoon chopped pimiento, 1 teaspoon chopped parsley and ¼ teaspoon onion juice. Blend thoroughly.

Club Dressing: To basic recipe add 3 tablespoons finely chopped scallions, 3 tablespoons tomato juice, 1 tablespoon Worcestershire sauce and 1 tablespoon sugar. Blend thoroughly.

Garden Dressing: To basic recipe add 6 large, finely chopped radishes; 2 sieved, hard-cooked eggs; ¼ green pepper, chopped; 2 tablespoons finely chopped onion; 2 tablespoons finely chopped parsley. Blend thoroughly.

Herb Dressing: To basic recipe, add 1 teaspoon salad herbs.

Cooked Salad Dressing

3 tablespoons cornstarch	Dash of cayenne
1 tablespoon sugar	½ teaspoon paprika
2 teaspoons powdered mustard	1¼ cups milk
	2 egg yolks
2 teaspoons salt	¼ cup vinegar
⅛ teaspoon pepper	½ cup salad oil

1. Mix cornstarch, sugar and seasonings in a small amount of the milk to make a smooth paste. Add remaining milk.
2. Cook over low heat, stirring constantly, until mixture thickens and boils.
3. Boil 2 minutes, stirring constantly.
4. Remove from heat; gradually beat in egg yolks.
5. Cook 2 minutes longer, stirring constantly.
6. Remove from heat and gradually beat in vinegar.
7. Add salad oil; beat until smooth.

Makes 2 cups dressing.

Mayonnaise

½ teaspoon powdered mustard	1 egg yolk
	2 tablespoons lemon juice or vinegar
½ teaspoon salt	1 cup salad oil
Dash of cayenne	
½ teaspoon sugar	

Mix together dry ingredients and add egg yolk. Mix well and stir in ½ teaspoon lemon juice or vinegar. Add oil gradually, drop by drop at first, then more quickly, beating vigorously. As mixture thickens, thin with remaining lemon juice or vinegar, and continue adding oil and beating until dressing is very stiff. Store in covered jar in refrigerator. Makes 1¼ cups.

Quick Russian Dressing

½ cup mayonnaise
1 hard-cooked egg,
   chopped

2 tablespoons chili sauce
2 tablespoons minced
   green pepper

Combine all ingredients and chill before serving. Makes 1 cup.

Creole Salad Dressing

1 cup mayonnaise
1 tablespoon prepared
   mustard
1 teaspoon horseradish

1 teaspoon Worcestershire
   sauce
½ cup chili sauce

Combine ingredients and chill before serving. Makes 1½ cups.

Pink Lemonade Dressing

½ cup lemon juice
½ cup salad oil
1 teaspoon salt

¼ cup honey
¼ cup red jelly or
   jam

Combine all ingredients and shake well in a tightly covered glass jar. Chill, and shake briskly before serving. Makes 1½ cups.

Honey Fruit Dressing

½ cup honey
¼ cup orange juice

¼ cup pineapple juice

Combine all ingredients and chill before serving. Makes 1 cup.

Sandwiches

Ever since the Earl of Sandwich ordered a "hand-food," a slice of meat between two pieces of bread, in order not to lose time from his play, sandwiches have been a favorite way of eating. They serve everyone—school children, laborers, picnickers.

Day-old bread is best for sandwiches because it is firmer in texture than very fresh bread. For sandwich variety, vary the bread as well as the filling. White, whole wheat, cracked wheat, rye, pumpernickel, crusty French, oatmeal, poppy-seed topped Vienna, Boston brown and raisin are all fine for sandwiches, as are homemade fruit and nut breads. Hamburger or frankfurter buns, poppy-seed rolls, bran or corn meal muffins and unsweetened crackers may be used for sandwiches, too.

To prevent soaking, spread both slices of bread with softened butter or margarine before adding filling. If sandwiches are made in advance, wrap or put in airtight plastic container, and refrigerate until time to serve or pack in the lunch box. If lettuce is used, add it to each sandwich just before serving.

Sliced Fillings

Use sliced, leftover cooked beef, pork, ham, veal, tongue, chicken or turkey; sliced American cheese, Swiss cheese or process cheese spread; sliced, canned luncheon meat, canned lunch tongue, canned veal loaf; or choose from the ready-to-eat sausages such as bologna, minced ham, cervelat and liverwurst. Spread sliced filling with seasoned spread or relish such as mustard, mayonnaise, salad dressing, pickle relish, chili sauce, catsup or horseradish. Add lettuce, if desired.

Combination Fillings

Liver and Bacon: Combine 1 cup finely chopped, cooked liver with 4 slices crisp cooked bacon, crumbled. Add 1 tablespoon chili sauce and 1 tablespoon mayonnaise. Fills 6 sandwiches.

Bacon and Egg: Combine 3 hard-cooked eggs, chopped, with 4 slices crisp cooked bacon, crumbled. Add ¼ teaspoon salt, dash of pepper and 2 tablespoons mayonnaise. Fills 6 sandwiches.

Egg salad: Make Egg Salad, page 217. Fills 8 sandwiches.

Ham Salad: Combine 1 cup chopped cooked ham, ½ cup chopped celery, 2 tablespoons sweet pickle relish, 2 tablespoons mayonnaise and 1 teaspoon prepared mustard. Add lettuce to each sandwich. Fills 6 sandwiches.

Chicken Salad: Combine 1 cup chopped cooked or canned chicken, ½ cup chopped celery, 1 tablespoon minced green pepper, ¼ teaspoon salt and 2 tablespoons mayonnaise. Add lettuce to each sandwich. Fills 6 sandwiches.

 Cut large sandwiches into quarters to make them easier for children to manage.

Fish Fillings

Tuna: Combine 1 can (6½ ozs.) tuna (flaked) with 2 teaspoons minced onion, 1 teaspoon lemon juice, 6 stuffed olives (sliced) and 3 tablespoons mayonnaise. Fills 8 sandwiches.

Tuna and Egg: Add 1 hard-cooked egg, chopped, to Tuna Sandwich Filling.

Sardine: Blend ¼ cup softened butter or margarine with 1 can (7 ozs.) sardines, drained and mashed. Add 1½ teaspoons lemon juice and 2 teaspoons minced onion. Fills 8 sandwiches.

Salmon: Combine 1 can (7¾ ozs.) salmon, 2 tablespoons sweet pickle relish, 2 teaspoons minced onion, 1 teaspoon lemon juice and 3 tablespoons mayonnaise. Fills 8 sandwiches.

Salmon and Eggs: Add 1 hard-cooked egg, chopped, to Salmon Sandwich Filling.

Salmon and Cucumber: Make Salmon Sandwich Filling, substituting ¼ cup chopped cucumber for pickle relish and onion.

Broiled Bacon Peanut Butter Sandwiches

6 slices white bread
½ cup peanut butter

6 slices bacon, finely diced

Toast bread on one side. Remove from heat and while bread is still warm, spread peanut butter on untoasted sides. Place bacon on peanut butter, allowing 1 slice bacon for each sandwich. Place open sandwiches under broiler heat until bacon is lightly crisped.

Baked Bean Sandwiches

1 cup baked beans, mashed
¼ teaspoon salt
2 slices crisp bacon, chopped

¼ cup catsup
8 slices Boston brown bread

Blend beans, salt, bacon and catsup. Spread over 4 thin slices of Boston brown bread. Top with remaining slices. Makes 4.

Corned Beef 'Burgers

1 can (12 ozs.) corned
    beef, finely chopped
¼ cup catsup

½ teaspoon salt
3 tablespoons mayonnaise
6 hamburger buns

Combine all ingredients except buns, mix thoroughly and season to taste. Shape into 6 patties and grill 10 minutes or until browned. Serve on split buns with a slice of tomato or cheese.

Fancy Party Sandwiches

1 package (8 ozs.) cream
    cheese
2 tablespoons light cream
    Dash of salt
    Food coloring

2 tablespoons minced
    chives
2 tablespoons minced olives
2 slices whole wheat bread
2 slices white bread

Blend cheese, cream and salt. Divide into three equal parts. Color one part pale pink; one part, pale green and add minced chives; add olives to the third. Spread 1 slice whole wheat bread with the pink cheese and top with a slice of white bread. Spread with pale green cheese; add a slice of whole wheat bread. Spread with cream cheese and olive mixture and top with white bread. Press stack together and slice crusts from all sides. Wrap in wax paper and moist cloth. Chill at least 4 hours, then cut in eight ½-inch slices. Cut each slice in thirds. Makes 24.

Easy Party Sandwiches, 1-2-3

1. Open Face Squares: Spread bread with butter or margarine, then with canned deviled ham or liver spread, or egg salad. Remove crusts; cut each bread slice into four squares. Top deviled ham with dab of chutney, liver paste with slices of stuffed olive, egg salad with bit of parsley.

2. **Shrimp Tomato Rounds:** Spread bread rounds with mayonnaise; add slice of tomato and top with whole, cooked shrimp and a dab of mayonnaise.

3. **Sardine Cucumber Rounds:** Spread bread rounds with butter or margarine. Top each with cucumber slice which has been marinated in French dressing. Add layer of mashed sardines which have been blended with lemon juice to taste. Garnish with bit of pimiento.

Hot Luncheon Meat Sandwiches

1 can (12 ozs.) luncheon
    meat
⅓ cup shredded cheese

½ cup mayonnaise
6 slices white bread

Cut luncheon meat into 12 thin slices. Lay slices in a shallow pan and heat in moderate oven (350°F.) until they start to curl. Mix cheese and mayonnaise. Remove hot meat slices, place on bread and spread each with cheese mixture. Return to oven and heat until cheese is partly melted. Makes 6 sandwiches.

French-toasted Cheese Sandwiches

1 egg, well beaten
½ cup evaporated milk
¼ cup water
½ teaspoon salt

Dash of pepper
8 slices bread
4 thick slices mild
    cheese

Combine first five ingredients in wide, flat-bottomed bowl. Top 4 slices of bread with the cheese slices, then top cheese with remaining 4 slices of bread. Dip sandwiches, one at a time, in the egg mixture. Brown both sides of sandwiches in hot fat, as in making French toast. Serve hot. Makes 4 sandwiches.

Grilled Ham 'n' Cheese Sandwiches

4 English muffins   8 thin slices cooked ham
  Butter   8 slices American cheese

Split muffins and spread with butter. Top each half with a slice
of ham and a slice of cheese. Slip under broiler until cheese melts
and browns slightly. Makes 4 servings of 2 halves each.

Prepared Sandwich Spreads

For sandwich variety, choose from the many ready-to-use canned
or packaged spreads such as these:

Cottage cheese   Cheese with bacon
Cream cheese, plain or   Canned liver spread
  flavored   Deviled ham
Pimiento cheese   Peanut butter
Pineapple cheese   Preserves
Cheddar cheese spread   Marmalade

For even greater variety, start with ready-to-use spreads and
add a pleasing complement. For example:

To cottage cheese, add any of the following: chopped nutmeats,
minced chives, grated carrot, chopped green pepper, sweet pickle
relish, shredded sharp cheese, well-drained crushed pineapple.
To cream cheese, add any of the following: minced chipped beef,
chopped raisins and nuts, stuffed olives, dried apricots or prunes,
liver spread, deviled ham, mashed sardines. Or spread one slice
of bread with cream cheese, the other with jam or marmalade.
To peanut butter, add any of the following: chopped raisins,
pitted dates, crisp bacon bits, mashed banana. Or spread one
slice of bread with peanut butter, the other with deviled ham.

Sauces

Many a good cook's reputation rests on her sauces. They add glamor to everyday foods and work magic with leftovers. White sauces, sometimes called cream sauces, are the basis for so many dishes that they should be mastered at an early date. Thin white sauce is used for creamed vegetables and cream soups; medium white sauce, for creamed chicken, seafood and scalloped dishes; thick white sauce, for croquettes.

Basic White Sauces

	Fat	Flour	Milk
THIN	1 tablespoon	1 tablespoon	1 cup
MEDIUM	2 tablespoons	2 tablespoons	1 cup
THICK	3 tablespoons	3 to 4 tablespoons	1 cup

1. Melt fat (butter, margarine or drippings) in a saucepan over low heat; add flour and blend.
2. Add milk slowly, stirring to blend.
3. Cook, stirring constantly, until sauce boils and thickens.
4. Stir in ¼ teaspoon salt and dash of pepper.
Makes 1 cup.

Variations of Basic Medium White Sauce

Cheese Sauce: Make Medium White Sauce, adding ¾ cup shredded or finely cut American cheese in Step 4. Continue to cook, stirring until cheese is melted and blended.

Mild Curry Sauce: Make Medium White Sauce, using 1 chicken bouillon cube dissolved in ½ cup boiling water for part of liquid. Add ½ teaspoon curry powder in Step 4.

Hard-cooked Egg Sauce: Make Medium White Sauce, adding 2 hard-cooked eggs, chopped, in Step 4.

Brown Gravy

2 cups hot water	Salt and pepper
¼ cup fat and drippings	Bottled concentrated
from roast meat	seasoning for gravy,
¼ cup flour	if desired

1. Remove meat from roasting pan to platter; keep warm while making gravy.
2. Pour off all fat and drippings from roasting pan into a cup.
3. Pour the hot water into roasting pan; scrape and stir to dissolve browned juices.
4. Heat the fat and drippings in a saucepan; blend in flour.
5. Cook over medium heat, stirring, until mixture is lightly browned.
6. Slowly stir in water from roaster, blending well. Continue to cook, stirring, until gravy boils and thickens.
7. Season with salt and pepper to taste.
8. For browner gravy, add enough bottled sauce to gravy to give desired color.

Makes about 2 cups.

NOTE: For a richer gravy, substitute light cream *or* 1½ cups evaporated milk plus ½ cup water for the liquid.

Mushroom Sauce

1 cup sliced fresh or
canned mushrooms
3 tablespoons butter
3 tablespoons flour
1½ cups milk *or* ¾ cup
evaporated milk
plus ¾ cup water

1 chicken bouillon
cube
1 teaspoon lemon juice
¼ teaspoon salt
Dash of pepper
Dash of nutmeg

Sauté mushrooms in butter until tender, 5 to 8 minutes. Blend in flour; gradually stir in milk. Add bouillon cube and cook, stirring constantly, until sauce thickens and bouillon cube is dissolved. Stir in lemon juice and seasonings. Makes about 2 cups.

Creamy Mustard Sauce

1½ teaspoons flour
1 tablespoon sugar
1½ teaspoons powdered
mustard

¼ teaspoon salt
½ cup milk
1 egg, beaten
2 tablespoons vinegar

Combine flour, sugar, mustard and salt in top of double boiler. Place over boiling water; gradually add milk, stirring constantly until thickened. Add egg and cook 2 to 3 minutes longer. Add vinegar and serve hot over fish or meat dishes. Makes ⅔ cup.

Quick Tomato Sauce

Empty 1 can (10½ ozs.) condensed tomato soup into saucepan; stir in 3 tablespoons water. Heat slowly to boiling point, stirring. Add 3 tablespoons butter or margarine. Makes ¾ cup.

Raisin Sauce

½ cup brown sugar
1 tablespoon flour
1½ cups water
2 tablespoons vinegar
2 tablespoons lemon
    juice

1 tablespoon butter or
    margarine
1 teaspoon powdered
    mustard
½ teaspoon salt
⅓ cup raisins

Mix together sugar and flour in saucepan; slowly stir in water. Cook over low heat, stirring, until mixture boils and thickens. Add remaining ingredients and cook 5 minutes longer, stirring constantly. Serve hot with ham or tongue. Makes about 2½ cups.

Spanish Sauce

1½ tablespoons salad oil
¼ cup chopped onion
¼ cup chopped green
    pepper
2 cups canned tomatoes

½ teaspoon salt
Dash of pepper
½ cup shredded American
    cheese

Heat salad oil in a skillet. Add onion and green pepper. Cook slowly until onion is golden. Add tomatoes and seasonings; heat. Pour over food to be sauced, sprinkle with cheese and brown quickly in very hot oven (450°F.). Makes 2½ cups.

Tartare Sauce

1 cup mayonnaise
½ teaspoon minced onion
    or chives

1 teaspoon minced parsley
2 tablespoons chopped
    dill pickle

Combine all ingredients, mixing well. Serve with broiled or fried fish or shellfish. Makes about 1 cup.

Parsley Lemon Butter Sauce

¼ cup butter or margarine   2 tablespoons chopped
Juice of ½ lemon   parsley

Melt butter, add lemon juice and parsley. Blend well and pour
over fish, lamb chops, or cooked vegetables such as broccoli or
cauliflower. Makes about ½ cup.

Orange Cranberry Sauce

1 pound cranberries,   1½ oranges, peel and all
  washed   2 cups sugar

Grind ingredients together in order given. This sauce improves
on standing and will keep two or three weeks in the refrigerator.
To keep longer, boil 5 minutes and seal with paraffin. Serve with
poultry, game, lamb, veal, ham. Makes about 1 quart.

Cranberry Sauce

2 cups sugar   1 quart cranberries,
1¾ cups water   washed

Boil sugar and water together 5 minutes. Add cranberries; cover
and simmer gently about 5 minutes or until berries pop. Remove
from heat. Serve chilled. Makes 1 quart.

*Keep a supply of ready-to-use sauces and sauce mixes
on hand. They're quick, easy and good.*

*Canned, condensed soups make flavorful, quick and
easy sauces. Heat in double boiler with 2 tablespoons
water and 2 tablespoons butter or margarine.*

Vegetable Sauces

Hollandaise Sauce

½ cup butter	½ teaspoon salt
2 egg yolks, slightly	Dash of cayenne
beaten	2 tablespoons lemon juice

Cream the butter and put ⅓ of it in a double boiler together with egg yolks, salt, cayenne and lemon juice. Cook very slowly over hot water, stirring constantly until mixture begins to thicken, about 3 minutes. Then add second third of the butter and, as it thickens, add the other third. Cook very slowly (or the sauce will curdle) until mixture coats a metal spoon. This will be about 20 minutes in all. Serve hot with asparagus, broccoli, cauliflower or artichokes. Makes 1 cup.

Sour Cream Sauce

2 egg yolks, slightly	½ teaspoon paprika
beaten	¾ cup dairy sour cream
¼ teaspoon salt	1 tablespoon vinegar

Combine egg yolks with salt, paprika, sour cream and vinegar in top of double boiler. Stir over hot, but not boiling, water until mixture is smooth and slightly thick. Makes 1 cup.

Vinaigrette Sauce

½ teaspoon salt	1 tablespoon minced
⅛ teaspoon pepper	parsley
½ teaspoon sugar	1 tablespoon minced onion
½ teaspoon paprika	1 tablespoon minced green
¼ cup salad oil	pepper or chopped
2 tablespoons vinegar	pickle

Mix together salt, pepper, sugar and paprika in small saucepan. Stir in oil and vinegar, and heat thoroughly but do not allow the sauce to boil. Add the remaining ingredients and serve over beets, spinach and other greens. Makes about ½ cup.

Spaghetti Sauce

½ cup butter or margarine
3 tablespoons olive oil
  or salad oil
⅓ cup chopped green
  pepper
⅓ cup chopped onion
½ cup chopped celery
1 clove garlic, minced
½ pound ground beef

1 can (8 ozs.) tomato
  sauce
2 cups diced, fresh
  tomatoes
1 teaspoon salt
⅛ teaspoon pepper
Dash of oregano
  (optional)

Melt the butter in a large, heavy skillet and add oil. Add vegetables and cook until lightly browned. Add ground meat and cook until redness disappears, stirring occasionally. Add tomato sauce, tomatoes and seasonings and mix thoroughly. Simmer, uncovered, over low heat for 1 hour. Makes about 1 quart.

Tomato Barbecue Sauce

¼ cup minced onion
2 cans (8 ozs. each)
  tomato sauce
1 cup water

1 tablespoon Worcester-
  shire sauce
1 teaspoon salt

Combine all ingredients in saucepan; bring to a boil and simmer 20 minutes. Makes about 2½ cups.

Dessert Sauces

Custard Sauce

3 tablespoons sugar   2 cups milk
2 eggs, beaten   ½ teaspoon vanilla
Dash of salt   extract

Combine sugar, eggs and salt in top of double boiler; stir in milk
and place over hot water. Cook, stirring constantly, until mixture
coats a metal spoon. Pour into a bowl, add vanilla and chill.
Makes 2 cups. Good on snow pudding or fruit or cake.

Hard Sauce

¼ cup butter or margarine   1 teaspoon boiling water
⅛ teaspoon salt   1 teaspoon vanilla extract
 1 cup confectioners' sugar

Cream butter thoroughly, add salt and gradually blend in sugar.
Add boiling water and vanilla, beating until smooth and fluffy.
Makes about 1¾ cups. Serve on plum pudding and cobblers.

Variations of Hard Sauce

Lemon Hard Sauce: Use 2 teaspoons grated lemon peel and 1
tablespoon lemon juice. Omit vanilla.
Golden Hard Sauce: Add 1 beaten egg yolk and ½ cup toasted,
blanched almond slivers.

 *Use the baby's canned puddings and strained fruits
as sauce for sliced fresh fruit, plain cake or gingerbread. For a crunchy sauce, fold in crushed peppermint stick candy or peanut brittle just before serving.*

Chocolate Sauce

2 squares (2 ozs.) unsweetened chocolate
6 tablespoons water
½ cup sugar

⅛ teaspoon salt
3 tablespoons butter or
  margarine
½ teaspoon vanilla extract

Combine first four ingredients in a saucepan. Cook over low heat, stirring constantly, until mixture boils, and chocolate is melted and blended. Remove from heat; stir in butter and vanilla. Makes about 1 cup.

Butterscotch Sauce

½ cup sugar
1 tablespoon light corn
  syrup
½ cup light cream or dairy
  half and half

½ cup brown sugar
2 tablespoons butter or
  margarine
½ teaspoon vanilla
  extract

Combine first four ingredients in saucepan. Bring to a boil, stirring until sugars dissolve; then cook without stirring 5 minutes. Remove from heat; stir in butter and vanilla. Makes 1½ cups.

Lemon Nutmeg Sauce

½ cup sugar
1 tablespoon cornstarch
1 cup boiling water
2 tablespoons butter or
  margarine

½ teaspoon grated lemon
  peel
1½ tablespoons lemon juice
Dash of salt
Dash of nutmeg

Combine sugar and cornstarch; add water gradually, stirring constantly. Boil 5 minutes, stirring as needed. Remove from heat and blend in remaining ingredients. Makes 1 cup.

Bing Cherry Sauce

1 can (1 lb.) Bing cherries   1 tablespoon cold water
2 teaspoons cornstarch   1 teaspoon sugar

Drain and pit cherries, saving the juice. Blend cornstarch with cold water and cherry juice. Heat to boiling point, stirring, until slightly thickened. Add sugar, if desired. Add cherries and serve the sauce warm on rice pudding or cake. Makes 2 cups.

Hot Brown Sugar Sauce

1 cup brown sugar   1 tablespoon butter or
⅛ teaspoon salt   margarine
⅔ cup water   1½ teaspoons vanilla
⅔ cup dark corn syrup   extract

Combine first four ingredients in a saucepan. Heat to boiling, stirring until sugar dissolves, and simmer gently 10 minutes. Remove from heat; stir in butter and vanilla. Serve warm with apple dumplings or baked apples. Makes about 1½ cups.

Melba Sauce

1 cup fresh or frozen   1 tablespoon cold water
   raspberries, mashed   ½ cup sugar
½ cup currant jelly   1 teaspoon cornstarch

Combine raspberries, jelly and water, and heat to boiling, stirring constantly. Add mixture of sugar and cornstarch, and cook, stirring, until thick and clear, about 10 minutes. Strain and cool. Serve over lemon sherbet, peach or vanilla ice cream or upside-down cake. Makes 1¾ cups.

NOTE: If frozen raspberries are used, omit sugar.

Soups

A joyful call of "Soup's on!" will get the family gathered at the dinner table quicker than any dinner bell ever invented.

So many delicious soups are available in canned, frozen or dry mix form that you could serve a different one every day for six months. If you started combining them to make new soups, you could go on for another six months. And if you tried slipping in extras, like deviled ham in cream of chicken or shrimp bits in cream of celery, the variety would be practically endless.

Although some homemade soups require leisurely cooking, many can be made in little more time than it takes to make a white sauce. And they're the perfect answer to what to do with water in which vegetables are cooked, with meat juices from roasts and pan frying, the outer leaves of salad greens and leftover meats and vegetables. Just put them all together, season with herbs and simmer in a covered pot. They'll ell GOOD SOUP every time.

Cream of Celery Soup

3 tablespoons butter
1 small onion, chopped
3 tablespoons flour
1½ teaspoons salt
    Dash of pepper

3 cups milk* or 1½ cups
    evaporated milk plus
    1½ cups water
2 cups cooked, diced
    celery

1. Melt butter in saucepan; add onion and cook until golden.
2. Blend in flour, salt and pepper.
3. Add milk slowly, stirring to blend.
4. Cook, stirring constantly, until mixture boils and thickens.
5. Add cooked celery. Season soup to taste.
Makes 6 servings.

* If available, substitute liquid drained from vegetables for up to 1 cup of the milk.

Variations of Cream of Celery Soup

Cream of Spinach Soup: Follow basic recipe, substituting 1½ cups chopped, cooked spinach for celery. Add ¼ teaspoon nutmeg.

Cream of Corn Soup: Follow basic recipe, substituting 1 can (1 lb.) cream-style golden sweet corn for celery.

Cream of Pea Soup: Follow basic recipe, substituting 1 can (1 lb.) peas, mashed, for celery, and using liquid drained from peas for part of the milk.

 Prepare soup vegetables over paper towel. When finished, parings can be bundled and discarded easily.

 Give extra flavor to cream soups by substituting 1 cup of meat stock (or 2 bouillon cubes dissolved in 1 cup water) for one cup of the milk.

Cream of Tomato Soup

2½ cups fresh, stewed or canned tomatoes	¼ teaspoon cinnamon
1 tablespoon minced onion	⅛ teaspoon baking soda
1 teaspoon sugar	3 tablespoons butter or margarine
1 teaspoon salt	3 tablespoons flour
½ bay leaf	1 teaspoon salt
	2½ cups milk

Combine first seven ingredients in a saucepan and simmer, uncovered, 5 minutes. Force through coarse strainer into a small bowl. Melt butter in saucepan; blend in flour and salt. Add milk gradually, stirring to blend. Cook, stirring, until mixture boils and thickens. Just before serving, stir tomato mixture gradually into hot sauce. Heat slowly, stirring constantly. If soup curdles, beat smooth. Makes 6 servings.

Cream of Mushroom Soup

2 cups chopped fresh mushrooms (about ½ pound)	3 cups milk
2 tablespoons chopped onion	1 cup beef stock or 2 beef bouillon cubes dissolved in 1 cup boiling water
¼ cup butter	1 teaspoon salt
3 tablespoons flour	⅛ teaspoon pepper

Sauté mushrooms and onion in butter until tender, 5 to 8 minutes, stirring occasionally. Blend in flour; add milk slowly and then beef stock, stirring to blend. Add salt and pepper, and cook, stirring constantly, until soup boils and thickens. Makes 6 to 8 servings.

Cream of Cheese Soup

2 tablespoons chopped
   onion
2 tablespoons butter
2 tablespoons flour
2 cups milk
¾ teaspoon salt

½ cup cooked carrot,
   minced
½ cup cooked celery,
   minced
1 cup shredded Cheddar
   cheese

Sauté onion lightly in butter. Add flour and milk to make a thin white sauce. Add salt, carrots, celery and cheese. Blend well and heat until steaming. Makes 4 servings.

Chicken Noodle Soup

2 pounds chicken necks
   and backs *or* carcass
   of roast chicken
2 quarts water
2 teaspoons salt
⅛ teaspoon pepper
⅛ teaspoon thyme

½ bay leaf
½ cup chopped onion
½ cup diced carrot
½ cup diced celery
1 cup uncooked egg
   noodles

1. Combine first six ingredients in large saucepan or kettle; cover and simmer 1 hour. Skim if necessary.
2. Add vegetables and simmer ½ hour longer.
3. Remove chicken bones.
4. Add noodles and cook 20 minutes or until noodles are tender.
5. Pick off any meat on chicken bones; chop and add to soup.
6. Season soup to taste (first adding 1 or 2 chicken bouillon cubes if richer flavor is desired), and reheat.

Makes 8 generous servings.

Variation: For Chicken Rice Soup, substitute ⅓ cup uncooked rice for the noodles. Cook 30 minutes after adding rice.

Split Pea Soup

1 cup dried split peas	2 teaspoons salt
1 ham bone or small	¼ teaspoon pepper
shank end	1 bay leaf
1 medium onion, chopped	6 cups water
½ cup chopped celery	
leaves	

1. Soak peas overnight in cold water to cover.
2. Put soaked peas in kettle with remaining ingredients; cover and simmer 1 hour, or until peas are tender, stirring occasionally.
3. Remove ham bone. Pick off any meat; chop it and return to soup, after straining the soup. (Push peas through strainer.)
4. If thinner soup is desired, add more water or milk. Season soup to taste and reheat.

Makes 6 servings.

Variations of Split Pea Soup

Lentil Soup: Follow basic recipe for Split Pea Soup, substituting 1 cup dried lentils for split peas.

Navy Bean Soup: Follow basic recipe, substituting 1 cup dried navy beans for split peas. Cook 2 to 3 hours, or until beans are tender, adding more water if necessary.

 Hot, nourishing soup is a welcome sight to lunchbox toters. If soup is piping hot when poured into the vacuum bottle, it will stay hot until lunch time.

Vegetable Soup

2 to 3 pounds soup bones
3 quarts water
1½ teaspoons salt
¼ teaspoon pepper
1 bay leaf
½ cup barley
1 cup diced carrots
1 cup diced potatoes

1 cup shelled peas or
    cut green beans
1 cup diced celery and
    leaves
½ cup chopped onion
2 cups shredded cabbage
1 can (1 lb.) tomatoes

1. Combine first five ingredients in a large kettle; cover and simmer 1 hour.
2. Add barley and continue to cook 1 hour.
3. Remove bones and skim fat, if necessary.
4. Add remaining ingredients and cook 1 hour longer.
5. Season to taste with additional salt and pepper, if desired.
Makes 8 to 10 servings.

Chilled Potato Onion Soup

2 tablespoons butter
1 onion, chopped
2 cups diced potatoes
1 cup chicken stock
2 cups milk

2 teaspoons salt
⅛ teaspoon pepper
1 cup light cream
2 tablespoons minced
    parsley or chives

Melt butter in large, heavy skillet. Add onion and sauté 5 minutes. Add potatoes, chicken stock, milk, salt and pepper, and cook over medium heat until potatoes are tender and soup is thickened. Remove from heat and cool. Combine with cream and chill in refrigerator. Garnish each serving with a sprinkling of minced parsley or chives. Makes 6 servings.

NOTE: Use 2 chicken bouillon cubes dissolved in 1 cup boiling water if chicken stock is not available.

French Onion Soup

¼ cup butter or margarine	½ teaspoon salt
6 medium onions, sliced	⅛ teaspoon pepper
5 beef bouillon cubes	3 slices toast, cubed
4 cups boiling water	¼ cup grated Parmesan or
½ teaspoon Worcester-	shredded sharp
shire sauce	Cheddar cheese

Melt butter in a saucepan and in it sauté onions over low heat until lightly browned. Dissolve bouillon cubes in boiling water. Add to onions along with Worcestershire sauce, salt and pepper. Cook until the onions are tender. Pour soup into an earthenware dish. Place toast cubes on top and sprinkle with cheese. Bake in hot oven (425°F.) until cheese is melted. Or, as a variation, toast may be placed on bottom of individual bowls, soup poured over, cheese sprinkled on, and the bowls placed under broiler until cheese forms brown crust. Makes 6 servings.

Southern Lentil Stew

1 cup dried lentils	1 large onion, sliced
1 quart cold water	3 medium carrots
2 teaspoons salt	2 tablespoons deviled ham
2 strips bacon	spread

Wash and pick over lentils; add water and soak 5 hours or overnight. Cook in water in which lentils were soaked. Place over medium heat, add salt, bring to a boil, then simmer until almost tender, about 45 minutes. Meanwhile cook bacon in skillet until crisp; remove bacon, crumble, and add to lentils. Put onion in skillet with bacon drippings and sauté until golden. Slice carrots about ⅓-inch thick. Add onion, carrots and deviled ham spread to lentils and cook until carrots are tender, about 15 minutes. Serve in soup bowls. Makes 6 servings.

Peanut Butter Bisque

6 tablespoons peanut   1 can condensed tomato
  butter   soup
3 tablespoons flour   3 cups milk

Heat peanut butter in top of double boiler; blend in flour. Gradually stir in soup and milk. Cook over hot water, stirring constantly, until thickened. Cover; cook 10 minutes longer. Serve with cheese crackers. Makes 6 servings.

Cabbage Chowder

1½ cups *or* ½ pound   2 tablespoons lemon
  smoked pork shoulder   juice
  butt, diced   1½ teaspoons brown
2 cups water   sugar
1½ cups shredded red or   Dash of allspice
  green cabbage   ½ teaspoon salt
2 tablespoons chopped   1 cup canned tomatoes
  onion

Place diced pork shoulder butt in a kettle with the water. Cover and simmer 1 hour or until tender. Add remaining ingredients; cover and simmer 45 minutes. Makes 4 servings.

Polka-dot Chowder

4 medium potatoes, diced   1 tablespoon butter
2 cups boiling, salted water   2 medium onions, chopped
1 tall can (1⅔ cups)   ½ teaspoon salt
  evaporated milk   ⅛ teaspoon pepper
1 can (1 lb.) cream-style   2 frankfurters, sliced
  corn   into circles

Cook potatoes in boiling, salted water until tender. Add evaporated milk and corn. Blend well and cook 5 minutes over low heat. Melt butter and sauté onions until yellow and clear. Add sautéed onions, salt, pepper and frankfurter circles to chowder. Cook until frankfurters are heated through. Makes 6 servings.

Fish Chowder

2 strips bacon	½ cup diced celery
½ cup chopped onion	2 large tomatoes
2 cups hot water	2 cups milk
2 medium potatoes, diced	¾ teaspoon salt
1 pound fish fillets	Dash of pepper

Cook bacon in soup kettle until crisp and brown. Remove bacon from kettle, crumble and set aside. Add onions to bacon fat and brown slightly. Add water and potatoes, and cook 10 minutes or until potatoes are partially tender. Cut fillets into 1-inch squares and add with celery. Cook until fish flakes easily when tested with a fork. Add tomatoes cut in thin wedges, milk and seasonings; heat thoroughly. Serve immediately. Makes 4 to 6 servings.

Scallop Vichyssoise

½ pound sea scallops, cooked	1 pint milk
2 cans (10¼ ozs. each) frozen condensed cream of potato soup	1 pint light cream
	Minced chives or chopped parsley

Cut any large scallops in half. Combine soup, milk and cream in a saucepan. Heat just until soup is thawed, then press through a sieve. Add scallops and heat thoroughly but do not boil. Garnish each serving with chives or parsley. Makes 6 servings.

Manhattan Clam Chowder

⅓ cup diced salt pork
1 cup chopped onion
¼ teaspoon thyme
2 cups diced potato
½ cup diced celery
1 can (1 lb.) tomatoes
2 teaspoons salt

⅛ teaspoon pepper
1 quart hot water
2 cans (10½ ozs. each)
    minced clams or 1½
    dozen steamed clams,
    chopped
Liquor from clams

Fry salt pork in a 4-quart saucepan or kettle until golden brown. Add onions and thyme, and sauté briefly. Add remaining vegetables, salt, pepper and water; simmer 45 minutes. Add clams and clam liquor and reheat. Makes 8 to 10 servings.

New England Clam Chowder

⅓ cup diced salt pork
½ cup finely chopped onion
3 cups diced potato
1 teaspoon salt
⅛ teaspoon pepper
2 cups hot water

2 cans (10½ ozs. each)
    minced clams or 1½
    dozen steamed clams,
    chopped
Liquor from clams
3 cups milk or 1½ cups
    evaporated milk plus
    1½ cups water

Fry salt pork in a 4-quart saucepan or kettle until golden brown; remove and save crisp bits. Add onion to pork fat and sauté briefly. Add potatoes, salt, pepper and water; cover and simmer 15 minutes. Add clams, clam liquor and milk; reheat to boiling point but do not boil. Garnish each serving with crisp salt pork bits. Makes 8 to 10 servings.

Oyster Stew

¼ cup butter or margarine ⅛ teaspoon pepper
1 pint oysters ¼ teaspoon paprika
1 quart milk 2 tablespoons chopped
1 teaspoon salt parsley

Melt butter, add oysters (in their liquor) and cook 8 minutes or until edges curl. Add milk and seasonings, and heat slowly to the boiling point but do not boil. Pour into soup bowls and sprinkle with parsley. Serve at once with oyster crackers. Makes 4 to 6 servings.

Soup Garnishes and Accompaniments

Avocado slices
Bread sticks
Caraway seeds
Cheese chips
Cheese, grated
Cheese popcorn
Cheese puffs
Chinese noodles
Chopped parsley, water cress, chives, celery or fresh herbs
Crisp crackers
Croutons—plain or garlic-flavored
Dash of paprika or cinnamon
Dusting of curry powder or nutmeg
Hamburger balls
Hard-cooked egg slices
Lemon slices with clove centers
Meat slivers
Melba toast
Mound of salted, whipped cream
Oyster crackers
Potato and corn chips
Puffed cereal
Raw onion slices
Ripe olive strips
Sieved egg yolk
Sliced or chopped, toasted nutmeats
Sliced Vienna sausage
Soda crackers
Sour cream
Stuffed olive slices
Thin rounds of frankfurters

Croutons

Spread day-old bread with softened butter or margarine and cut into small cubes. Spread out in a shallow baking pan; bake in a slow oven (325°F.) until golden brown, stirring occasionally. Or sauté unbuttered cubes in a small amount of butter or margarine, turning frequently to brown evenly. Float on soup.

Vegetables, Salads and Breads

The importance of vegetables in the diet can hardly be over-emphasized. They are rich sources of the vitamins and minerals essential to good health and supply much of the bulk necessary for adequate elimination.

Because vegetables are highly perishable they should be selected carefully for freshness and stored to preserve it. Economizing on quality is unwise, but a considerable saving can be realized by buying vegetables in season and using more of those vegetables in plentiful supply.

Most vegetables should be cooked, covered, in as little water as possible to preserve both nutrients and flavor. Too frequently they are overcooked, losing not only food value but also the attractive appearance so important when children are being encouraged to sample.

Butter, salt and pepper are all the seasoning needed for most vegetables. For variety, melt the butter first, brown slightly and flavor with just a hint of garlic or curry powder, horseradish, mustard, lemon, parsley or chives. Or top hot cooked vegetables with one of the sauces suggested on page 236.

How to Prepare, Cook and Serve Fresh Vegetables

Artichokes: Wash and cut off stem end and any discolored leaves. Cook, covered, in small amount of boiling, salted water, or, uncovered, in boiling, salted water to cover, 30 to 45 minutes. Drain upside down. Serve at once with melted butter, mayonnaise or Hollandaise Sauce.

Asparagus: Break off tough ends, remove scales and wash thoroughly. Cook whole or cut into 3-inch lengths. Tie stalks into bunches of 6 to 8, keeping ends even. Stand upright in 1 inch boiling, salted water in deep kettle or coffeepot. Cook 15 to 20 minutes covered, or cook stalks 12 to 15 minutes in 1 inch boiling, salted water in covered pan. (Stalk pieces may be cooked 5 minutes before adding tips.) Drain by lifting whole stalks from water with tongs. Season with salt, pepper, butter or margarine; or serve with Hollandaise Sauce, Vinaigrette Sauce or White Sauce.

Beans—Green—Wax: Remove stem ends and strings. Wash. Break into 1-inch lengths or slice lengthwise. Cook 10 to 12 minutes (broken) or 10 to 15 minutes (sliced) in 1 inch boiling, salted water in covered pan. Drain. Season with salt, pepper and butter; or serve with White Sauce or Vinaigrette Sauce.

Beans—Lima: Shell and wash. Cook 20 to 30 minutes in 1 inch boiling, salted water in covered pan. Drain. Season.

Beets: Cut off stems, leaving 1 inch of stems and roots. Scrub thoroughly. Cut big beets in half, cook small ones whole. Cook 30 to 50 minutes (depending on age) in 1 inch boiling, salted water in covered pan. Drain. Remove skins. Season with salt, pepper, and butter or margarine.

Beet Greens: Cut off very tough stems. Wash greens in several waters, lifting out of the water each time. Cook 5 to 15 minutes in 1 inch boiling, salted water in covered pan. Drain. Chop coarsely; drain again. Season with salt, pepper, and butter or margarine; or serve with White Sauce.

Broccoli: Discard big leaves and tough stalk ends. Wash thoroughly. Slit big end of stalk up 2 to 3 inches. Cook 15 to 20 minutes in 1 inch boiling, salted water in covered pan. Drain by lifting stalks out of water with tongs. Season with salt, pepper, butter or margarine and a little lemon juice; or serve with Hollandaise Sauce.

Brussels Sprouts: Discard wilted leaves. Wash. Cook 10 to 20 minutes in 1 inch boiling, salted water in covered pan. Drain. Season with salt, pepper, and butter or margarine; or serve with Hollandaise Sauce.

Cabbage—Green or Red: Discard wilted outside leaves. Cut in quarters or sixths, removing most of the core. Cook in wedges or shreds. Cook 7 to 15 minutes (wedges) or 4 to 8 minutes (shredded) in 1 inch boiling, salted water in covered pan. Drain thoroughly. Season with salt, pepper, and butter or margarine. Or serve in hot thin cream or White Sauce.

Carrots: Wash; pare or scrape, removing slice at stem and root end. Cook small carrots whole; split large ones lengthwise, or slice. Cook 15 to 25 minutes (halves or small whole) or 10 to 15 minutes (sliced) in 1 inch boiling, salted water in covered pan. Drain. Season with salt, pepper, and butter or margarine; or serve with White Sauce.

Cauliflower: Discard leaves; cut out woody base and any discolored portion. Cook whole or break into flowerets. Cook 20 to 25 minutes (whole) or 10 to 12 minutes (flowerets) in 1 inch boiling, salted water in covered pan. Drain. Season with salt, pepper, and butter or margarine; or serve with White Sauce, Cheese Sauce or Hollandaise Sauce.

Celery: Cut off leaves. Scrub each stalk; remove tough strings and any discolored portion. Cut into ½-inch pieces. Cook 10 to 15 minutes in 1 inch boiling, salted water in covered pan. Drain. Season with salt, pepper, and butter or margarine; or serve with White Sauce.

Chard: Wash thoroughly. Separate leaves from stalks. Cook stalks in 1 inch boiling, salted water in covered pan 15 minutes; add leaves and continue cooking 5 to 10 minutes. Drain thoroughly. Chop coarsely; drain again. Season with salt, pepper, and butter or margarine; or serve with White Sauce.

Corn on the Cob: Husk fresh corn; remove silks; cut off discolored or unkerneled portions. Cook 5 to 8 minutes in large quantity boiling, salted water in covered kettle. (Cook in batches: 1 ear per person in each batch.) Drain by lifting ears out of water with tongs. Serve at once, passing salt, pepper, and butter or margarine.

Kale: Cut out and discard tough stalks. Wash thoroughly in several waters, lifting out of the water each time. Cook 10 to 15 minutes in a very small amount of salted milk in covered pan. Drain thoroughly. Chop coarsely; drain again. Season with salt, pepper, and butter or margarine; or serve with White Sauce.

Kohlrabi: Cut off stems and leaves. Wash; pare. Cook sliced or cut in quarters. Cook 25 to 30 minutes in 1 inch boiling, salted water in covered pan. Drain. Season with salt, pepper, and butter or margarine; or serve with White Sauce.

Okra: Wash thoroughly; cut off stem ends. Cook whole 10 to 15 minutes (depending on age) in 1 inch boiling, salted water in covered pan. Drain. Season with salt, pepper, and butter or margarine, and a little lemon juice or vinegar; or serve with Hollandaise Sauce.

Onions: Peel under running water; cut slice from stem and root ends. Halve or quarter large onions; leave small ones whole. Cook 25 to 35 minutes (depending on size) in 1 inch boiling, salted water in covered pan. Drain. Season with salt, pepper, and butter or margarine; or serve with White Sauce.

Parsnips: Pare; cut slice off stem and root ends. Cook sliced or cut in quarters. Cook 10 to 20 minutes in 1 inch boiling, salted water in covered pan. Drain. Season with salt, pepper, and butter or margarine; or mash before seasoning and beat until fluffy.

Peas: Shell and wash. Cook 10 to 25 minutes (depending upon age) in 1 inch boiling, salted water in covered pan. Drain. Season with salt, pepper, and butter or margarine; or reheat in thin cream or serve with White Sauce.

Potatoes—Sweet, boiled: Scrub thoroughly; remove woody portions but do not pare. Halve large sweet potatoes, cook small ones whole. Cook 25 to 35 minutes in 1 inch boiling, salted water in covered pan. Drain. Holding each potato on a fork, peel off skin. Season with salt, pepper, butter or margarine; or mash before seasonings are added, and beat with a little milk until fluffy.

Potatoes—White, boiled: Scrub thoroughly. Cook in skins or pare thinly. Halve or quarter large potatoes, cook small ones whole. Cook 20 to 30 minutes (depending on size of pieces) in 1 inch boiling, salted water in covered pan. Drain.

Rutabaga: Wash and pare. Slice or cut into cubes. Cook 25 to 35 minutes in 1 inch boiling, salted water in covered pan. Drain. Season and mash until fluffy.

Spinach: Discard roots and wilted leaves. Wash thoroughly in several waters, lifting out of the water each time. Cook 8 to 10 minutes in ½ inch boiling, salted water in covered pan. Drain thoroughly. Chop coarsely; drain again. Season, or serve with White Sauce with a dash of nutmeg or with grated Parmesan.

Squash—Hubbard: Wash and pare. Remove seeds and stringy portion. Cut into 2-inch pieces. Cook 25 to 35 minutes in 1 inch boiling, salted water in covered pan. Drain, mash, season, add margarine and a little milk, and beat until light and fluffy.

Squash—Summer and Zucchini: Scrub; cut off discolored portion and stem end. Do not pare if young and tender. Cube or slice thinly. Cook 15 to 20 minutes in 1 inch boiling, salted water in covered pan. Drain well. Season with salt, pepper, butter or margarine; or mash and drain again before seasoning.

Turnips: Wash; pare. Remove slice at stem and root ends. Cube or slice. Cook 15 to 20 minutes in 1 inch boiling, salted water in covered pan. Drain. Season with salt, pepper, butter or margarine, and a little chopped parsley; or mash before adding seasonings, and beat until fluffy.

Turnip Greens: Cut off very tough stems. Wash thoroughly in several waters, lifting greens out of the water each time. Cook 8 to 15 minutes in ½ inch boiling, salted water in covered pan. Drain. Chop coarsely; drain again. Season with salt, pepper, and butter or margarine; or serve with White Sauce.

To peel tomatoes, put them in boiling water for about 1 minute until skins wrinkle. Drain, then rub off skins. Or hold each tomato on a fork over heat until the skins burst. Remove peel with sharp knife.

Old Fashioned Baked Beans

2 cups navy or pea beans
5 cups water
1 teaspoon powdered
  mustard
2 teaspoons salt
¼ teaspoon pepper

¼ cup brown sugar
¼ cup molasses
2 small onions,
  quartered
¼ pound salt pork

Wash beans; place in saucepan with water and soak 8 hours or overnight. Bring to a boil and cook, covered, ½ hour or until skins begin to burst. Add next 6 ingredients, mixing lightly. Cut salt pork into four pieces; place in bottom of greased 2-quart bean pot. Add bean mixture. Cover and bake in very slow oven (250°F.) 6 to 8 hours, adding more water if necessary during baking. Makes 6 to 8 servings.

NOTE: To speed preparation of beans for baking, cover washed beans with the water, bring to boiling point and boil rapidly for 2 minutes. Remove from heat, cover and let stand 1 hour. Beans are then ready to cook using same water in which they were soaked.

Spanish Lima Beans

4 strips bacon
2 medium onions
1 green pepper
1½ cups cooked tomatoes

2 cups cooked lima
  beans
1 tablespoon sugar
½ teaspoon salt

Cook bacon in saucepan but do not crisp; remove bacon. Slice onions and pepper thinly, and cook in bacon fat until onion is transparent. Add tomatoes and simmer 5 minutes. Then add lima beans, bacon, sugar and salt; mix well and cook slowly for 20 minutes. Makes 4 servings.

Harvard Beets

2 tablespoons butter   ½ teaspoon salt
2 tablespoons flour   ⅛ teaspoon pepper
¼ cup boiling water   ⅛ teaspoon ground cloves
¼ cup vinegar   2½ cups diced, cooked
⅓ cup brown sugar   beets

Melt butter and stir in flour. Gradually add boiling water and cook until thickened, stirring constantly. Add vinegar, sugar and seasonings; mix well until sugar dissolves. Add beets and cook until thoroughly heated. If canned beets are used, substitute ¼ cup beet liquid for the water. Makes 6 servings.

Panned Green Cabbage

2 to 3 tablespoons butter   1 quart shredded green
    or margarine or bacon   cabbage, tightly packed
    drippings   Salt and pepper

Melt butter in a heavy saucepan, add the cabbage and cover to hold in the steam. Cook slowly until just tender, about 8 minutes. Season to taste. Makes 6 servings.

Crumbed Carrots

8 medium carrots   3 tablespoons butter or
1 egg, slightly beaten   margarine
    Fine cracker crumbs

Cook whole carrots in small amount of boiling, salted water until tender. Drain. Cut carrots lengthwise into strips. Roll carrots in egg, then in cracker crumbs. Brown lightly in hot butter. Makes 4 to 6 servings.

Honey-glazed Carrots

12 small carrots *or* 6 large
   carrots, halved
¼ cup butter or margarine
 1 tablespoon brown sugar
 2 tablespoons honey

¼ teaspoon grated
   orange peel
3 tablespoons finely
   minced parsley

Cook carrots in small amount boiling, salted water until tender, about 15 minutes. Melt butter in a skillet, add sugar. honey, orange peel and drained carrots. Cook over low heat, turning carrots until well glazed. Remove from pan and roll in parsley. Makes 4 to 6 servings.

French Green Beans

2 pkgs. (10 ozs. each)
   frozen French-cut green
   beans, cooked and
   drained

1 can condensed cream of
   mushroom soup
½ can (3½ ozs.) French
   fried onions

Combine beans and soup in a shallow 1-quart baking dish. Sprinkle onions over the top and heat in moderate oven (350°F.) about 30 minutes. Makes 6 servings.

Dress up vegetables with a garnish of thinly sliced almonds sautéed in butter.

Save the liquid drained from canned or home-cooked vegetables to add extra flavor and food value to soups, sauces and gravies.

Cauliflower au Gratin

1 medium cauliflower	1 tablespoon butter or
1 cup Medium White	margarine
Sauce, page 231	¼ cup shredded
¼ cup bread crumbs	American cheese

Cook cauliflower according to directions, page 255; drain (reserving liquid) and place in a greased 1½-quart casserole. Make Medium White Sauce, using water from cauliflower for part of liquid. Brown bread crumbs in hot butter; mix with shredded cheese. Pour sauce over cauliflower and sprinkle with crumb-cheese mixture. Bake in moderate oven (350°F.) 15 to 20 minutes. Makes 6 servings.

Corn Pudding

1 cup Thick White Sauce,	1 teaspoon salt
page 231	1 tablespoon sugar
2 cups canned corn	2 teaspoons butter
2 eggs, beaten	1 cup corn flakes

Make White Sauce and add corn, eggs, salt and sugar. Stir well and pour into a greased 1½-quart baking dish. Melt butter and combine with corn flakes. Sprinkle corn flakes mixture over pudding. Set in pan of hot water and bake in moderate oven (350°F.) 30 to 35 minutes. Makes 4 to 6 servings.

Panned Eggplant

1 large eggplant	3 medium tomatoes,
1 green pepper, chopped	peeled and chopped
1 small onion, chopped	1½ teaspoons salt
2 tablespoons salad oil	

Peel eggplant and cut into 1-inch cubes. Sauté green pepper and onion in salad oil until tender. Add eggplant, tomatoes and salt. Cover and cook over medium heat 5 to 10 minutes, stirring occasionally, until eggplant is just tender. Makes 6 servings.

Lettuce with Hot Bacon Dressing

4 strips bacon	½ teaspoon salt
2 teaspoons sugar	¼ cup vinegar
½ teaspoon powdered mustard	1 medium head lettuce

Cook bacon over low heat until crisp. Remove and crumble. Combine sugar, mustard, salt and vinegar, and add to hot bacon drippings in skillet. Break lettuce into small pieces and sprinkle with bacon. Pour hot dressing over lettuce. Toss and serve immediately. Makes 4 to 6 servings.

Mushrooms Sauté

1 pound fresh mushrooms	¾ teaspoon salt
¼ cup butter	⅛ teaspoon pepper

Wash mushrooms; slice ¼-inch thick. Melt butter in a large skillet; add mushrooms, and sprinkle with salt and pepper. Sauté gently 5 to 8 minutes or until mushrooms are tender, turning often. Remove from heat and let stand 5 minutes to absorb juices. Makes 6 servings.

Scalloped Onions

2 pounds small white onions	½ cup fine dry bread crumbs
1 cup Medium White Sauce, page 230	2 tablespoons butter or margarine

Cook onions according to directions, page 257; drain (reserving liquid) and place in a greased 1½-quart casserole. Make Medium White Sauce, using water from onions for part of liquid. Brown crumbs in hot fat. Pour white sauce over onions, sprinkle with crumbs. Bake, uncovered, in moderate oven (350°F.) 15 to 20 minutes. Makes 6 servings.

French Fried Onion Rings

4 large white onions   ½ cup flour
1 cup fat for frying   ¼ teaspoon salt
⅔ cup milk   Dash of pepper

Wash and peel onions. Cut into ¼-inch slices and separate into rings. Heat fat to 375°F. or to the point where a cube of day-old bread browns in 1 minute. Dip onion rings in milk, and then in the flour seasoned with salt and pepper. Fry onions, a few at a time, for 2 to 3 minutes or until lightly browned. Remove and drain on absorbent paper. Makes 6 servings.

Tuna-stuffed Baked Potatoes

4 large, hot baked   Salt and pepper
   potatoes   1 tablespoon minced
2 tablespoons butter or   onion
   margarine   1 can (6½ ozs.) tuna
½ cup hot milk

Cut lengthwise slice from top of each baked potato; scoop out inside with a spoon and mash. Beat in butter and hot milk. Season to taste. Add minced onion and flaked tuna; mix. Pile tuna mixture lightly into potato shells. Place on cookie sheet or in shallow baking dish, and bake in very hot oven (450°F.) 10 minutes or until lightly browned. Makes 4 servings.

Country-style Potatoes

3 tablespoons bacon
    drippings or salad oil
¼ cup finely cut scallions
    with tops, or onions
3 cups peeled, finely diced
    potatoes

3 tablespoons flour
1 teaspoon salt
⅛ teaspoon pepper
¼ cup milk

Heat 1 tablespoon of the bacon drippings over low heat in a heavy skillet. Add scallions or onions and sauté until tender, but not brown, about 5 minutes. Put potatoes in mixing bowl, sprinkle with flour, salt and pepper, and mix thoroughly. Add scallions and milk, mix until distributed. Heat remaining bacon drippings in skillet. Turn potato mixture into skillet and press down with a large spatula. Cook over low heat about 20 minutes, or until crisp and browned on the bottom. Turn and brown other side. Makes 4 to 6 servings.

Scalloped Potatoes

2½ tablespoons butter or
    margarine
2½ tablespoons flour
1 teaspoon salt

2 cups milk
6 medium potatoes, pared
    and thinly sliced

Melt butter in a saucepan, stir in flour and salt. Add milk slowly, stirring constantly until sauce boils and thickens. Add potatoes. Heat, stirring occasionally. Pour into a greased 2-quart casserole, cover, and bake in moderate oven (350°F.) 30 minutes or until done. Makes 6 servings.

Candied Sweet Potatoes

6 medium sweet potatoes   ⅓ cup butter or margarine
¼ cup orange juice   ½ teaspoon salt
¾ cup brown sugar

Cook potatoes according to directions, page 257. Peel, halve lengthwise, and arrange in a greased, shallow baking dish. Combine remaining ingredients in saucepan and heat to boiling, stirring until sugar dissolves. Pour over sweet potatoes. Bake in moderate oven (375°F.) 30 minutes, basting with syrup once or twice. Makes 6 servings.

Sweet Potatoes Hawaiian

6 medium sweet potatoes   ¼ teaspoon ginger
3 tablespoons butter or   ⅛ teaspoon ground cloves
    margarine   ¼ cup sugar
1½ teaspoons salt   ⅔ cup pineapple juice

Cook potatoes according to directions, page 257; peel. Mash thoroughly. Add remaining ingredients and beat until light and fluffy. Reheat over boiling water. Makes 6 servings.

Stuffed Baked Sweet Potatoes

6 sweet potatoes, baked   ½ teaspoon salt
3 tablespoons butter   ¼ cup raisins
⅓ cup hot milk   ½ cup broken pecans

Cut baked sweet potatoes in halves lengthwise. Scoop out the insides and mash with butter, milk and salt. Add more milk if not as moist as desired. Add raisins and pecans. Heap lightly into sweet potato shells and reheat. Makes 6 servings.

Spinach au Gratin

3 pounds fresh spinach
1 cup Medium White
  Sauce, page 231
½ cup shredded sharp
  American cheese

½ cup fine dry bread
  crumbs
2 tablespoons butter,
  margarine or
  bacon fat

Cook spinach according to directions, page 257; drain (save liquid) and chop. Make Medium White Sauce, using water from spinach for part of liquid. Add cheese to hot sauce and cook, stirring, until cheese is melted and blended. Combine chopped spinach with sauce; pour into a greased 1½-quart casserole. Brown crumbs in hot butter; sprinkle over spinach. Bake in moderate oven (350°F.) 15 to 20 minutes. Makes 6 servings.

Baked Acorn Squash

3 medium acorn
  squash
Salt and pepper

1 cup dark corn syrup,
  maple syrup or honey
2 tablespoons butter

Cut squash in halves, remove seeds and scrape out all loose pulp. Sprinkle each half with a little salt and pepper. Place skin side down in large pan and put equal amounts of syrup or honey in each of the squash cavities. Dot with butter and pour water in pan to depth of 1 inch. Bake in moderate oven (350°F.) 1 hour. Makes 6 servings.

Zucchini, Italian-style

2½ pounds zucchini
¼ cup salad oil
3 medium onions, sliced
1½ teaspoons salt

¼ teaspoon pepper
½ bay leaf
3 cups tomato juice

Scrub zucchini, cut off ends. Cut crosswise into 1-inch slices. Heat oil in a large skillet; add zucchini and brown on both sides. Add remaining ingredients, cover, and simmer 30 minutes or until tomato juice forms a thick sauce. Makes 6 servings.

Grilled Tomatoes

4 ripe, medium tomatoes
  Salt and pepper

¼ cup buttered bread
  crumbs

Wash tomatoes. Cut out stem end and cut in halves crosswise. Arrange, cut side up, in baking pan; sprinkle with salt and pepper, then crumbs. Broil 10 to 15 minutes. Makes 4 to 6 servings.

Scalloped Tomatoes

1 can (1 lb. 13 ozs.)
  tomatoes
2 tablespoons chopped
  onion
1 tablespoon chopped
  green pepper
3 tablespoons chopped
  celery

3 tablespoons flour
4 teaspoons sugar
1 teaspoon salt
¼ teaspoon pepper
½ cup soft bread
  crumbs
2 tablespoons butter

Combine vegetables in mixing bowl. Mix together flour, sugar, salt and pepper; stir into vegetables. Turn into greased 1½-quart baking dish; top with bread crumbs and dot with butter. Bake in moderate oven (350°F.) 45 minutes. Makes 6 servings.

 Top creamed vegetables with packaged bread stuffing mix. Sprinkle with shredded cheese, dot with butter and bake in moderate oven until delicately browned.

Frozen Foods

You can serve your family better meals more easily, in less time and at a lower cost when you take full advantage of frozen foods and make your home freezer work for you.

When you have a home freezer and use it to the fullest, you can:

• Plan your meals around frozen foods to have more free time for the children, community activities and just plain fun.

• Avoid frequent trips to market by stocking frozen foods, staples and canned foods once a month.

• Be prepared for any mealtime emergency—whether it be a sick child that keeps you from going to market or your husband phoning at five o'clock that he's bringing an important customer home to dinner.

• Cook when you have the time and freeze the food for use when your time is precious.

• Cook in cool weather and freeze the food for meals during the summer heat.

• Save time and fuel by making favorite family dishes in quantity and freezing the extras for future use.

• Minimize muss and fuss after each meal because fewer pots and pans are needed when precooked frozen foods are used. Just pop in oven and serve.

• Plan, prepare, label and freeze complete meals that can be readied for serving in specific times as, for example, 20-minute lunches, 30-minute dinners and so forth.

• Come home late from a PTA meeting or Ladies' Aid tea and be able to have a complete, nutritious meal on the table easily in half an hour.

• Return from a vacation trip, and, without a hurried shopping stop, serve a meal fit to climax a happy family outing.

• Buy or make up frozen low-calorie dinners to serve weight watchers in your family so the rest of the family won't have to diet just because they do.

• Assemble frozen foods that combine to make a meal for your family, put them together in a large polyethylene bag and slip in step-by-step instructions for your husband or an older child to follow in case you must be away from home at mealtime.

• Bake one day a week and stock the home freezer with bread one week, cake the next, pie the third and prepared dishes the following—each category to last a month or more. It's almost as easy, when you have all supplies and utensils out and the oven on, to double or triple a recipe as to make just one.

• Save and enjoy leftovers that would otherwise go to waste. Such ready-to-eat tidbits can be used for lunchbox fillers or midnight snacks. Take, for instance, the last two pieces of cherry pie and store in the freezer until someone says, "Gee, I wish I had a piece of your cherry pie tonight."

• Buy meat wholesale, have it packaged to order the way your family likes it and frozen at a locker plant.

• Prepare and freeze half a dozen chickens on a free day, then sit back and enjoy them for many a day.

- Use ice cube trays to freeze a number of foods that are convenient to have on hand in small amounts. For example, you can freeze concentrated meat and poultry broths in ice cube trays, remove cubes and store labeled in polyethylene bags ready to add zest to soups, sauces and gravies. Likewise use double strength coffee cubes for a quick glass of iced coffee, frozen fruit juice cubes to chill a fruit drink.

- Please your fisherman husband by freezing his catch, thus coupling future good eating for the entire family with happy memories for him. Same practice applies to the ardent sportsman and his game.

- Treat your family to a variety of breads every meal. Just buy a loaf each of three or four different breads, then make up and freeze family size packets containing a few slices of each kind.

- Enjoy many commercially frozen foreign, regional and unusual foods that you don't know how to make or might not take the time to prepare.

- Avoid the daily struggle with the ice cube tray by keeping a generous supply of ice cubes in plastic freezer bags to remove easily as needed.

- Store a supply of extra ice cubes and crushed ice to have on hand for party service.

- Make all sorts of fancy dishes and dramatic desserts to stash away for impromptu entertaining.

- Buy ice cream economically in half-gallon containers and keep the freezer stocked with a choice of two or more flavors. Ice cream is wonderful to have on hand for a cooling summer snack, a nourishing family dessert or a special occasion concoction. Among ice cream specialties which can be bought commercially prepared are spumone, éclairs, ice cream pies, sponge cake rolls and fancy pastry molds.

- Save leftover sweetened whipped cream by swirling it into individual toppings and freezing on wax paper on a cookie sheet.

Remove and wrap each swirl separately before storing in the freezer, ready to pop onto a dessert or cup of hot cocoa later.

• Pop lots of corn at a time and freeze the extra. Heat before serving and it's as crisp as when freshly popped.

• Cook and freeze foods for church bazaars and suppers so you'll be free to work at the church the day of the affair. Baked beans, cakes and so forth can be frozen in the same attractive aluminum containers in which they are to be sold or served.

• Make and freeze holiday food gifts such as special holiday breads, batches of fancy cookies, fresh fruit jam and candies at your leisure.

• Prepare fruit for holiday fruitcakes and freeze it until you are ready to make and bake the cakes. The most time-consuming part will be over with.

• Give parties with less fatigue and more personal pleasure because foods requiring time-consuming preparation are ready in your freezer. It's like having a built-in catering service.

• Avoid menu monotony. Instead of having the remains of a roast day after day, just freeze the leftovers to eat when in the mood.

• Have family fun preparing food for the freezer production-line fashion. For example, 20 pounds of ground meat will make 6 two-pound meat loaves, 16 patties, 40 meat balls and leave enough meat for a gallon of spaghetti meat sauce. Package patties, meat balls and sauce in portions just right for one meal each.

 Shop where the frozen food cabinet is kept neat and attractive and where the temperature indicators show zero degrees or below—the only safe storage temperature for frozen foods.

How to Freeze Foods at Home

There are three essentials for successful home freezing. The food to be frozen must be fresh and carefully prepared. Freezing does not improve quality, only preserves it. It must be properly packaged to exclude air so the food does not dry out during storage, with consequent loss of flavor, color and appeal. It must be frozen quickly at a temperature of zero or below. Freezing should not be attempted in the ice cube compartment of a refrigerator.

For consistently good results, follow the directions in your freezer manual. The following tips may also help you:

When preparing casseroles and similar main dishes for freezing, the general rule is to undercook slightly and also to underseason. Reheating will finish the cooking time. Additional seasoning may be added later if necessary.

Before freezing meat, remove as much bone as practical in order to save valuable freezer space. Make soup stock from the bones and freeze to use many ways. Cover individual portions of cooked meat and poultry to be frozen with a gravy to prevent drying out when reheated.

Almost all types of pie can be frozen successfully at home. If the pies are frozen unbaked, do not cut vent holes in the upper crust until just before baking. If a frozen pie is to be topped with meringue, it is better to remove pie from freezer and add meringue just before baking.

When freezing unbaked fruit pies, add an extra teaspoon or two of tapioca or cornstarch to take up the juice drawn from the fruit during freezing. Be sparing with spices because they tend to become stronger on freezing.

There doesn't seem to be much difference between frosting a cake before or after freezing. However, if a cake is frosted, it is best to freeze it before wrapping.

How Long to Store?

The length of time frozen food may be held at its prime depends on many factors. These include the type of food, original quality and freshness, care taken in preparing and packaging, speed of freezing and constancy of the storage temperature.

A few foods, such as homogenized milk, cream, ice cream, butter, dishes made with gelatin and cooked prepared dishes, should not be stored over a month. Most other foods keep well for six to eight months. Exceptions are ham, bacon, sausage, fatty fish and unbaked products, which should not be held over three months. These may not spoil but their flavor will be impaired

Whenever homemakers talk about frozen foods one question is sure to be asked. Is it safe to refreeze food? According to food technologist Donald K. Tressler, an authority on frozen foods, there is no danger in refreezing foods that have not been allowed to warm above 40°F. The danger comes when thawed foods are allowed to start spoiling, then are refrozen. However, refrozen foods do not taste so good as once-frozen foods.

Although the management of the frozen food supply varies from family to family, some type of system is needed to assure an assortment of foods and to aid in menu planning.

If you are chart-minded, make one so you can tell at a glance the location of all foods, what is available and what needs replenishing. Otherwise keep a working inventory to use as a marketing guide, crossing off foods as used, and noting quality of bought frozen foods for future reference. Be sure first foods in the freezer are first used.

Good Lunches
for Children

Home Lunches

School children who go home for lunch get more than food. Mother is there, and she can help solve the morning's problems before you can say "lunch is served." She can, that is, if she has planned for this important break in the school day.

Many mothers find that the only way they can be sure of serving lunch on time and giving their undivided attention to the children is to partially prepare lunch as soon as the children leave for school in the morning. If this preliminary work is done right after breakfast, the utensils used can be washed with the breakfast dishes, saving both work and clutter.

Other mothers prefer to serve quick dishes that can be made just a few minutes before the children come home. The Shirred Eggs with Cheese, in the September Lunch Calendar, page 285, is a good example. The basic preparation is as simple as breaking eggs into baking cups, yet the dish has excellent food value and appetite appeal for hungry youngsters.

Lunch, which should furnish one-third of the day's nutrients, is the balance wheel of the day. If eggs were absent from the morning meal, lunch can make room for them. If fruit was neglected at breakfast, it can be used in a luncheon salad or dessert. If cereal or toast was left untouched, there are many good ways to use a cereal or bread in the noon meal.

Lunch Calendar

The following calendar is a guide to varied, nutritious, appetite-appealing lunches. Make it work for you in suggesting different ways to serve foods. Switch the menus around to suit your convenience. Get some fun out of dressing up the leftovers so the children will switch from "I don't want that cold ham," to "Gee, Mom, this ham 'n' spinach pie is super!"

NOTE: Serve milk or a milk drink with these lunches and add a breadstuff if needed.

January

MONDAY	TUESDAY	WEDNESDAY	THURSDAY	FRIDAY
		Chicken Noodle Soup Toasted Cheese Sandwiches Sponge Cake	Chickenburgers Cranberry Sauce Broccoli Banana Pudding	Creamed Tuna and Peas on Toast Grapefruit Sections with Honey
Vegetable Soup Deviled Ham Sandwiches Fruit Compote	Hot Broth Pear and Cottage Cheese Salad Raisin Rice Pudding	Chicken Livers on Toast Fresh Pears Date Bars	Peanut Butter and Raisin Sandwiches Carrot Sticks Strawberry Ice Cream	Baked Beans and Brown Bread Sandwiches Baked Apple
Broiled Kidneys Creamed Potatoes Canned Peach Halves	Bacon and Lettuce Sandwiches Banana Ambrosia Molasses Cookies	Macaroni and Cheese Lettuce Wedges Floating Island Vanilla Wafers	Leftover Beef Stew Hot Baking Powder Biscuits Waldorf Salad	Creamed Eggs on Toast Raw Vegetable Salad Stewed Apricots
Scrambled Eggs with Frizzled Dried Beef Celery Sticks Brownies	Corned Beef Hash Buttered Beets Fruit Gelatin	Chicken Shortcake with Mushroom Soup Sauce Apple	Leftover Meat Baked Potatoes Baked Custard with Fruit Sauce	Codfish Cakes Buttered Carrots Fruit Tapioca
Cream of Tomato Soup Liver Patties Tangerines Oatmeal Cookies	Spanish Rice Coleslaw Butterscotch Pudding	Celery Soup Cottage Cheese Salad Sliced Bananas in Pineapple Juice	Finger Vegetables Spaghetti with Meat Sauce Choice of Fresh Fruit	

February

MONDAY	TUESDAY	WEDNESDAY	THURSDAY	FRIDAY
				Pea Soup Scrambled Egg Toastwiches Fruit Gelatin
Luncheon Quickie Pear Cranberry Compote Animal Crackers	Tomato Juice Sardine Sandwiches Carrot and Celery Sticks Apple Betty	Frankfurters Sauerkraut Strawberry Rennet Custard	Cream of Celery Soup Peanut Butter and B:con Sandwiches Tangerines	Scalloped Salmon Buttered Peas Corn Muffins Chocolate Pudding
Canned Pork and Beans Lettuce Wedges Lemon Pudding	Sweet Potato and Sausage Casserole Stewed Figs Sugar Cookies	Creamed Dried Beef on Toast or Rusk Vegetable Salad Baked Apple	Cream of Tomato Soup Cottage Cheese Salad Raspberry Rennet Valentine Cookies	Asparagus Soup Chopped Egg and Mushroom Sandwiches Orange Ambrosia
Veal-stuffed Cabbage Rolls Butterscotch Pudding	Clam Chowder Peanut Butter—Chili-sauce Sandwichettes Fruit Cocktail	Ham Cornucopias with Hot Potato Salad Lettuce Wedges Tapioca Pudding	Creamed Eggs on Noodles Bran Muffins Apple	Grilled Cheese Sandwiches Mixed Cabbage Salad Cherry Gelatin
Corned Beef Hash Buttered Kale Grapes or Bananas Oatmeal Cookies	Buckwheat Pancakes with Syrup Applesauce Ginger Cookies	Toasted Tuna Sandwiches Carrot Raisin Slaw Rice Pudding	Chicken Noodle Soup Green Salad Dried Fruit Compote	Codfish Cakes Tomato Sauce Raw Vegetable Sticks Custard Pudding

March

MONDAY	TUESDAY	WEDNESDAY	THURSDAY	FRIDAY
Cheese Omelet Bran Muffins Vanilla Pudding with Peach Sauce	Cabbage Chowder Corn Muffins Apricot Whip Brownies	Creamed Vegetables on a Crisp Cereal Cheese-spread Buns Canned Plums	Baked Bean Sandwiches, Coleslaw Apple Cranberry Sauce Molasses Cookies	Tuna Vegetable Pie Green Salad Coconut Cream Pudding
Onion Soup Peanut Butter and Bacon Sandwiches Stewed Fruit	Cream of Mushroom Soup Ham Toastwiches Fruit Gelatin Chocolate Cookies	Deviled Eggs on Macaroni Bows with Celery Soup Sauce Orange Rennet	Cream of Tomato Soup Cottage Cheese Pancakes Canned Pears	Cheese 'Burgers Spinach Banana Cereal Cookies
Irish Stew Celery Stalks Lime Fruit Gelatin Molasses Cookies	Tomato Juice Open Liver Celery Sandwiches Caramel Cup Custard	Clam Chowder Wheat Crackers Fruit Cup Pound Cake	Spaghetti Meat Sauce Cabbage Salad Apples	Cottage Cheese and Raisin Sandwiches Celery Sticks Pineapple Slices
Open Hot Meat Loaf Sandwiches Carrot Slaw Chocolate Pudding	Beef Lentil Stew Tangerines Peanut Butter Cookies	Scrambled Eggs and Bologna Spring Green Salad Cherry Tapioca	Cream of Asparagus Soup Salmon Sandwiches Orange Snow	Tuna Macaroni Casserole Carrot Sticks Strawberry Gelatin
Hot Vegetable Juice Chicken Celery Salad Hot Biscuits with Honey				

April

MONDAY	TUESDAY	WEDNESDAY	THURSDAY	FRIDAY
	Chicken Broth Sardine Sandwiches Fruited Gelatin Brownies	Eggs Goldenrod on Fluffy Rice Raw Vegetable Salad Vanilla Custard	Cream of Tomato Soup Cottage Cheese and Raisin Sandwiches Stewed Apricots	Scrambled Egg Sand- wiches Spring Vegetables Chocolate Pudding
Canned Beef Stew Coleslaw Pineapple Wedges Oatmeal Cookies	Hot Vegetable Juice Ham Sandwiches Bananas Vanilla Wafers	Baked Omelet Canned Green Beans Fruit on Cereal with Cream	Vegetable Chowder Cheese Crackers Canned Plums Sugar Cookies	Macaroni and Cheese Shredded Lettuce with French Dressing Apple Betty
Baked Ham Patties Cooked Vegetable Salad Farina Pudding	Beef Noodle Soup Carrot, Celery, Apple and Ground Peanut Salad Butterscotch Pudding	Spanish Rice Green Salad Sliced Oranges Macaroons	Asparagus Soup Cream Cheese on Raisin Bread Bananas	Creamed Tuna on Corn Chips Cranberry Sauce Maple Rennet
Leftover Meat and Vegetable Pie Gingerbread with Whipped Cream	Peanut Butter and Jelly Sandwiches Carrot Sticks Orange and Prune Cup	Broiled Hamburgers Creamed Potatoes Grapefruit Sections Chocolate Cookies	Chili Con Carne Watermelon Pickle Baked Custard with Peach Sauce	Codfish Cakes with Tomato Sauce Buttered Cabbage Peppermint Stick Tapioca
Corn Meal Waffles Honey or Jelly Bacon Curls Canned Pears	Creamed Chipped Beef on Toast Buttered Asparagus Apple Crisp	Green Pea Soup Soda Crackers Fruit Cup Molasses Cookies		

May

MONDAY	TUESDAY	WEDNESDAY	THURSDAY	FRIDAY
			Grilled Hamburgers on Toasted Buns Finger Vegetables Butterscotch Pudding	French Toast with Hot Applesauce Celery Sticks Strawberry Yogurt
Noodles with Mild Cheese Sauce Grapefruit and Prune Salad Sugar Cookies	Scotch Broth Chopped Liver Sandwiches Lemon Rennet	Scalloped Lima Beans and Tomatoes Pear Salad Peanut Butter Cookies	Cream of Celery Soup Open Face Grilled Cheese Sandwiches Stewed Prunes	Scrambled Eggs Sweet Pickles Sliced Banana in Orange Juice
Vegetable Meat Pie Orange and Coconut Salad Raisin Cookies	Hard-cooked Eggs with Tomato Sauce Canned Peaches Oatmeal Cookies	Junior Veal Casserole Cheese Crackers Stewed Prunes and Pineapple Chunks	Mushroom Soup Shredded Lettuce and Carrot Salad Caramel Custard	Flaked Salmon with Egg Sauce Green Salad Fruit Gelatin
Scalloped Potato and Ham Casserole Carrot Curls Molasses Cookies	Hot Tomato Juice Bacon and Cottage Cheese Sandwiches Chocolate Nut Pudding	Chicken Gumbo Soup Egg Salad Sandwiches Baked Apple with Cream	Hot Tongue Sandwiches Coleslaw Peanut Butter Tapioca	Macaroni and Cheese Casserole Mixed Raw Vegetables Butter Cookies
Vegetable Soufflé with Saltines Fruit Milkshake Cereal Cookies	Hot Apple Juice Cottage Cheese and Carrot Sandwiches Junior Pineapple Pudding	Cream of Chicken Soup Peanut Butter Sandwiches Apple Betty	Cream of Asparagus Soup Bacon and Lettuce Sandwiches Orange Sections	Poached Eggs on Spinach Bread Pudding with Strawberry Sauce

June

MONDAY	TUESDAY	WEDNESDAY	THURSDAY	FRIDAY
Broiled Cheese and Tomato Sandwiches with Crisp Bacon Caramel Custard	Toasted Peanut Butter and Jelly Sandwiches Waldorf Salad Toll House Cookies	Celery Soup Grated Carrot Raisin Mayonnaise Sandwiches Chocolate Pudding	Grilled Hamburgers Creamed Potatoes Canned Sliced Peaches Sugar Cookies	Sardine Sandwiches Tomato Slices Strawberries with Milk or Cream
Cooked Vegetable Plate Pineapple Chunks Raisin Cookies	Cabbage and Egg Scallop Sliced Beets Apricot and Rice Pudding	Cream of Asparagus Soup Deviled Ham Sandwiches Apples	Chili Con Carne Fresh Fruit Brownies	Cheese Noodles Carrot Sticks Fruit Gelatin Vanilla Wafers
Chopped Chicken Liver Sandwiches Baked Apple Butter Cookies	Tomato Soup Egg Salad Sandwiches Raspberry Rennet Oatmeal Cookies	Creamed Chicken and Vegetables on Toast Cherry Tarts	Asparagus with Melted Cheese Sauce Cantaloupe Lemon Cookies	Tuna Salad and Lettuce Sandwiches Mixed Fruit Peanut Butter Cookies
Split Pea Soup Cottage Cheese and Olive Sandwiches Apricot Sherbet	Bacon and Jelly Sandwiches Mixed Vegetable Salad Fresh Cherries	Tomato Cheese Rice Fresh Green Peas Bananas with Dairy Half and half	Chopped Ham and Vegetable Salad Potato Chips Applesauce with Cinnamon Sugar	Scrambled Eggs Finger Vegetables Ice Cream with Strawberry Sauce
Vegetable Soup Cheese Crackers Sliced Oranges Molasses Cookies				

July

MONDAY	TUESDAY	WEDNESDAY	THURSDAY	FRIDAY
	Sliced Ham and Relish Sandwiches Spring Salad Blueberry Cupcakes	Hamburgers in Buns Potato Chips Carrot Sticks Ice Cream Cones	Chicken in the Rough Hot Buttered Biscuits Slices of Watermelon	Deviled Eggs with Cheese Sauce on Toast Cantaloupe
Tomato Juice Liverwurst and Chopped Celery in Rolls Bananas	Cream Cheese and Jelly Sandwiches Celery Sticks Gingerbread Cupcakes	Chilled Pea Soup Peanut Butter and Bacon in Buns Cantaloupe Wedges	Grilled Frankfurters in Toasted Buns Baked Beans Fresh Peaches	Chopped Egg and Celery Salad Sandwiches Ice Cream Cup Fig Bars
Liver Sausage Spread Sandwiches Potato Chips Pineapple Spears	Chopped Raw Vegetable Salad Sandwiches Marble Cake	Leftover Meat and Noodle Salad Cherry Tomatoes Fresh Raspberries	Cheese Burgers in Toasted Buns Lettuce Wedges Chocolate Ice Cream	Nutted Cream Cheese on Raisin Bread Carrot Sticks Radishes Half Cantaloupe
Leftover Meat and Vegetable Sandwiches Butterscotch Brownies	Chilled Grape Juice Ham Salad Sandwiches Chocolate Jumbles	Peanut Butter and Honey Sandwiches Shredded Coleslaw Ice Cream Cones	Sliced Chicken Sandwiches Fresh Cherries Lemon Wafers	Sardine Sandwiches Cucumber Wedges Fruit Cup Molasses Cookies
Pineapple Juice Chopped Egg and Olives in Rolls Fresh Strawberries	Meat Loaf Sandwiches Tomatoes, Pickles Sugar Cookies	Grilled Cheese on English Muffins Lettuce Wedges Plums	Cold Boiled Ham Potato Salad Cup Custard Grapes	

August

MONDAY	TUESDAY	WEDNESDAY	THURSDAY	FRIDAY
		Veal Loaf Sandwiches Coleslaw Orange Pudding Brownies	Mushroom Soup Liver Celery Spread on Crackers Three-melon Cup	Salmon Salad Hot Corn Muffins Banana Milk Punch
Jellied Consommé Egg and Tuna Salad on Bun Halves Fruit Compote	Frankfurters Sweet Corn Raspberries Sugar Cookies	Tomato Juice Grilled Sardine Sandwiches Fresh Fruit Cup	Fruit and Ginger Ale Mold Raisin Toast Cocoa	Fish Chowder Saltines Honeydew Fig Cookies
Tomato-egg Salad Hot Gingerbread Buttermilk	Celery Soup Pimiento-cheese Sandwiches Fruit Gelatin	Ham and Cheese Sandwiches Celery Relishes Peach Tapioca	Vegetable Juice Hot Potato Salad in Bologna Cups Raspberries	Creamed Vegetables on Toast Orange Ice Macaroons
Peanut Butter and Raisin Sandwiches Carrot Sticks Ice Cream	Chilled Beet Soup Cream Cheese and Chive Sandwiches Apricot Betty	Hamburgers on Buns Sliced Tomato Peach Melba	Chicken à la King on Toasted Muffins Fresh Plums Vanilla Wafers	Southern Bisque Peanut Butter on Cheese Crackers Pineapple Gelatin
Fruit Salad Bowl Hot Bran Muffins Butterscotch Pudding	Tuna Turnovers Green Salad Blueberries and Cream	Summer-vegetable Casserole Brown Bread Watermelon	Asparagus Soup Egg Salad Sandwiches Lemon Pudding	Macaroni and Cheese Tomato Wedges Cantaloupe Sundae

September

MONDAY	TUESDAY	WEDNESDAY	THURSDAY	FRIDAY
	Celery Soup Peanut Butter and Bacon Sandwiches Fruit Cup	Tomato Stuffed with Ham Salad Potato Chips Cup Custard	Grilled Cheese and Bacon Sandwiches Waldorf Salad Melon Cookies	Fresh Tomato 'n' Fish Chowder Toasted Muffins Stewed Prunes
Scotch Broth Tuna Sandwiches Banana Pineapple Ambrosia	Fresh Succotash Bacon Pear Slices in Orange Juice	Cream of Spinach Soup Pimiento-cheese Sandwiches Grapes Brownies	Bologna Sandwiches Buttered Cabbage Ice Cream on Apple-sauce Cake	Shirred Eggs with Cheese Chilled Fresh Pears Molasses Cookies
Vegetable Plate Bran Muffins Cantaloupe	Cream of Mushroom Soup Deviled Egg Salad Cranberry Snow	Creamed Chicken on Toast Sliced Tomato Plum Cobbler	Corn Chowder American Cheese Sandwichettes Orange Pudding	Codfish Cakes Buttered Carrots Fruit Tapioca Chocolate Snaps
Cauliflower Soup Peanut Butter on Whole Wheat Toast Fruit Gelatin	Tongue Sandwiches Lima Beans Sliced Peaches Milkshake	Tuna Omelet Buttered Toast Rice Pudding	Macaroni and Cheese Coleslaw Peach Tapioca	Cottage Cheese and Fresh Fruit Salad Date Nut Bread Hot Cocoa

October

MONDAY	TUESDAY	WEDNESDAY	THURSDAY	FRIDAY
Baked Chicken Croquettes Buttered Peas Orange and Cranberry Gelatin	Grilled Cheese Sandwiches Celery Sticks Hot Gingerbread Whipped Cream	Tomato Soup Bran Muffins with Cream Cheese Fruit Compote	Chopped Bologna Relish Sandwiches Floating Island Vanilla Wafers	Fish Chowder Corn Bread Strawberry Jam Apples and Cheese
Chili Con Carne Crackers, Pickles Cooked Rice Cereal with Fruit	Vegetable Soup Peanut Butter on Raisin Bread Vanilla Pudding	Cabbage Meat Rollups Bran Muffins Lime Pear Gelatin	Carrot Soup Egg Salad Sand-wiches Bananas	Scalloped Salmon, Peas and Potatoes Corn Muffins Fruit Cup
Split-pea Soup Ham Loaf Sandwiches Cherry Tapioca	Sardine Salad Poppy Seed Rolls Apple Snow with Custard Sauce	Pork Pancake Special Fruit Sundae Oatmeal Cookies	Chicken Soup Liver Spread on Crackers Gelatin Fruit Whip	Creamed Tuna on Leftover Waffles Carrot Salad Maple Sundae
Cream of Celery Soup Peanut Butter and Bacon Sandwiches Fruit Cup Cookies	Creamed Vegetables on Noodles Sweet Potato and Prune Pudding	Pea Soup Turkey Sandwiches Grapes	Corned Beef Hash Cabbage Wedges Baked Apple Peanut Cookies	Potato Soup Deviled Egg Salad Date Nut Bread with Cream Cheese
Scrambled Eggs with Ham Mashed Yams Fruit Salad	Baked Beans on Brown Bread Coleslaw Baked Apples			

November

MONDAY	TUESDAY	WEDNESDAY	THURSDAY	FRIDAY
			Tomato Rice Soup Tongue Sandwiches Stewed Prunes and Apricots	Oyster Stew Oyster Crackers Coleslaw Chocolate Pudding
Creamed Chipped Beef on Toast Celery Carrots Baked Apples	Chicken Noodle Soup Fruit Salad Hot Gingerbread	Leftover Meat Honey-glazed Carrots Fruit Compote	Vegetable Soup Peanut Butter on Toast Prune Whip	Cheese Fondue Green Beans Fruit Tapioca
Meat Sandwiches Finger Vegetables Applesauce on Leftover Cake	Beef Heart Burgers Waldorf Salad Oatmeal Date Cookies	Mushroom Soup Sardine Egg Salad Sliced Oranges Peanut Cookies	French Toast with Bacon Maple Syrup Fruit Gelatin	Tomato Juice Tunaburgers with Cheese Sauce Indian Pudding
Split Pea Soup Cheese Sandwiches Maple Bread Pudding	Spaghetti with Meat Sauce Green Salad Fresh Fruit Cup	Grilled Franks Molasses Baked Beans Apple Betty	HAPPY THANKSGIVING!	Cottage Cheese and Dried Fruit Salad Honey Bran Muffins Pumpkin Pie
Creamed Eggs on Noodles Buttered Peas Bananas	Peanut Butter and Bacon Sandwiches Carrot Raisin Salad Toll House Cookies	Asparagus Soup Grilled Cheese Sandwichettes Butterscotch Pudding	Cream of Tomato Soup Ham and Cheese Sandwiches Lime Pear Gelatin	Salmon on Biscuit Rolls Celery Sticks Lemon Pudding

December

MONDAY	TUESDAY	WEDNESDAY	THURSDAY	FRIDAY
Banana, Peanut and Cottage Cheese Salad Hot Baking Powder Biscuits, Honey	Tomato Soup Liverwurst Sandwiches Canned Pears Chocolate Cookies	Toasted Cheese and Bacon Sandwiches Carrot Sticks Fruit Gelatin	Frankfurter Chowder Lettuce Wedge with Thousand Island Dressing Spice Cookies	Vegetable Soup Sardine Sandwiches Sliced Oranges and Prunes
Cream of Potato and Chive Soup Ham Sandwiches Butterscotch Cookies	Spanish Rice Mixed Green Salad Baked Custard	Cream of Asparagus Soup Potato Chips Fruit Cup	Canadian Bacon and Corn Casserole Red Cabbage Slaw Apple Muffins	Cheese Fondue Cooked Vegetable Salad Fruit Gelatin
Creamed Chicken on Waffles Relish Plate Mince Tarts	Ham Balls on Pineapple Rings Coconut Cream Pudding	Chicken Salad Rolls Cranberry Sauce Prune Whip	Eggs Goldenrod Buttered Toast Waldorf Salad Macaroons	Vegetable Soup Cheese Crackers Gingerbread with Raisin Sauce
Tomato Soup Grilled Cheese Sandwiches Orange Ambrosia	MERRY CHRISTMAS!	Creamed Dried Beef on Toasted English Muffins Coleslaw Fruitcake	Turkey Noodle Soup Peanut Butter and Jelly Sandwiches Apple Tapioca	Spanish Omelet Fruited Gelatin Salad Peanut Butter Cookies

Pack-and-carry Lunches

If your child takes his lunch to school, you pack more than 150 lunches each year, which adds up to quite a job. It's a job with special problems, too. Lunch-box meals must be easy to eat, with a minimum of dishes and spoons to carry; they must have plenty of taste and eye appeal, and they must be varied enough to keep youngsters looking forward eagerly to lunch each day. Most important, a lunch-box meal should be every bit as filling and nutritious as a noon meal at home.

Before planning lunch-box meals, ask for ideas from those who are going to eat the lunches. If you pack what they like as well as what you know they should have, you can be pretty sure they'll eat it. Furthermore, you may create enough interest to make them want to help pack it as well.

If sandwiches are the mainstay of the lunch box, vary the fillings each day to keep them from becoming tiresome. If you must repeat a filling the second day, add another food to it to change the texture.

Vary the sandwich breads, too, using rye, whole wheat, graham, enriched white, cracked wheat, raisin, pumpernickel, Boston brown bread, fruit and nut breads, muffins and rolls. Hard rolls, crisp crackers and corn bread are also a welcome change.

Try to include milk in some way. It can be carried in the vacuum bottle, cold, as it comes from the container, or hot in cocoa or soup. Cheese sandwich fillings are another way to include extra milk in the children's lunches. Add nonfat dry milk to sandwich spreads for a calcium dividend.

Crisp, moist vegetables go well with sandwiches. Children like to munch on easy-to-eat carrot sticks, celery stalks (plain or cheese-stuffed) and cucumber wedges. Lettuce leaves, a section of green or red cabbage, green pepper rings and firm, whole tomatoes are also popular. Wrap carefully to preserve freshness.

Fruits, both fresh and dried, are an ideal lunch-box dessert. Apples, oranges, pears, peaches, plums, bananas, tangerines and grapes all pack and travel well and may be eaten out of hand. Raisins, prunes, dates and figs are also lunch-box favorites.

The protein foods—meat, poultry, fish, eggs and cheese—may be used in sandwich fillings. Occasionally tuck in cold fried chicken, a deviled egg or sticks of cheese or luncheon meat to be eaten with the fingers.

Include something sweet and satisfying in every lunch box. Cookies, cupcakes or squares of cake carry well. So do fruit gelatin, sliced sugared fruits and stewed fruits, if packed in covered jars, plastic containers or paper cups with lids.

The actual packing job will go quickly if you have all lunch-making equipment in one place, all ingredients on hand, and some of the work done ahead of time. Here are some pointers:

1. Clean the lunch box the night before and let it air. At the same time, scald the vacuum bottle and let it drain.

2. Keep handy in one place: sandwich bags, saran, paper napkins, aluminum foil, paper cups or small jars or plastic dishes with tight-fitting lids for packing salads, puddings, sliced fruit, etc. It's

 For easy packing and eating, cut a small ripe tomato almost through into 6 or 8 wedges. Sprinkle with salt and close into original shape before wrapping in saran or foil for the lunch box.

a good idea to have three small shakers filled with sugar, salt and pepper, labeled and sealed, ready to go into the lunch box when needed.

3. Spread butter or margarine all the way to the edge of each slice of bread to keep the filling from soaking in. Mayonnaise, mustard, catsup, chili sauce or pickle relish help keep sandwiches from becoming dry. Lettuce leaves lose their crispness in sandwiches not eaten right away, so it's better to wrap well-drained leaves separately to be added to sandwiches at lunch time.

4. To speed sandwich-making, keep on hand a variety of sandwich-filling ingredients: canned meat or fish, sliced cheese or cheese spreads, peanut butter, jelly. Mixed sandwich fillings such as egg salad, ham salad, and chopped raisins and carrots with mayonnaise can be made ahead of time and stored in covered jars in the refrigerator to use next day.

5. Prepare vegetable relishes the night before, wrap and store in refrigerator. A three-day supply of carrot sticks, celery stalks and other fresh vegetables may be prepared at one time and stored until needed.

6. Be lunch-box minded when preparing other meals. Dinner leftovers, whether soup, meat, salad, vegetable or dessert, can taste mighty good at lunch next day. When baking cupcakes, save a couple for the lunch box. When making pudding, spoon an extra serving into a paper cup for tomorrow's lunch box.

7. Take advantage of canned and packaged foods to save time and fuss. It takes only a few minutes to heat canned soup and

If you have a freezer, and school-age children who carry their lunches, prepare a supply of box lunches and freeze them for future use.

pour it into a vacuum bottle. Canned chili, spaghetti or baked beans can go into a vacuum bottle, too. Canned fruit or vegetable juices make refreshing lunch time beverages on warm days.

8. If you are rushed for time in the morning, you can do *all* the work the night before. Place the entire lunch box except the hot food, in the refrigerator overnight.

9. Be sure to put heavy items such as fruits and foods in paper or plastic containers at the bottom of the lunch box, then add sandwiches, cookies and other lighter foods. Line the lunch box with a festive napkin; an attractive lunch looks more inviting and will be more readily eaten by the children.

10. Every lunch carrier likes a surprise; some reminder that his lunch was packed with loving care. Dried fruits, nuts, marshmallows, gumdrops and chocolate mints are sure to please.

Parties, Picnics and Barbecues

Pre-school Birthday Parties

The birthday child gets a thrill out of making the invitations and then dropping them into the mailbox or delivering them in person. Even a three-year-old enjoys helping with refreshments and decorations.

The party's high spot is food and favors. Identical gifts avoid rivalries. Gay hats, bright balloons, lollipops, rate high.

Cake, ice cream and "soda" are traditional, but cookies with fruit gelatin or tapioca pudding and chocolate milk served in varied colored paper cups are good party fare, too, and a little easier for children of this age to handle. Out of consideration for small tummies, leave candy off the party table. Instead, give each child a little bag or party cup of candies to take home and share with his family.

School-age Holiday Parties

School-age children like more sophisticated parties, complete with games, contests and prizes. Take the party's theme from a holiday near at hand and use appropriate decorations and foods.

Cake and ice cream, served with fruit punch, ginger ale, chocolate milk or hot cocoa, are perfect refreshments for almost any party and any time of the year. For a Valentine party, bake the birthday cake in heart-shaped pans or decorate it with red candy hearts on white frosting. For St. Patrick's Day, serve pistachio ice cream and use pale green frosting on the cake. On Halloween, serve orange sherbet and chocolate cake with orange-tinted frosting. For Easter, cover sides and top of freshly frosted cake with green-tinted coconut. Make an Easter-bunny nest of coconut and fill with jelly-bean "eggs."

For an Independence Day party, roll cardboard into a cylinder and cover with red crepe paper to make a giant firecracker centerpiece. Fill firecracker with birthday "poppers," each tied to a crepe paper steamer leading to a place at the table. For a Christmas party centerpiece, make a sugarplum tree hung with fancy cookies, miniature popcorn balls, candy canes, lollipops and gumdrop men.

Teen-age Parties

By the time boys and girls reach high school, party favors and games have lost their attraction. Teen-agers are an active lot and their parties usually center around dancing or sports. They like to meet at someone's house for a snack after a roller skating party, basketball game or school dance. Food is important to them, and lots of it! These menus are sure to please:

AFTER-THE-GAME-SPREAD

Pizza pie
Ice cream or sherbet
Chocolate brownies
Bottled soft drinks

Pizza Pie

1 package or cake yeast,
   active dry or
   compressed
¾ cup very warm water
2½ cups biscuit mix
1 can (1 lb.) peeled
   tomatoes, drained
   and chopped
1 can (8 ozs.) tomato
   sauce
1 clove garlic, minced

½ teaspoon salt
⅛ teaspoon pepper
½ cup grated Parmesan
   cheese
2 packages (6 ozs. each)
   sliced Mozzarella or
   process American
   cheese, cut in quarters
1½ teaspoons dried
   oregano
5 teaspoons olive oil

Sprinkle or crumble yeast into very warm water in a large bowl and stir until dissolved. Add biscuit mix and stir vigorously to make a dough. Knead dough about 20 times on a surface well dusted with biscuit mix. Divide dough in 5 parts; roll each part into an 8-inch circle and place on ungreased cookie sheet. No rising is necessary and unbaked pizzas may stand safely while others are baking. Combine tomatoes, tomato sauce, garlic, salt and pepper. Sprinkle dough with Parmesan cheese, arrange ⅓ of sliced cheese on it, then drizzle with tomato mixture; arrange remaining sliced cheese on top, and sprinkle with oregano. Drizzle 1 teaspoon olive oil over each pizza. Bake in hot oven (425°F.) 15 to 20 minutes until filling is bubbly and crust lightly browned. Cut each pizza into 6 wedges and serve immediately.

COME-AND-GET-IT SNACK

Frankfurter roll-ups

Mustard   Pickles   Potato chips

Ice cream sundaes (assorted ice cream flavors with bowls of chocolate sauce, butterscotch sauce, fruit sauce, chopped nuts, etc.)

Frankfurter Roll-ups

6 slices bread   6 frankfurters

3 tablespoons prepared   3 tablespoons soft
   mustard   butter

Spread each slice of bread with mustard. Place frankfurter on mustard and roll up. Fasten bread with a wooden pick and brush outside with butter. Broil about 10 minutes, turning once, or bake in hot oven (400°F.) about 20 minutes. Makes 6 servings.

Adult Parties

When children reach school age, a bridge luncheon is a pleasant way for Mother to entertain her friends. The morning will be free for party preparations and the guests will be ready to leave soon after the children come home from school in the afternoon. Tables may be set up and places laid before the guests arrive; then, when the tables are cleared after lunch, the game may begin at once. It's a good idea to arrange food on plates in the kitchen, passing only dressings or sauces and hot breads during the meal. The food should be as pretty to look at as it is good to eat, and not too hearty.

A bridge luncheon is difficult to manage if your youngsters come home from school for the noon meal. In that case, why not ask friends for dessert at one-thirty, followed by bridge? Serve a festive dessert with tea or coffee, candies and salted nuts.

A tea or open house on a week-end afternoon or evening is a pleasant way to entertain a large group of friends. Arrange a buffet table, with coffee service at one end and tea at the other, cookies and tiny cakes on your handsomest trays, candies and salted nuts in bonbon dishes. On a warm day, substitute an iced fruit punch for either the coffee or tea. For an open house during the winter holidays, eggnog or hot mulled cider might replace the tea or coffee.

For a more elaborate party, add trays of fancy sandwiches to the buffet table. These may be made early in the day and stored in the refrigerator until serving time.

Home dinner parties are ideal for entertaining a small group of friends, but it isn't easy to have guests for dinner when there are young children in the house. Early evening is the busiest part of a mother's day: the children must have their supper, party or no, and the problem is even more complicated when there is an infant to be fed and put to bed.

Dinner parties can be managed happily, however, if the menu is chosen carefully so that most of the food can be prepared in advance. The solution is to prepare and cook dinner on a split-work schedule, part before five o'clock and part after six, with the children's supper sandwiched neatly between.

A main-dish casserole can be put together in the afternoon and then baked while the children are being fed. A main-dish salad improves when chilled several hours in the refrigerator. Even a tossed green salad can be made ahead of time; the prepared greens will stay crisp in covered salad bowl or refrigerator bag, ready to be tossed with dressing just before serving.

Meats that need long cooking can be started early; those that cook quickly may be cooked in the half-hour before dinner. Most desserts can be made well in advance. Cake mixes, hot bread mixes, frozen fruits and vegetables are great timesavers. Here are two dinner parties planned for a split-work schedule:

EASY DINNER PARTY

Orange-glazed baked ham, page 160
Scalloped potatoes   Buttered lima beans
Mixed green salad
Hot rolls
Pineapple upside-down cake, page 61

Check Chart for Roasting Meat, page 158, and set the alarm clock for time to start in order to have ham done on schedule. At 4 P.M. make the upside-down cake (packaged cake mix saves time). Oven will be preheated for ham. Prepare salad vegetables and return to refrigerator. Make sauce for scalloped potatoes; pare and thinly slice potatoes and add to sauce in pan.

At 6 P.M. heat potatoes and sauce to boiling; pour into greased casserole and place in oven to bake. Spread ham with orange mixture and return to oven for glazing. Then cook the frozen lima beans and toss the salad with dressing. And don't forget to put the rolls in the oven to heat!

CASSEROLE DINNER PARTY

Chicken casserole de luxe, page 144
Marinated tomato and cucumber slices
Corn on the cob   French bread
Chocolate cream pie, page 206

In the morning, cook chicken for casserole (skip this step if using canned chicken). Make the pie (pie-crust mix makes short work of the crust; chocolate-pudding mix makes a quick filling).

At 4 P.M. slice tomatoes and cucumbers into a bowl, pour on French dressing almost to cover; place, covered, in refrigerator. Slice French bread at 1-inch intervals, but do not slice through. Spread both sides of each slice with softened butter or margarine. Make chicken casserole and put in oven to bake.

At 6 P.M., the children's supper out of the way, you go into

action again. Shuck the corn. Whip cream for the pie; return
to refrigerator. Put the children to bed. Set the table. Freshen
up and dress. Later, while the corn cooks, put French bread in
the oven to crisp.

When guests come for a game of cards or an evening of good
conversation, simple refreshments are in order. Nice to serve
throughout the evening are iced drinks, with bowls of popcorn,
pretzels, potato chips or other tidbits.

When a heartier snack is called for, choose foods that need
little last-minute preparation. Nothing mars a party like having
the hostess disappear into the kitchen for long periods. Consider
the following suggestions, to be served with tea, coffee or cocoa.

1. **Cheese Tray:** A small Edam or Gouda cheese makes a colorful centerpiece: cut a slice off the top, then cut off triangles of the
red jacket all around for a scalloped effect. Surround with slices
of Swiss and sharp American cheese; wedges of Roquefort or
blue cheese, Camembert and Gruyere; blocks or wedges of cream
cheese. Border the tray with one or two kinds of crackers, rye
wafers, melba toast, thin slices of rye bread.

2. **Sandwich Platter:** Make several kinds of sandwiches, pages
228-230, using white, whole wheat, rye and nut breads for
variety. Put in air-tight container and store in refrigerator. At
serving time, remove crusts, if desired, and arrange cut sandwiches on platter. Serve with relish tray of dill and sweet pickles,
green and ripe olives, crisp vegetables.

3. **Choose-your-own Snack Tray:** Arrange bowls of deviled ham,
liver spread, packaged cheese spreads and mixed sandwich fillings on tray, or fill sections of divided snack server with spreads.
Sandwich spreads such as chopped egg and bacon; fish, chicken
or ham salad; and sardine spread may be made in advance and
stored, covered, in the refrigerator until serving time. Serve with
crackers, rye wafers, melba toast and thin slices of rye bread.

Picnics

"Mother, please may we have a picnic?" It's a plea every mother hears often during the summer months, for eating outdoors has a special appeal for children. Setting out in the car or on foot with a basket of lunch is the beginning of adventure. And to young appetites, sharpened by fresh air and sunshine, simple picnic food tastes more delicious than the most elaborate dinner at home.

A picnic kit that's always ready to go, avoids most of the fuss of preparing for a picnic. It saves bustling around to assemble everything needed and prevents discovering, when it's time to open a tin, that the can opener was left at home.

You can buy completely outfitted picnic hampers but you will be more likely to have just what you want by assembling your own. Start with a deep basket—one with a hinged lid and handles to sling over the arm—and put into it all the things you usually take on your picnics: tablecloth, napkins, plates and cups, knives and forks, salt and pepper, matches, can-and-bottle opener. You will probably want to use paper tablecloths and napkins. Plates and cups may be of the disposable variety, too, or you may prefer inexpensive plastic ones. The knives and forks may be the oldest ones in the kitchen drawer or they may be from the dime store; the important thing is to keep them in the hamper for picnic use only. After each picnic, clean out the basket and replace all supplies so that everything will be ready for the next picnic.

Here is a check list to follow:

Basic Supplies

Hamper or basket
Insulated carriers
Vacuum bottles or picnic jugs
    to keep cold things cold and
    hot things hot
Aluminum foil, wax paper,
    saran
Paper plates, cups, napkins
Eating utensils
Can-and-bottle opener
Table covering, if desired
Paper towels for cleaning up

Cooking Equipment

Portable grill
Lighter fluid
Matches
Newspaper to help start fire
Coffeepot
Skillet
Soup kettle
Old cookie sheet to hold foods
    set by the fire to warm
Long-handled grill for broiling
Long-handled fork, spoon,
    tongs
Meat turner
Cutting and paring knives
Potholder or asbestos mitt
Steel wool to scour grill, etc.

Food Accompaniments, Comforts and Conveniences

Salt and pepper
Catsup, mustard, relishes
Worcestershire sauce
Sugar and cream for coffee
Drinking water if you are not
    sure of a supply at the picnic
    site
Canned or bottled beverages
Marshmallows to toast over
    the embers
Blanket to sit on or for the
    baby's nap
Camera and film
Portable radio
Playthings for the children
Reading material for adults
First-aid kit
Insect repellent
Sunglasses
Suntan oil
Sweaters, in case it gets cool
Soap
Washcloth
Big pail for carrying water

Sandwiches outrank all other picnic foods in popularity because they travel well and may be eaten without plate or utensil. Wrap sandwiches individually, put in sandwich bags, or stack and wrap sandwiches of one kind together. When taking more than one kind of sandwich, label each to save confusion and handling at mealtime. Make sandwiches a few hours before setting out so that they may be chilled in the refrigerator. For suggestions and recipes, see Sandwiches, pages 225-230.

If you picnic in the backyard or at a spot not too far from home, a salad or a casserole dish is a nice addition to the usual picnic fare. Chill salad greens thoroughly beforehand; carry in a jar and add to the salad just before serving. Casseroles taken hot from the oven will stay hot for an hour or two when wrapped in several thicknesses of newspaper. Newspaper wrapping will help keep salads cold, too.

If beverages cannot be purchased at the picnic site, a vacuum jug or bottle will keep hot beverages hot and cold ones cold from home to mealtime. If you don't have a vacuum bottle, pack bottled beverages or milk in a bucket of ice.

Picnics can be enjoyed by the whole family even when there's an infant in the house. A baby can't have the usual picnic fare, of course, but you can take along a jar or two of baby food and a bottle for him. The bottle of milk or formula can be carried in one of the insulated containers made for that purpose: placed in the container boiling hot, it will drop to feeding temperature in four hours. Baby won't mind having his prepared vegetables and fruits spooned into his mouth right from the jar or can. And if it's cereal he is expecting, take baby cereal in a small covered jar and add milk or formula at feeding time. Infants can enjoy the outing, awake or asleep, in a basket or car bed placed in a shady spot. For an active toddler, there are portable playpens.

Backyard Barbecues

There's an extra thrill in eating outdoors when part of the meal is cooked over an open fire. The crackle and warmth of the fire and the smell of wood smoke adds zest to the occasion, and whets the appetite.

The job of making the fire is usually left to Dad, so be sure to give him the go-ahead about three-quarters of an hour before you want to begin cooking. It is best to build a big fire at the start so that no wood or charcoal need be added later. Let the fire burn down to a hot bed of coals at least three inches deep which will stay hot all through the cooking period. The fire is not ready for cooking as long as flames are still visible.

If your outdoor fireplace has no work space at the sides, it's a good idea to set up a table nearby to hold the food to be cooked, the sauces, seasonings and cooking equipment. Most meats can be cooked right on the fireplace grill. Two-sided grills of wire mesh with long handles are practical for cooking frankfurters and hamburgers because a number of servings may be turned over in one operation. The cook will need a long-handled fork, pot holder or asbestos gloves, and a cover-all apron. When steak is on the menu, set out a carving board and a sharp knife. A piece of clean cloth tied around the end of a long stick is useful for applying barbecue sauce.

Barbecue Menus

I   Barbecued spareribs
    Roasted potatoes
    Grilled tomatoes, page 268   Pumpernickel
    Apple pie, page 200, with cheese

Barbecued Spareribs

Allow 1 side of spareribs per person. Wipe ribs with a damp cloth; brush thoroughly with Tomato Barbecue Sauce, page 237. Place on grill, meaty side down, and cook slowly over hot coals until brown. Brush again with sauce, turn and continue to broil slowly until meat is very tender, brushing frequently with sauce. Cooking time will be 1 to 1½ hours, depending upon heat of the fire and distance between food and the coals.

Roasted Potatoes

Scrub medium-size baking potatoes. Wrap each potato in a square of aluminum foil, folding edges over and pinching to seal; then repeat with another piece of aluminum foil so that each potato is wrapped in two separate covers. About half an hour before spareribs are done, place prepared potatoes on hot coals (around edge of fireplace so that spareribs will continue to have full heat of fire). Cook 12 to 15 minutes; then turn and cook 12 to 15 minutes longer. Remove foil wrappings, serve in jackets.

II Grilled frankfurters
 Toasted rolls   Pickle relish   Catsup   Mustard
 Baked macaroni and cheese, page 141
 Chef's salad bowl, page 213
 Doughnuts   Apples   Toasted marshmallows

Teen-agers are always getting together for a frankfurter roast. The next time one is scheduled for your backyard, stand by with a few tips but let them do most of the work. Grilled frankfurters are best when cooked slowly so they are hot all the way through with no charring on the outside. Cook them on the fireplace grill or in two-sided wire grills with long handles. If it's every man for himself, provide long-handled forks or long sticks of green wood with pointed ends. (These can be used for the marsh-mallows later.) Split the frankfurter rolls, spread with softened butter or margarine, and toast, cut side down, on the grill about five minutes before the frankfurters are done. The baked beans should go to the table hot from the oven; the salad in a chilled bowl from the refrigerator. Set out a tray of doughnuts, a bowl of red apples and marshmallows, and let everyone go to it.

III Barbecued chicken
French fried potatoes
Mixed green salad, page 212   Toasted garlic bread
Chocolate refrigerator cake

This is an easy company picnic-style dinner because most of the food can be prepared in advance. Make the cake the day before; chill in the refrigerator until serving time. Before guests arrive, prepare salad vegetables and chill in bowl in refrigerator; prepare garlic bread. While chicken is broiling, spread frozen French fried potatoes in shallow baking pan. Heat potatoes and bread on outdoor grill if it is large enough; otherwise heat in kitchen oven. Toss salad with dressing at the table.

Barbecued Chicken

Have broiling chickens split in half. Allow ½ chicken per person. Brush all over with Barbecue Sauce, page 237; place on grill, cut side down. Cook until lightly browned on underside; brush with sauce, turn and brown on other side. Continue to cook, turning frequently and brushing with barbecue sauce as needed. Cook skin side down about as long as cut side down. Total cooking time will be 30 to 45 minutes. Chicken is done when meat at thickest part of leg is tender.

Toasted Garlic Bread

Mince 1 garlic clove very fine; blend thoroughly into 5 table-spoons butter or margarine. Slice French bread into thick slices, taking care not to cut through bottom of loaf, and spread both sides of each slice with garlic butter. Wrap in heavy duty aluminum foil. Heat on outdoor grill (but not directly over coals) 15 minutes, turning frequently.

IV   Garlic-broiled steak
     Toasted buns   Roasted corn on the cob
     Green salad, page 212, with tomato and cucumber
     Fruit shortcake, page 119

If your fireplace is large enough, steak, buns and corn may all be cooked outdoors. Otherwise toast buns and cook corn indoors. Split buns, spread with softened butter or margarine, and toast on grill, cut side down, for 5 minutes.

Garlic-broiled Steak

Have sirloin or porterhouse steak cut 1½ to 2-inches thick, allowing ½ to ¾ pound per person. Remove from refrigerator 1 hour before cooking. Just before cooking, rub steak with cut clove of garlic, brush with salad oil and sprinkle generously with salt. Brush hot grill with oil; place steak on grill and broil 1 minute on each side to seal in juices. Then cook 5 minutes on each side for rare steak, 10 minutes on each side for medium-well done. For best results, coals should be very hot.

Roasted Corn on the Cob

Pull down husks of corn part way; remove blemishes with sharp knife, then replace husks. Moisten husks by soaking ears in salted water; drain. About 20 minutes before steak is done, arrange corn ears on bed of coals (around edges of fireplace so steak will continue to receive full heat). Cook 10 to 15 minutes, turning frequently so husks do not burn all the way through. Peel down husks and break off along with stem end. Serve corn with butter or margarine and salt.

V   Barbecued ham steaks   Grilled hamburgers
      Mustard   Piccalilli   Catsup   Sliced onions
      Potato salad   Coleslaw   Toasted buns
      Chilled watermelon   Bottled soft drinks

This menu is particularly good for a neighborhood get-together, where work is parcelled out and the expense is shared. The hostess can double as purchasing agent; buying meat, buns, and watermelon and keeping a record of the costs. Let one neighbor bring potato salad, another coleslaw. The third might provide relishes and condiments, paper plates and napkins. If your outdoor fireplace isn't large enough to cook for a crowd, ask guests who have portable grills to bring them. While the menfolk build the fire and set up tables and chairs, the women can make hamburger patties, split and butter the buns, and set the table.

Barbecued Ham Steaks

Have center slices of tenderized ham cut 1-inch thick, allowing ½ pound per person. Brush hot grill with salad oil; place ham on grill and brown lightly on both sides. Brush with barbecue sauce, page 237, and continue to cook, turning occasionally, 20 to 30 minutes or until meat is very tender.

Grilled Hamburgers

2 pounds ground beef,   1 tablespoon thick bottled
  chuck or round   meat sauce
2 eggs   1 teaspoon prepared
1 teaspoon salt   mustard

Combine all ingredients and mix lightly. Form into 8 patties.
Brush hot grill with salad oil; place patties on grill and cook over
hot coals 5 to 10 minutes on each side, turning once only.

VI Lamb kebabs, page 170
    Pilau   Hot French bread   Roast bananas

Pilau

5 tablespoons butter or   3 cans (10½ ozs. each) beef
  margarine   broth *or* 4 bouillon
1½ cups uncooked   cubes dissolved in 4
  rice   cups boiling water

Melt butter in heavy skillet; add rice and stir over medium heat
until golden brown. Slowly stir in broth. Cover and cook slowly
25 minutes or until rice is tender, adding water if needed. Add
salt, if necessary. Makes 6 servings.

Roast Bananas

Select not-quite-ripe bananas; do not peel. Place unpeeled
bananas on grill and cook over hot coals, turning often, until skin
is brown all over. Split each banana open lengthwise with a
sharp knife; sprinkle with cinnamon and sugar. Eat from skins
with a spoon.

Special Diets

Using the Basic 4 Food Groups on pages 2 and 3 as a guide to family meal planning is pretty good assurance that special diets will not be necessary. However, there are times in most households when modifications of the normal diet are in order. The information in this chapter is for just such times.

On the following pages there's a Calorie Counter's Guide for weight watchers, suggestions for diet changes during pregnancy and lactation, and help in feeding children with food allergies. In addition, there's information on diets commonly prescribed for a sick youngster—whether for an upset stomach or convalescence from a more serious ailment.

A Calorie Counter's Guide*

Approximate calories provided by average servings of common foods

FOOD	SIZE OF SERVING	CALORIES
Almonds, shelled, unblanched	18 medium	130
Apple, raw	1 medium	75
Applesauce, canned, sweetened	1 cup	185
Asparagus, canned	6 spears	20
Avocado, raw	½ peeled	280
Bacon	4 small slices	355
Banana	1 medium	90
Beans, green, string, cooked	¾ cup	45
Beans, lima, cooked	1 cup	150
Beans, navy, dried, cooked	½ cup	125
Beef, chuck, without bone	3 ounces	265
Beef, corned beef hash	3 ounces	120
Beef, hamburger	3 ounces	315
Beef, sirloin	3 ounces	255
Beef-vegetable stew	1 cup	250
Beet greens, cooked	¾ cup	35
Beets, cooked, diced	1 cup	70
Biscuits, baking-powder	1 biscuit	130
Blueberries, raw	1 cup	85
Bouillon	1 cube	2
Bran flakes	1 cup	115
Bread, corn	1 slice	105
Bread, white, enriched	1 slice	65
Bread, whole-wheat or rye	1 slice	55
Broccoli, cooked	1 cup	45
Brussels sprouts, cooked	1 cup	60
Butter	1 tablespoon	100
Buttermilk	1 cup	85
Cabbage, cooked	1 cup	40
Cabbage, raw	1 cup	25

* Adapted from *Composition of Foods*, United States Department of Agriculture, Handbook No. 8.

FOOD	SIZE OF SERVING	CALORIES
Cake, angel food	1 average serving	110
Cake, frosted and filled	1 average serving	400-450
Cake, plain	1 average serving	130
Cake, sponge	1 average serving	115
Candy, caramels	1 ounce	120
Candy, chocolate	1 ounce	145
Cantaloupe	½ cantaloupe	35
Carbonated beverages	1 cup	80-105
Carrots	1 cup	45
Cauliflower, cooked	1 cup	30
Celery, raw, diced	1 cup	20
Cheese, American or Cheddar	1 ounce	115
Cheese, cottage (not creamed)	1 ounce	25
Cheese, cream	1 ounce	105
Cheese, Swiss	1 ounce	105
Cherries, pitted, raw	1 cup	65
Chicken	1 average serving	100
Chicken soup	1 cup	75
Chocolate milk	1 cup	215
Cookies, plain and assorted	1 3-inch cookie	110
Corn	1 ear	85
Corn, canned	1 cup	170
Corn flakes	1 cup	95
Corn grits, cooked	½ cup	60
Cream, heavy	1 tablespoon	50
Cream, light	1 tablespoon	30
Cucumber	6 slices	5
Custard, baked	1 cup	285
Doughnut	1 medium	135
Eggs	1 egg	75
Farina, enriched, cooked	1 cup	105
Frankfurter	1 average	125
Fruit cocktail, canned	1 cup	180
Gelatin, flavored	½ cup	80
Grapefruit	1 cup sections	75
Grapefruit juice, unsweetened	1 cup	90
Grapes	1 cup	85
Halibut, broiled	1 steak (4 x 3 x 1½)	230
Ham, cured, cooked	3 ounces	340

FOOD	SIZE OF SERVING	CALORIES
Heart, beef	3 ounces	90
Honey, strained	1 tablespoon	60
Honeydew melon	1 average serving	50
Ice cream, plain	⅛ of quart brick	145
Jams, marmalades, preserves	1 tablespoon	55
Lamb, chop	3 ounces	355
Lamb, leg roast	3 ounces	230
Lemon	1 medium	20
Lettuce	2 large leaves	5
Liver, beef, fried	2 ounces	120
Luncheon meats	2 ounces	125-150
Macaroni, cooked	1 cup	210
Margarine	1 tablespoon	100
Milk, malted	1 cup	280
Milk, nonfat or skim	1 cup	85
Milk, whole	1 cup	165
Molasses	1 tablespoon	50
Muffins	1 muffin	135
Mushrooms, canned	½ cup	15
Noodles, containing egg	1 cup	105
Oatmeal, cooked	1 cup	150
Oils, salad or cooking	1 tablespoon	125
Olives, green	2	15
Onions, raw	1 medium	50
Oranges	1 medium	70
Orange juice, fresh	1 cup	110
Pancakes	1 4-inch cake	60
Peaches, canned	1 cup	175
Peaches, raw	1 medium	45
Peanut butter	1 tablespoon	90
Pears, raw	1 medium	95
Peas, green, cooked	1 cup	110
Pickle, dill	1 large	15
Pie, apple	1 average serving	330
Pie, coconut custard	1 average serving	265
Pie, lemon meringue	1 average serving	300
Pineapple, canned in syrup	½ cup	100
Pineapple juice	1 cup	120

FOOD	SIZE OF SERVING	CALORIES
Pork, loin or chops, cooked	3 ounces	285
Potato chips	5 medium	55
Potatoes, baked	1 medium	95
Potatoes, French fried	8 pieces	155
Pretzels	5 small	18
Prunes	4 medium	75
Pudding, vanilla	1 cup	275
Raisins	½ cup	215
Raspberries, red, raw	1 cup	70
Rice, cooked	1 cup	200
Rice, puffed	1 cup	55
Rolls, plain	1 roll	120
Salad dressing, French	1 tablespoon	60
Salad dressing, mayonnaise	1 tablespoon	90
Salmon, canned, pink	3 ounces	120
Sardines, canned, drained solids	3 ounces	180
Sherbet	½ cup	120
Shrimp, canned	3 ounces	110
Sour cream	½ cup	245
Spaghetti, cooked, unenriched	1 cup	220
Spinach, cooked	1 cup	45
Strawberries, frozen	3 ounces	90
Strawberries, raw	1 cup	55
Sugar, granulated or brown	1 tablespoon	50
Sweet potatoes, baked	1 medium	185
Tangerines	1 medium	35
Tomato catsup	1 tablespoon	15
Tomato juice, canned	1 cup	50
Tomato soup	1 cup	90
Tomatoes, canned or cooked	1 cup	45
Tomatoes, raw	1 medium	30
Tuna, drained solids	3 ounces	170
Turnips, cooked, diced	1 cup	40
Veal cutlets, cooked	3 ounces	185
Waffles	1 5-inch waffle	215
Walnuts	8-15 halves	100
Watermelon	½ slice	45
Wheat germ	1 tablespoon	15

Diets for Mothers-to-be and New Mothers

The expectant mother is like an athlete training for the Olympics. She must live according to certain time-tested rules which best prepare her for the Big Event. Perhaps the most important of these rules concerns her diet. For the right foods in the right amounts not only safeguard her own health, they also help to ensure a strong, healthy baby at birth and during infancy. Furthermore, hospital records show that mothers who have had excellent diets during pregnancy are more likely to be able to nurse their babies satisfactorily, have less complications, healthier babies.

Actually, a good prenatal diet is not very different from a good daily diet. But those differences are all-important. During pregnancy, a woman needs more protein, minerals and vitamins; fewer fat and carbohydrate foods. Also, her doctor may recommend that she take a vitamin D supplement, and, if not already, iodized salt.

It's not easy to stick to a sound pregnancy diet unless proper eating has become a habit. Knowing the what and why of food needs, as explained in Chapter One, helps. So does making a game of checking the foods eaten each day against the sample menus *below* planned for a pregnant woman whose weight is no problem. This menu provides about 2500 calories.

Of course, any diet changes should be made only with a doctor's approval and there should be some leeway for enjoying those luscious concoctions served at baby showers.

Sample Day's Menus for Expectant Mothers

BREAKFAST   Orange juice—8 ounces
Oatmeal or other enriched or whole grain cooked
    cereal—½ cup* *or* ready-to-eat cereal—¾ cup*
Egg—1, cooked without fat
Toast—1 slice   Butter or margarine—1 teaspoon
Coffee or tea—Use sugar and cream sparingly
Milk—8 ounces

* With whole milk and 1 teaspoon sugar

LUNCH   Soup—1 cup consommé
Sandwich made of:
    Bread—2 slices enriched or whole wheat
    Butter or margarine—1 teaspoon
    Filling of lean meat, poultry, Cheddar cheese,
        cottage cheese or peanut butter—1 to 2 ounces
Lettuce and tomato salad—2 teaspoons dressing
Stewed apricots—½ cup
Milk—8 ounces

DINNER   Beef pot roast—a slice about 4x3x½"
Baked potato—1 medium
Carrots—½ cup   Broccoli—½ cup
Waldorf salad with raisins—½ cup
Baked custard or milk pudding*—½ cup
Milk—8 ounces

*If milk quota has been met, substitute a fruit.

Whether a mother-to-be is on a maintenance or a reducing diet, the number of servings from each of the Basic 4 Food Groups remains the same. It's best to cut down, not out, during weight control—eliminate foods with little nutrients and lots of calories.

All pregnant women need 1 quart of milk a day. However, if weight is a problem, some or all of the milk may be taken as skim milk or buttermilk, or as nonfat dry milk added to other foods. Today, fluid nonfat milk is fortified with vitamins A and D. In some cases doctors advise calcium tablets and vitamin supplements in lieu of part of the milk quota.

Weight-watching expectant mothers need at least as many servings of fruits and vegetables as recommended in the basic diet. They provide important vitamins and minerals at a very small cost in calories. To cut down on calories, fruit juices should be unsweetened; canned fruits in light syrup or dietetic pack. Vegetables should be served without butter, margarine and rich sauces; never fried. High-calorie dried beans, lima beans, corn, peas, sweet potatoes and parsnips should be avoided. Between-meal nibbles should be limited to low-calorie raw vegetables and fruits. For example, three small stalks of celery yield only 9 calories; half an orange, only 32 calories.

Underweight mothers-to-be who do not have the appetite for large servings at mealtime should make a practice of eating protein-rich snacks. For example, they might eat a wedge of Cheddar cheese and a pear with a glass of milk in the midmorning, and a peanut butter sandwich or a cup custard in the midafternoon.

Nursing mothers need about 1000 extra calories a day. It takes from 500 to 700 calories to form the milk necessary for the infant. The remaining 300 to 500 calories are needed for extra activity involved in taking care of the infant.

The lactating mother needs one and one-half quarts of milk in order to meet the calcium and phosphorus needs of the infant without undue drain on her own supply. Part of this should be taken between meals; perhaps, for variety, in cocoa or soup.

During lactation some mothers find it wise to avoid such vegetables as cabbage, cucumbers, radishes and onions.

Allergy Diets

How can a child exist without wheat, milk or eggs in his diet? Believe it or not, it *is* possible, but it takes some doing, particularly in the sweet line which allergic children miss most of all. The first two recipes are wheatless, milkless and eggless; the next, milkless and eggless; the other, eggless. It's best to have allergy identified by a doctor before modifying diet; consult him on diet changes.

Rye Apple Crisp

3 cups pared and sliced
    cooking apples
1 tablespoon lemon juice
½ cup rye cracker crumbs

½ cup brown sugar
½ teaspoon cinnamon
½ teaspoon nutmeg
¼ cup soft butter

Arrange apples in buttered 8-inch square baking pan. Sprinkle with lemon juice. Combine crumbs, brown sugar, cinnamon and nutmeg; cut in the butter. Spread crumb mixture over apples and bake in moderate oven (375° F.) 20 to 25 minutes. Makes 6 servings.

Rice Drops

1 cup butterscotch pieces
¼ cup corn syrup, light or
    dark

1¾ cups bite-size shredded
    rice biscuit cereal
¼ cup flaked coconut

Melt butterscotch pieces with corn syrup over hot water in top of double boiler; blend well. Remove from heat but keep over hot water. Stir in cereal and coconut until well coated. Drop by teaspoonfuls onto wax paper. Cool. Makes 2 dozen.

Shortbread Squares

2 cups sifted flour   ⅓ cup sugar
⅛ teaspoon salt   2 tablespoons water
⅔ cup butter or margarine   1 teaspoon vanilla extract

Sift together flour and salt. Cream butter; add sugar and blend well. Gradually add 1 cup of the flour to creamed mixture, then add remaining flour alternately with water and vanilla. Blend well. Place dough between two sheets of wax paper and roll into an 8 x 12-inch rectangle. Peel off top piece of wax paper, turn dough over onto ungreased cookie sheet and peel off second piece of wax paper. Mark dough into 2-inch squares and prick each square with a fork. Bake in slow oven (325° F.) 30 minutes. Cut along marked lines while hot. Makes 2 dozen.

Eggless White Cake

¼ cup butter or margarine   3 teaspoons baking powder
1 cup sugar   ¾ cup milk
2 cups sifted flour   1 teaspoon vanilla extract
½ teaspoon salt

Cream butter; add sugar and beat well. Sift together flour, salt and baking powder. Add to creamed mixture alternately with milk. Stir in vanilla. Spread batter in greased and lined 8-inch square pan and bake in moderate oven (350° F.) 30 minutes. (This cake sags a little and is hard to frost but children like it anyway.)

For a speedy eggless cake, select a cake mix that contains no egg and prepare as directed, substituting 1 teaspoon baking powder for each egg called for on label.

Feeding the Convalescent Child

While Johnny is in the hospital having his appendix out he has a whole staff of nurses, doctors, and dietitians to look after him. But when he comes home, he's *your* baby. When Sue-Ellen has the measles, it's up to you to carry out the doctor's orders, to prepare the food she needs, to keep her quiet and happy in bed. You must triple as nurse, dietitian and play therapist—no easy job when there's a family and a house to take care of besides.

Many childhood illnesses such as colds and digestive upsets are not serious enough to warrant a physician's care. And even when your child is under the care of a doctor, much is left to your own judgment. Doctors are such busy people they simply don't have time to go over a diet in detail and explain its preparation. Instead they usually prescribe a liquid diet or a soft one and outline it so quickly that even a shorthand expert would have difficulty getting it all down. The three diets outlined here will serve as helpful guides and may be adapted to any special instructions from your doctor.

The Liquid Diet

During illness, particularly when fever is present, the patient needs plenty of fluids to replace those lost in vomiting, diarrhea and perspiration. He needs foods that are easy to eat and easily digested. This liquid diet fulfills these requirements.

Milk: Plain and in beverages, soups and desserts
Cereal: Thin gruels
Eggs: Beaten raw, mixed with milk or a fruit juice
Fruit juices: plain or in beverages and desserts
Vegetable juices: plain or in soups
Meats: Strained meats
Soups: Meat or chicken bouillon
Desserts: Plain ice cream, milk or water sherbets, fruit-juice gelatins, custards, simple rennet puddings

Juices and cereal gruels in the liquid diet should be strained. The strained fruits and vegetables prepared for babies may be used, and prepared baby cereals thinned with milk make suitable gruels. Meat and chicken bouillon may be made quickly by dissolving bouillon cubes in hot water. For extra nourishment, strained fruit juice may replace part or all of the water when making gelatin desserts.

When the patient is on a liquid diet, food should be given at two or three-hour intervals. If the patient cannot sit up, a bent-glass drinking tube is a great help. In any case, colored straws and glasses make liquid foods more appealing to children.

The Soft Diet

As the name implies, the soft diet is made up of foods which require little or no chewing. The patient still needs plenty of fluids but he can handle more solid nourishment, too. He needs extra amounts of body building and protective foods: protein to rebuild wasted tissue, vitamin C to fulfill the increased requirement of this vitamin during infections, and vitamin B_1 to restore the appetite.

When the doctor prescribes a soft diet, your patient can have all of the foods on the liquid diet plus the following:

Bread: Enriched white bread, zwieback, plain crackers
Cereals: Cooked enriched cereal, rice and macaroni products
Cheese: Cottage, pot or cream cheese
Eggs: Soft-cooked, poached or scrambled in a minimum of fat
Fruit: Cooked purées or raw ripe banana, alone or with cereal
Vegetables: Cooked purées, alone or in soup; baked or boiled mashed potato
Meats: Strained and junior meats
Desserts: Cornstarch or rice pudding; sponge or angel cake

The change from a liquid to a soft diet should be gradual, with cooked cereals and soft-cooked eggs the first soft foods added. Strained fruits and vegetables prepared for babies are useful on this diet, too.

When the patient is on a soft diet, plan three small meals a day, with extra feedings between meals and at bedtime.

The following menu provides adequate nourishment and makes attractive tray meals. Notice the contrast in colors and shapes of the food. If your child cannot feed himself, be sure to place the tray so he can see what he is eating. Give him small bites and alternate the foods to make eating more interesting. Allow time for chewing but do not let him dawdle through the meal.

A Day's Soft-diet Menus

BREAKFAST	Farina mixed with puréed apricots
	Milk
MORNING SNACK	Orange juice
DINNER	Poached egg on toast strips
	Puréed peas
	Strawberry Ice Cream
	Milk
AFTERNOON SNACK	Zwieback and milk
SUPPER	Cream of tomato soup with crackers
	Baked potato
	Lemon sherbet
	Milk

The Light or Convalescent Diet

Convalescence is a time of rebuilding, so a light diet does not mean a skimpy one. The convalescent needs well-balanced meals made up of simple, easily digested foods. Besides the foods in the liquid and soft diets, the convalescent diet includes:

Meat: Lean beef, lamb and liver
Cheese: Cheddar cheese, Swiss cheese and process cheese spread
Vegetables: Any fresh or raw vegetable except shell beans, dried beans, cabbage, onions, turnips, cucumbers, radishes, corn
Fruits: Any fresh, cooked or canned fruit except melons
Desserts: Plain unfrosted cakes, simple cookies
Soups: Any soup except those which contain forbidden vegetables
Cereals: All cereals including whole-grain cooked and packaged ready-to-eat varieties

By the time your patient is on a convalescent diet, he should have three regular meals a day. Between-meal snacks are all right provided they don't affect the appetite for regular meals.

A Day's Convalescent-diet Menus

BREAKFAST   Stewed prunes
Whole wheat flakes with milk
Buttered toast
Hot cocoa

DINNER   Chopped beef patty
Mashed potato   Chopped spinach
Fruit gelatin
Milk

AFTERNOON SNACK   Tomato juice and crackers

SUPPER   Cheese omelet
Tomato and lettuce salad
Whole wheat bread and butter
Sliced banana with cream
Milk

When your child has a cold, fluids are of utmost importance, particularly when the cold is accompanied by a fever. Give plenty of fruit and vegetable juices, bouillon, milk, ginger ale and water. When the cold is severe, it is wise to feed a liquid diet for the first day or until the fever subsides. Then give a soft diet and change gradually to a convalescent diet as the appetite returns.

When your child has a digestive upset, the most important thing is to give the digestive tract a rest. Give nothing but cool water at first, just three or four tablespoons each hour, then offer clear fluids such as weak tea, ginger ale and bouillon. Sometimes fruit juices are omitted if they seem to irritate an already upset digestive system. When the appetite begins to revive, offer other foods on the liquid diet (still omitting fruits and their juices), changing gradually to the soft diet. Fats, such as cream, margarine, butter, hard for an upset stomach to handle, and roughage foods such as whole grain cereals, raw vegetables and unpeeled fruits, should be added slowly following recovery.

Meals on a Tray

When you are accustomed to preparing food for a healthy and hungry family, the finicky appetite of a convalescent child presents new problems. Here are some suggestions to make eating come more easily to a child confined to bed:

1. Use a tray small enough for a child to manage easily. A small tray may be used if main course and dessert are served separately. A tray with folding legs is nice because it keeps the weight of the tray off the child's lap.

2. Make each tray an attractive place setting. Bright-colored pottery or plastic dishes from the dime store may be used along with regular dinnerware. Colorful place mats and napkins— paper ones are fine—add a cheerful note.

3. Keep servings small. Too much food can discourage a faltering appetite.

4. Serve food in a form that is easy to eat. Cut meat into

small pieces, scoop out baked potato, cut toast into strips. Don't fill cups and glasses too full.

5. Stick to familiar foods. A child may form a lasting dislike for a new food introduced during illness.

6. Go easy on sugar, jams and jellies, rich desserts, fried and highly seasoned foods even after the patient has progressed to the convalescent diet.

7. For older children, serve cold foods cold; hot foods hot and on heated plates. Very young children usually prefer foods neither very cold nor very hot.

8. Never beg or bribe a sick child to eat. When he says he is finished, simply remove the tray without comment. Too much concern over food during an illness can lead to lasting feeding problems.

9. Never discuss a child's lack of appetite in his hearing. He may try to starve himself to keep up his intriguing reputation of "eating like a bird."

10. Sometimes a young patient enjoys choosing his meals in advance, especially if Mother makes up a master menu giving foods fanciful names. Usually though, it's best to keep the contents of each tray a secret until it appears at mealtime.

Children Can Cook

Memo to Mothers:

Children like to cook. Even a two-year-old wants to pour the milk on his cereal and spread his own bread. Older children love to help mother measure and mix long before they can read a recipe.

Cooking together, like this, can be a source of much pleasure to children and mothers alike. Habits of cleanliness, accuracy, and neatness are important by-products of teaching a child to cook, and there is no better way to learn the rules of good nutrition than by helping to plan meals at an early age. Most important of all, cooking gives a child a sense of self-reliance and satisfaction.

How early can cooking lessons start? As soon as a child begins

to show an interest in food preparation. A three or four-year-old
will enjoy trying his hand at some of these:

Eggnog. He can beat the egg while you add sugar and milk.
Baked Potatoes. He can help pick out potatoes of the right
size, scrub them and rub the jackets with fat.
Soft-cooked Egg. He can carefully lower egg on a spoon into a
pan of hot water, then watch an egg timer and tell you when the
egg is "done."
Sandwiches. He can spread bread with butter and add filling
if you set out all ingredients.
Canned Soup. He can turn crank of wall-type can opener, add
milk or water to the soup and stir until smooth.
Gelatin Pudding. He can stir gelatin while you add water; can
fold fruit into the pudding after it is cool.
Cocoa. He can stir chocolate syrup into hot milk.

The recipes in the next chapter, planned especially for young
cooks, start out in simple fashion and grow progressively more
demanding as your apprentice cook gains in skill. The first ones
are easy enough for a first or second-grader to make with mother's
help or for an older child to tackle with just a little supervision.
Others were planned for youngsters who can read the recipes but
need help with the measuring and mixing. Still others were
written for more advanced cooks (although not necessarily older
ones) who can do everything themselves, from reading the recipe
to serving the finished dish.

Before you and your child embark on the adventure of cooking
together, here are a few tips to ensure smooth sailing:

1. For the earliest cooking lessons, choose a time when you are
not busy. Very young cooks need patient instruction.
2. Make cooking fun. It should be considered a privilege,
never a duty. Don't nag about cleaning up afterward; rather
encourage pride in a neat kitchen.

3. In the beginning, teach everyday skills such as beating eggs, whipping cream, paring vegetables, greasing pans. Then when you are busy in the kitchen you can let your youngster help, instead of shooing him away.

4. Don't be afraid to let your child use the range and oven. Learning the proper way to use them is the best safety measure. Always stress how careful *you* are when handling hot pans, opening the oven, pouring hot liquids.

5. Store cooking utensils the child can use within his reach, if possible. A step-stool is handy for a child to use in reaching utensils and foods in high cupboards.

6. Don't try to correct every mistake. They are part of learning. If your young cook forgets the baking powder, a flat soggy cake is an object lesson he'll remember.

7. Praise often. Even if the finished product is not perfect, the young cook will be pleased with it.

8. Take time to answer questions. Very young children are interested in results, but school-age cooks want to know why you do things in a certain way.

9. When your young chef acquires enough skill, let him cook alone. It takes courage to walk out of the kitchen saying, "Just call me if you need me," but it's another important step in letting your youngster grow up.

10. Don't expect your child's cooking to save you time and work. It won't, at least not for a long time. Your reward is in his pride in achievement, his feeling of satisfaction and self-confidence. Then some day you will discover how nice it is to have an assistant cook to take over in the kitchen when you are ill or busy with some household task!

A Child's Cookbook

This chapter of mother's cookbook was written for you because you want to learn to cook.

Mother is going to be a big help to you as you learn. Listen to everything she tells you and watch carefully when she shows you what to do. Pretty soon you will be able to cook all by yourself and maybe even cook a whole lunch or breakfast for the family. That would be fun, wouldn't it?

How to Get Ready to Cook

Here are 5 *be sures* to start you off right:

1. *Be sure* to dress properly. Clean dungarees or overalls are fine, or perhaps you girls will want to wear a clean cotton dress. Short-sleeved shirts or dresses are best, particularly when it comes to washing-up. An apron will keep your clothes clean. Maybe mother will get you a plastic one that can be wiped clean and needs no washing or ironing.

2. *Be sure* to wash your hands and dry them on paper toweling

or a clean hand towel. Use warm water and plenty of soap and scrub those finger nails. You don't want any dirt or germs to get into the food you cook.

3. *Be sure* to ask mother what you can cook that would help her most. Ask her to help you choose an easy recipe.

4. *Be sure* to read the recipe carefully. Ask mother to explain anything you don't understand.

5. *Be sure* to get out all the foods the recipe calls for, and also the pans, cups, spoons and bowls you need before you start. Put them together on the kitchen counter or work table. This will save time when you begin to cook. It will also keep the kitchen from getting messy and make it easier to clean up afterward.

Now you are ready to cook. But if this is your first adventure in the kitchen, better read the rest of this before you begin.

How to Clean Up after Cooking

After you have finished cooking, clean up the kitchen so mother will let you cook again soon. If you make something that bakes in the oven, you can do most of the cleaning up while it is baking. There are 5 *be sures* for cleaning up.

1. *Be sure* to wash all the pans and cups and other utensils you have used and put them away. Hang up the dish towel to dry.

2. *Be sure* to put away all of the food packages you have used. If you don't know where they belong, ask mother and then remember for the next time.

3. *Be sure* to wipe off the kitchen counter or work table and the top of the range if you used it.

4. *Be sure,* if you spilled anything on the floor, to wipe it up with the cloth or mop mother uses for the floor. Or sweep the floor, brush the dirt onto a dustpan and empty it where mother does.

5. *Be sure* to turn off the oven, if you used it.

How to Measure

I know you want to start cooking right away, but there is one more thing you should know—*how to measure*. If you want your recipes to turn out good every time, you must measure everything exactly and in the right way.

First set in one place the equipment you will need for measuring ingredients (the food that goes into the recipe):

1. A measuring cup which has the 1 cup mark at the rim and a nest of 4 cups consisting of ¼ cup, ⅓ cup, ½ cup and 1 cup.

2. A set of measuring spoons including ¼ teaspoon, ½ teaspoon, 1 teaspoon and 1 tablespoon.

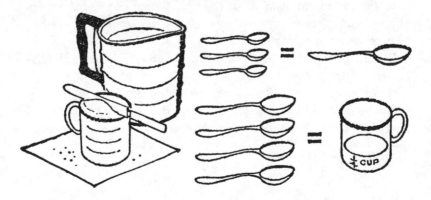

All recipes use level measurements unless the directions state differently. So, if your recipe calls for 1 cup of flour, it means a cup leveled off at the rim, not a heaping cup.

Here's how to measure flour. Today many flour companies are advocating using all-purpose flour without sifting; follow package directions. To measure sifted flour, sift flour onto wax paper. With a spoon, pile sifted flour into measuring cup. (Be careful not to pack the flour.) Now draw a spatula or the straight edge of a table knife across the rim of the cup to level off the flour. For ⅓ or ½ cup, use the proper size from the nest of graduated cups. If you need less than 1 cup of flour and you do not have a nest of cups, you can use a set of spoons to measure. There are 4 tablespoons in ¼ cup, 5 tablespoons and 1 teaspoon in ⅓ cup and 8 tablespoons in ½ cup.

Here's how to measure sugar. You measure granulated sugar as you do flour, except that you do not sift it unless it seems lumpy. Spoon sugar into the cup and level off with a spatula or straight knife edge. For brown sugar, first roll out the lumps on wax paper with a rolling pin. Then *pack* it into the measuring cup.

Here's how to measure baking powder, salt and spices. Select measuring spoon of the correct size. Dip the spoon into the can or package until spoon is piled high. Then level off the ingredients with spatula or straight edge of a table knife. When leveling, be sure to hold the spoon over the can or box to catch what is scraped off.

Here's how to measure butter, margarine or other fat. This guide will help you:

$$
\begin{aligned}
4 \text{ bars} \quad (1 \text{ pound}) &= 2 \text{ cups} \\
2 \text{ bars} \quad (½ \text{ pound}) &= 1 \text{ cup} \\
1 \text{ bar} \quad (¼ \text{ pound}) &= ½ \text{ cup} \\
½ \text{ bar} \quad (⅛ \text{ pound}) &= ¼ \text{ cup}
\end{aligned}
$$

So if a recipe calls for ½ cup of shortening, you can use ¼-pound bar of butter or margarine. If you need ¼ cup, simply cut a ¼-pound bar in two and use half.

If you are using tub butter or fat from a can, you can use a measuring spoon or one of the cups from a nest. Be sure to pack the fat solidly on the spoon or in the cup, then level off with spatula or straight edge of knife.

Here's how to measure water, milk and other liquids. For water or milk, set a glass measuring cup on a table and slowly pour into it the amount of liquid called for in the recipe. Then bend until your eye is on a level with the side of the cup and check to be sure the liquid is level with the mark on the cup.

Vanilla extract and other flavorings are usually used in small amounts and therefore are measured by the spoonful. Select the right spoon from the measuring set and pour the flavoring in slowly until level with edge of the spoon.

To measure a sticky liquid like molasses or syrup, lightly grease the inside of the spoon or cup with a fat before pouring in the liquid. This will prevent sticking and make it easier to pour from the measuring cup or spoon.

Now, if you have taken care of the first 5 "be sures" on page 328, you are ready to cook. Here are 12 easy recipes:

Chocolate Milk Shake

YOU WILL NEED
THESE UTENSILS:
    tight screw-capped jar
    measuring spoons
    measuring cup

AND THESE FOODS:
    2 cups cold milk
    2 tablespoons chocolate
      syrup

Here's what you do:

1. Pour milk and chocolate syrup into jar, and screw on lid.
2. Shake jar until milk and chocolate are well mixed and frothy.
3. Pour into two glasses and serve.
    Makes two refreshing servings.

NOTE: For a frosted drink, first put a spoonful of ice cream into each glass, then pour milk shake over ice cream.

Cinnamon Toast

YOU WILL NEED
THESE UTENSILS:
    cup
    measuring spoons
    toaster
    knife

AND THESE FOODS:
    1 teaspoon cinnamon
    4 tablespoons sugar
    4 slices bread
    Butter or margarine

Here's what you do:

1. Mix cinnamon and sugar together in cup.
2. Toast bread in toaster.
3. While toast is still hot, butter quickly.
4. Now sprinkle cinnamon-sugar mixture over hot buttered toast.
    Makes four warm, spicy slices.

NOTE: Each slice may be cut into three strips on a cutting board and served at snack time or to mother at tea time.

Lettuce Salad with French Dressing

YOU WILL NEED

THESE UTENSILS: AND THESE FOODS:
  cutting board   1 head of lettuce
  knife   ½ cup prepared French
  paper toweling   dressing
  wax paper
  6 serving dishes
  measuring cup

Here's what you do:

1. Strip off all outside and bruised lettuce leaves.
2. Wash the head of lettuce well to remove all sand.
3. Place lettuce on cutting board. Cut head in half and cut each
   half into 3 equal wedges or sections.
4. Pat gently between paper toweling to remove all excess water.
5. Put lettuce in refrigerator crisper; or wrap in wax paper or
   saran and chill.
6. When ready to serve, arrange lettuce wedges on plates.
7. Just before serving, pour French Dressing over each lettuce
   wedge.
   Makes six healthy servings.

 To Vary: Shred your lettuce wedges by slicing them into ¼-inch pieces and tossing with your favorite bottled dressing. Toss bacon bits, or cheese cubes or sliced eggs with your lettuce leaves.

To Serve: Top an open faced sliced chicken sandwich with the shredded lettuce salad or serve your lettuce wedge salad by alternating wedges with slices of ham and cheese and topping with French dressing.

Fruit Gelatin

**YOU WILL NEED
THESE UTENSILS:**

teakettle
mixing bowl
wooden spoon
can opener
strainer and bowl
measuring cup
6 serving dishes

AND THESE FOODS:

1 cup water
1 package flavored
    gelatin
1 can (1 lb. 13 ozs.) fruit
    cocktail

Here's what you do:

1. Put water in teakettle and bring to bubbling boil.
2. Empty gelatin into bowl.
3. Pour 1 cup boiling water over gelatin.
4. Stir with wooden spoon until gelatin is all dissolved.
5. Let it stand until cool.
6. Open can of fruit cocktail and empty into strainer placed over a bowl.
7. Measure 1 cup of syrup from fruit cocktail and add it to gelatin.
8. Add fruit cocktail and stir.
9. Pour the fruit gelatin into 6 serving dishes.
10. Set dishes in refrigerator for 3 hours to gel (become firm).

Makes six servings of colorful fruit gelatin. May be served with light cream or whipped cream.

To Vary: Change the shape by chilling in a 3-cup mold. A ring mold can be filled with slices of fresh or canned peaches, pineapple or apricots, ice cream or flavored yogurt.

To Serve: Top with marshmallow cream, ice cream or crumbled sugar wafers.

Hot Cocoa

YOU WILL NEED

THESE UTENSILS: AND THESE FOODS:
  measuring cup   4 tablespoons cocoa
  measuring spoons   4 tablespoons sugar
  1-quart saucepan   ⅓ cup water
  wooden spoon   3 cups milk
  4 serving cups   4 marshmallows

Here's what you do:

1. Put cocoa and sugar in pan; mix with the spoon.
2. Add water and mix all together.
3. Place pan over heat on top of range. Better keep stirring until
   sugar dissolves.
4. Boil for 3 minutes.
5. Stir in milk. Cook 5 minutes more, but do not let cocoa boil.
   Turn off heat.
6. Put a marshmallow in each cup and pour in cocoa. (If you
   haven't any marshmallows, don't worry. Cocoa is mighty good
   served plain.)
   Makes four delicious cups of cocoa.

NOTE: To make a cocoa sauce, stop with step 4. Cool cocoa mixture and store in refrigerator. Then for delicious cocoa milk just
add ¾ cup cold milk to 2 tablespoons cold sauce and mix well.

 To Vary: Top each cup with one of the following:
a dab of whipped cream
sprinkling of cinnamon or nutmeg
a dab of strawberry jam
a cream-filled sandwich cookie
a scoop of vanilla ice cream

Scrambled Eggs

YOU WILL NEED

THESE UTENSILS:	AND THESE FOODS:
mixing bowl	2 eggs
measuring spoons	½ teaspoon salt
egg beater	¼ teaspoon pepper
skillet	2 tablespoons light
fork	cream
serving spoon	1 tablespoon butter or
	margarine

Here's what you do:

1. Break eggs into bowl.
2. Add salt, pepper and cream to eggs.
3. Beat eggs lightly with egg beater until whites and yolks are mixed.
4. Melt butter in skillet on top of range over low heat.
5. When butter is melted, pour eggs into skillet and stir quickly with fork. (Otherwise you might have an omelet instead of scrambled eggs.)
6. When eggs are in large, light, fluffy pieces, they are done.
7. Turn off heat and serve immediately, while piping hot.

Makes two light and fluffy servings. A morning delight with hot buttered toast.

To Vary: Add to your egg mixture: crumbled bacon, chopped cooked ham, buttered toasted bread cubes, cheese cubes or chunks of brown and serve sausages.

To Serve: Top halves of English, corn or bran muffins; fill individual, hollowed out hero rolls; sprinkle with paprika or dab with barbecue sauce or catsup.

French Toast

YOU WILL NEED

THESE UTENSILS: AND THESE FOODS:

mixing bowl   2 eggs
egg beater   ¾ cup milk
measuring cup   ½ teaspoon salt
measuring spoons   6 slices day-old bread
skillet   2 tablespoons butter
pancake turner

Here's what you do:

1. Break eggs into bowl and beat with egg beater.
2. Add milk and salt, and beat together.
3. Now dip bread slices in egg mixture until both sides are coated with mixture.
4. Melt butter in skillet on top of range.
5. When butter is melted, put coated bread slices into skillet, using pancake turner.
6. Fry to a light golden brown color on bottom side of bread, turn with pancake turner and brown on other side.
7. Turn off heat. Serve hot.

Makes three golden brown servings of two slices each. Oh, so good with butter, maple syrup, jam or marmalade.

 To Vary: Use 1-inch thick diagonal slices of French bread or English muffins instead of white bread.

To Serve: Top with a sprinkling of cinnamon, nutmeg, cinnamon sugar, or apple pie spice. Or 3 slices of canned peaches or 2 pear halves. Make a sandwich with a cream cheese, raisins, or date mixture or orange marmalade as the filling.

Baked Potatoes

YOU WILL NEED
THESE UTENSILS:

AND THESE FOODS:

vegetable brush
paper toweling
wax paper
pot holder
long-handled fork
paring knife
measuring spoons

4 Idaho baking potatoes
1 teaspoon vegetable fat
4 teaspoons butter or
  margarine
4 dashes of salt
4 dashes of paprika

Here's what you do:

1. Set oven for 400°F. (mother will help you).
2. Wash and scrub potatoes clean with vegetable brush.
3. Dry potatoes with a paper towel.
4. Take a small piece of wax paper, put some vegetable fat on it and rub fat over each potato.
5. Place potatoes on oven rack so they do not touch each other.
6. Bake for about 1 hour or until done.
7. Test to see if they are done by pulling rack out, using a pot holder, and squeezing potatoes with fingers protected by a paper towel. If they are soft, they are finished. (Careful of the hot oven!)
8. Turn off oven and remove potatoes from oven rack with long-handled fork.
9. Now cut a cross on top of each potato with paring knife. Press gently on each side of potato to open the cross a little.
10. Place a teaspoon of butter or margarine on open potato cross.
11. Sprinkle each potato with salt and paprika.

   Makes four buttery baked potatoes. You might garnish your plate of potatoes with some colorful parsley sprigs.

 To Vary: Halve; sprinkle with Parmesan cheese; broil.

Buttered Peas

YOU WILL NEED
THESE UTENSILS: AND THESE FOODS:
  colander   2 pounds fresh peas
  measuring cup   ½ cup water
  saucepan with lid   1 teaspoon salt
  measuring spoons   1 tablespoon butter or
  serving dish   margarine

Here's what you do:

1. Shell the peas into colander just before cooking. Rinse peas lightly in colander.
2. Put ½ cup water into saucepan.
3. Add salt to water; put pan over heat on top of range. Bring water to bubbling boil.
4. Now add peas to boiling water; cover tightly with saucepan lid.
5. Let cook for 15 minutes.
6. To see if peas are tender, test a big pea by spooning it out of pan, blowing on it (it will be hot), and eating it.
7. If tender, turn off heat and remove pan from range.
8. Place peas in serving dish, add butter; serve immediately. Makes four servings of hot, buttery peas.

 To Vary: Add to your boiling water ½ teaspoon dried mint, oregano or ginger. Instead of 1 teaspoon salt, add 1 teaspoon garlic, onion, or celery salt.

To Combine: Add to cooked rice, mushrooms, lima beans, slivered almonds, bean sprouts, water chestnuts.

To Serve: Fill scooped out halves of 2 or 3 tomatoes with the peas; mix cooked peas with mashed potatoes or mashed carrots and sprinkle with cinnamon.

Hamburger Patties

YOU WILL NEED

THESE UTENSILS:
  measuring spoons
  mixing bowl
  skillet
  spatula

AND THESE FOODS:
  ¾ pound ground beef
  ½ teaspoon salt
  ⅛ teaspoon pepper
  1 tablespoon salad oil

Here's what you do:

1. Mix the ground beef, salt and pepper in bowl with your freshly washed hands.
2. Divide ground beef into 4 parts.
3. Shape each part gently into a flat cake. Do not pack too tightly.
4. Heat oil in skillet on top of range.
5. Lay patties in pan. (Careful! The fat might spatter.)
6. In a few minutes the under side will be browned; turn meat with spatula and brown the other side. Turn off heat.

Makes four hamburger patties. Delicious with warm hamburger buns for lunch or served with potatoes and vegetables on a plate at suppertime.

To Vary: Add to meat mixture one of these:
  ½ cup cooked peas or cooked carrots
  1 hard cooked egg, cut into chunks
  ½ cup raisins

Top with one of the following:
  Barbecue, soy or sweet and sour sauce
  Canned cream of mushroom or asparagus soup; heated

Applesauce with Raisins

YOU WILL NEED
THESE UTENSILS: AND THESE FOODS:
  paring knife   6 apples
  cutting board   1 cup water (about)
  large saucepan   1 cup sugar
  wooden spoon   ½ cup raisins
  strainer   4 dashes of cinnamon
  mixing bowl
  measuring cups
  4 serving dishes

Here's what you do:

1. Wash apples clean but do not peel them.
2. Cut each apple into 4 sections; cut away any seeds or brown spots.
3. Now cut apples into smaller parts on cutting board.
4. Put apples into saucepan; add enough water to just cover apples.
5. Cook about 20 minutes, stirring once in a while.
6. When apples are soft but not mushy, pour into strainer. Mash them through strainer into bowl with wooden spoon.
7. When applesauce is all strained into bowl, add sugar and stir.
8. Put applesauce back into pan, add raisins and heat again. Then turn off heat.
9. Serve hot with a sprinkling of cinnamon on top.

Makes four spicy, warm dishes of applesauce. Also delicious when served cold.

To Vary: Add ½ cup gum drops instead of raisins. or top with yogurt, crushed graham crackers or ice cream.

To Serve: Place in ready-baked tart shells.

Peanut Butter Cookies

YOU WILL NEED
THESE UTENSILS: AND THESE FOODS:

2 mixing bowls   2 eggs
egg beater   1 cup sugar
measuring spoons   1 cup brown sugar
measuring cups   1 cup shortening
wooden spoon   1 cup peanut butter
flour sifter   1 teaspoon vanilla
wax paper   extract
cookie sheets   2 cups flour
fork   1 teaspoon baking soda
pot holders   ½ teaspoon salt
spatula   1 teaspoon shortening

Here's what you do:

1. Set oven for 350°F.
2. Break eggs into one bowl and beat with egg beater until fluffy and light; then set bowl aside.
3. Put sugars and shortening into another bowl and stir with wooden spoon until sugar is all blended with the shortening.
4. Add peanut butter and mix it in.
5. Add eggs and vanilla to bowl with peanut butter and mix well.
6. Put flour, baking soda and salt into sifter set on wax paper and sift them into bowl; mix all together.
7. Put teaspoon of shortening on a small piece of wax paper and rub over cookie sheet.
8. Now roll 1 tablespoon of dough into a ball and place it on cookie sheet. Press it down and crisscross with a fork dipped into flour. Repeat until all dough is used.

 To Vary: Add peanuts, coconut, or chocolate pieces.

9. Slide cookie sheets into oven and bake cookies 12 to 15 minutes. Then turn off oven.
10. Remove cookie sheets from oven with pot holders.
11. Let cookies cool slightly, then take them off with spatula.

Do not overbake. Ask mother to help you decide when they are done. Makes 25 crunchy cookies.

Look What You've Done

With the recipes you have learned to make, you can now cook a whole day's meals. This is how your menu might look.

BREAKFAST Pineapple juice
Scrambled eggs
Cinnamon toast
Hot cocoa

DINNER Hamburger patties
Baked potato
Buttered peas
Lettuce salad with French dressing
Peanut butter cookies
Milk

SUPPER French toast
Applesauce with raisins
Fruit gelatin
Chocolate milkshake

Now you are ready to use the rest of this cookbook, with your mother's help of course. Have fun!

Quick and Easy

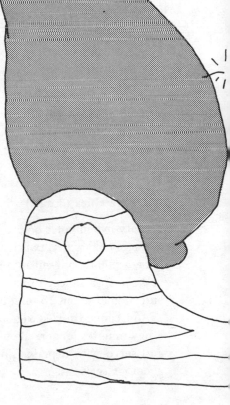

Fortunately, for the busy mother, new convenience foods are appearing on supermarket shelves each day. Take advantage of them.

This does not mean you should heat and serve—ring in variations of your own to personalize the dish. Mix and match for new taste treats. You'll feel extremely creative the day you adapt traditional recipes to convenience foods.

Children can start cooking earlier and cook often with these quick-to-fix products. Because there is less clean up to do and less preparation, the time the child spends in the kitchen with mother or on his own, will be sweeter, too.

Here we present a collection of easy, quick to make recipes—some featuring convenience foods, some without.

Avocado Cheese Soup

1 large avocado
1 can (10¾ ozs.) condensed
   Cheddar cheese soup,
   undiluted

1 can (14½ ozs.) evapo-
   rated milk, undiluted
6 thin slices tomato *or*
   chopped chives *or*
   chopped dill weed

Ten minutes before serving, halve, seed, pare and dice avocado.
Combine soup and evaporated milk. Stir over low heat until smooth. Add diced avocado and continue heating just until heated through. Do not boil.

Top each serving with a slice of tomato and pass the seasoned pepper. Makes 4 to 6 servings.

Quick Fish Chowder

1 medium-sized fish fillet
1 small potato
1 cup water
Dash of salt
1 small can mixed
   vegetables (1 cup)

1 teaspoon butter or
   margarine
½ cup milk
Parsley

Twenty-five minutes before serving, check fish carefully for bones. Rinse in cold water, pat dry and cut into small pieces.

Pare potato and cut into small cubes. Place fish, potato, water and salt in a saucepan and bring to a boil, then turn down heat and simmer about 15 minutes or until potato is tender.

Add canned mixed vegetables, including the liquid, and cook a few minutes longer. Remove from heat, stir in butter and milk and serve with a perky sprig of parsley. Makes 3½ cups or 2 generous servings.

Oyster Noodle Stew

4 ounces egg noodles
1 can (10 ozs.) frozen
   oyster stew, undiluted

1 soup can milk
Salt and pepper
Paprika and butter

Fifteen minutes before serving, cook egg noodles as directed on the package. Drain.

Heat oyster stew and milk. Add noodles and season to taste. Serve in soup bowl topped with a dash of paprika and a pat of butter. Makes 4 servings.

Vegetables, Salads and Breads

Beans and Bean Sprouts

¼ cup margarine
1 can (1 lb.) French-style
   green beans, drained

1 can (1 lb.) bean sprouts,
   well drained
¼ cup soy sauce

About five minutes before serving, melt margarine in skillet. Add green beans, bean sprouts, and soy sauce. Cover and cook just until hot. Makes 6 servings.

Spinach Supreme

2 packages (10 ozs. each)
   frozen chopped
   spinach
½ cup dairy sour cream

½ cup seasoned day-old
   bread crumbs
2 tablespoons butter or
   margarine, melted

Fifteen minutes before serving, cook spinach according to package directions. Drain and turn into 1½-quart casserole.

Hot Macaroni Salad

2 cups elbow macaroni
2 cups diced cooked green beans
¾ cup diced American cheese
2 cups thin fully cooked
  ham strips

¼ cup mayonnaise
1 tablespoon minced onion
¼ cup bottled chili sauce
1 teaspoon salt
¼ teaspoon pepper

Twenty-five minutes before serving, cook macaroni according to package directions and drain.

Combine hot macaroni with remaining ingredients except the salad greens. Let stand 5 minutes then serve on crisp salad greens. Makes 6 servings.

Tuna-Onion-Orange Salad

Fresh spinach leaves
2 Bermuda or other sweet
  onions
4 navel oranges

1 can (6½- or 7-ounce) tuna
Lemon French Dressing
  (below)

Do ahead and refrigerate. Wash and drain spinach leaves, tear into smaller pieces, if desired, and crisp in refrigerator.

Peel onions and cut into thin slices. Peel oranges and cut into thick cartwheel slices. Chill separately until needed.

At serving time, arrange spinach, onion and orange slices attractively on salad platter. Open can of tuna, drain and invert on platter, leaving tuna in circular shape. Let each assemble his salad. Pass dressing. Makes 4 servings.

Lemon French Dressing

¼ cup lemon juice
½ cup salad oil
2 tablespoons sugar

½ teaspoon salt
1 teaspoon paprika
¼ teaspoon pepper

Combine all ingredients and chill before serving. Makes ¾ cup.

Savory Cheese Biscuits

2 packages (4 ozs. each)   ½ cup grated sharp
   buttermilk biscuit mix   American cheese
                      ½ teaspoon celery salt

Add cheese and celery salt to a biscuit mix before adding liquid as label directs. Roll dough ¼″ thick and cut into squares with a floured knife. Bake as directed on package. Makes 10 to 12 biscuits.

Deviled Ham Gems

1 package (14 ozs.) corn   1 can (2¼ or 3 ozs.) deviled
   muffin mix   ham

Twenty minutes before serving, prepare muffin mix following package directions for 9 muffins. Spoon into greased muffin pans until two-thirds full. Indent each muffin with back of spoon and drop in a spoonful of deviled ham. Bake in hot oven (400°F.) 15 minutes or until done. Makes 9 muffins.

Meats

Meat Ball Stewganoff

2 medium onions   1 can (1 lb., 14 ozs.) meat
½ pound fresh mushrooms   ball stew
3 tablespoons butter   ⅓ cup dairy sour cream

Fifteen minutes before serving, peel onions and slice thinly.

Remove stem ends and slice mushrooms.

Melt butter in large skillet. Add onions and mushrooms; cook until onions are tender and remove from skillet.

Put canned meat ball stew in skillet and heat thoroughly. Add onions and mushroom slices and heat 2 or 3 minutes. Stir in sour cream. Heat thoroughly, but do not boil. Makes 4 servings.

Quick Beef Stew

1 lb. beef, cut in stew-size
  pieces
Meat tenderizer
2 tablespoons bacon fat
½ teaspoon paprika
6 or more onions
6 or more carrots, cut in
  half
6 or more potatoes, un-
  peeled
2 teaspoons salt
¼ teaspoon pepper
1 cup vegetable stock *or*
  water
1 can (6 ozs.) tomato paste

Thirty minutes before serving, sprinkle beef with tenderizer as directed on the container. Brown in fat in pressure cooker, sprinkle with paprika and add remaining ingredients.

Cook for 15 minutes after 10-pound pressure is reached. Let pressure go down gradually while you set table and call family together. Makes 4 servings.

Stuffed Green Peppers California Style

4 green peppers
1 can (1½ lbs.) chili with
  beans
¾ cup shredded pasteurized
  process cheese
¼ cup fine dry bread
  crumbs
1 teaspoon chili powder
  (optional)
Monterey Jack or
  Mozzarella cheese,
  crumbled or cubed

Forty minutes before serving, start heating oven to 350°F. Split green peppers in half lengthwise and remove seeds and membrane. Parboil 5 minutes.

Meanwhile, mix together chili and process cheese. Stuff pepper halves with this mixture.

Combine crumbs and chili powder, and sprinkle on tops of pepper halves. Bake at 350°F. 30 minutes. Remove from oven and sprinkle with cheese. Makes 4 servings.

Enchiladas

4 canned or frozen tortillas
¼ cup fat
1 can (1 lb. 4 ozs.) chili
   con carne

6 tablespoons grated
   Cheddar cheese
1 small onion, sliced
¼ teaspoon salt

Twenty minutes before serving, heat tortillas in fat.

Spread with half of the hot chili con carne, roll up and place in baking dish, folded side down.

Pour rest of chili con carne over rolled tortillas and sprinkle with cheese. Place in oven just long enough to melt cheese.

Add onion slices and sprinkle with salt and chili powder, if desired. Makes 4 servings.

Oriental Skillet Supper

1½ pounds flank steak, top
   round or other tender
   beef, thinly sliced
   and cut into strips
1 cup sliced onions
2 cups sliced celery
½ pound mushrooms, sliced

2 cups fresh spinach,
   washed and drained
1 bunch green onions,
   cut in 2-inch lengths
1 can (1 lb.) bean sprouts
2 tablespoons salad oil
   Sauce (below)

Fifteen minutes before serving, arrange meat and vegetables attractively on a large platter or in separate bowls.

Heat skillet, add 2 tablespoons oil and sear meat on both sides, about 1 minute. Remove meat to a bowl.

Add vegetables and sauce to pan and cook quickly over high heat for about 3 minutes. Stir gently, keeping ingredients separated as much as possible. When almost done, push vegetables (still crisp) to side of pan, add meat; simmer a minute or two.

Serve at once with hot rice. Makes 6 servings.

Sukiyaki Sauce: Combine 2 tablespoons sugar, ½ cup soy sauce and ½ cup beef stock or half a can of consommé.

Roast Beef Hashburgers

1 can (15 ozs.) roast beef
  hash
4 hamburger buns, split and
  toasted

3 tablespoons shredded
  cheese
1 onion, sliced into rings
1 can (8 ozs.) tomato sauce
  with mushrooms, heated

Twenty minutes before serving, start heating broiler. Remove both ends from can of hash; push out contents in one piece. Slice hash into 8 patties.

Place one patty on each toasted bun half and sprinkle with cheese.

Slip patties under broiler to heat through and to melt cheese.

Top each patty with an onion ring and fill ring with tomato sauce. Makes 4 servings.

Southern Goulash

½ pound ground beef
2 cans (15¼ ozs. each)
  spaghetti with tomato
  sauce and cheese

½ pound Cheddar cheese

Forty-five minutes before serving, start heating oven to 350°F. Cook ground beef in a skillet until well browned. Mix with spaghetti.

Cut cheese into thin slices. Line bottom and sides of a 2-quart casserole or baking dish with cheese slices, reserving some for the top. Turn spaghetti mixture into cheese-lined casserole and top with remaining cheese. Bake at 350°F. 30 minutes or until spaghetti is hot and bubbling. Makes 8 servings.

Sesame Chicken Noodles

2 pkgs. chicken noodle
    dinner
1 can (1 lb.) peas
1 can (6 ozs.) boned
    chicken, diced

2 tablespoons sliced
    pimiento
Toasted sesame seeds

About thirty minutes before serving, follow package directions for preparing the chicken noodle dinner.

After combining cooked egg noodles and chicken sauce mix, add peas, chicken and pimiento. Heat and serve with a liberal garnish of toasted sesame seeds. Makes 6 to 8 servings.

Turkey Tetrazzini

8 ozs. uncooked noodles
2 cans (10½ ozs. each)
    chicken both, diluted
¼ lb. fresh mushrooms,
    button or sliced
5 tablespoons margarine
2 tablespoons flour

1 cup light cream
2 cups cooked turkey
    chunks
2 tablespoons sherry (if
    desired, not necessary)
Grated Parmesan cheese

Forty minutes before serving, start heating oven to 350°F. Cook noodles in chicken broth until just tender, about 9 minutes. Drain and reserve 2 cups broth.

Meanwhile, sauté mushrooms in margarine until browned, stir in flour and add broth as in making a white sauce; cook until thickened.

Add cream, turkey, noodles and sherry, if used. Mix well, pour into greased 1½-quart casserole and sprinkle with cheese. Bake at 350°F. 30 minutes. Makes 4 to 6 servings.

Mock Chicken Divan

4 slices buttered toast
Sliced cooked chicken
1 can (1 lb.) asparagus
   spears *or* 1 package
   (10 ozs.) frozen
   broccoli, cooked

1 can (10¾ ozs.) Cheddar
   cheese soup, undiluted
½ soup can milk
1 tablespoon grated Par-
   mesan cheese

Twenty-five minutes before serving, lay toast slices flat in shallow baking dish. Top each slice with 2 or 3 chicken slices and asparagus spears.

Blend cheese soup and milk, and pour over top. Sprinkle with cheese. Heat at 400°F. 15 minutes or until sauce is hot and bubbly. Makes 4 servings (2 for father).

Glazed Chicken

1 3½ to 4½ pound
   roasting chicken
½ cup bottled barbecue
   sauce
½ cup melted butter or
   margarine

4 teaspoons lemon juice
½ teaspoon paprika
2 tablespoons sugar

While roasting chicken, combine barbecue sauce and butter.

Add lemon juice, paprika, and sugar. Mix thoroughly until the sugar is dissolved.

Roast (or broil) the chicken as usual. About 15 or 20 minutes before the chicken is done, spread with sauce mixture. Continue cooking for remainder of time. This sauce will give a tantalizing rich glaze. Makes 4 to 6 servings.

Swiss Cheese Fondue

3 tablespoons butter or
   margarine
3 tablespoons all-purpose
   flour
1 teaspoon salt
2 cups milk

1 pound Swiss cheese,
   shredded
Salt, pepper, cayenne
1 loaf unsliced bread, cut
   into one-inch cubes and
   toasted

Fifteen minutes before serving, melt butter in chafing dish or electric skillet. Stir in flour and salt until thoroughly blended.

And milk and cook, stirring constantly until sauce thickens and is smooth.

Add cheese and stir until it melts. Season to taste with salt, pepper and cayenne.

Dunk toast cubes in fondue. Makes 4 or 5 servings.

Tip: ½ cup beer or white wine may be substituted for ½ cup of the milk in which case, it is stirred in just before serving. And, should there be any fondue left, refrigerate it It makes a delectable spread for cracker snacks. It can also be reheated with a little milk and served over toast for the children's lunch.

Catsup Poached Eggs

2 tablespoons butter or
   margarine

¼ cup catsup
4 eggs

Melt butter in skillet. Add catsup and stir until hot. Break eggs separately into catsup, cover and cook at low heat to desired doneness.

Remove each egg to a slice of buttered toast. Makes 2 to 4 servings.

Heavenly Baked Eggs

4 slices bread, crumbled
3 tablespoons melted
   butter
¼ cup shredded American
   cheese
4 eggs

½ cup cream or evaporated
   milk
½ teaspoon thyme or savory
½ teaspoon salt
Dash of pepper

Twenty-five minutes before serving cover bottom of shallow pie pan with crumbled bread. Drizzle butter over crumbs and toast in a moderate oven (350°F.) until golden, stirring occasionally.

Sprinkle with cheese and, with the bowl of a spoon, make four little hollows for the eggs. Break an egg into each hollow.

Return to oven and bake about 15 minutes or until eggs are cooked as desired. Makes 2 to 4 servings.

Fish Potato Roll-ups

1 pound fish fillets
1 tablespoon dried
   parsley flakes
1½ teaspoons salt
¼ teaspoon coarsely
   ground pepper

1 package (9 ozs.) frozen
   French fried potatoes
2 tablespoons butter
1 can (8 ozs.) tomato sauce

Thirty-five minutes before serving, heat oven to 350°F. Separate or cut fish fillets into six portions. Sprinkle with parsley, salt, and pepper.

Roll fish around French fries, making six bundles.

Melt butter in small baking dish, place bundles with potatoes upright in dish. Pour on tomato sauce. Bake at 350°F. 25 minutes. Makes 4 servings.

Scallipops

1 package (7 ozs.) frozen
   breaded scallops
½ cup seasoned bread
   crumbs
¼ cup tomato sauce or
   mayonnaise

2 tablespoons prepared
   horseradish
¼ cup shredded Cheddar
   Wooden skewers or
   picks
   Paprika

About thirty minutes before serving, cut scallops into bite-size pieces and bake following package directions. During last five minutes of baking, sprinkle bread crumbs in flat pan and place in oven to brown lightly, stirring as needed.

Combine tomato sauce and horseradish. Roll scallops in tomato sauce mixture, then roll half of them in crumbs, half in cheese. Insert skewers. Dust tops with paprika. Serve hot. Makes 3 to 4 servings.

Tip: For a party, serve plain baked scallops on skewers with an assortment of dips and dunks.

Small Fry Favorite

6 small fish such as butter-
   fish, smelts, croakers or
   dabs (½ to ¾ lb. each)
⅔ cup corn meal

1½ teaspoons salt
1½ teaspoons paprika
6 slices bacon

Thirty minutes before serving, heat oven to 400°F. Dredge each fish with mixture of corn meal, salt and paprika. Arrange on aluminum foil in baking dish.

Top each fish with a slice of bacon. Bake at 400°F. 15 to 20 minutes. Makes 6 servings.

Baked Bananas Melba

4 bananas	¼ cup brown sugar
Melted butter or	Nutmeg
margarine	Mock Melba Sauce
2 tablespoons orange juice	(*below*)

Twenty-five minutes before serving, start heating oven to 350°F. Peel bananas, cut in half lengthwise and place in buttered baking dish.

Brush bananas with melted butter and sprinkle first with orange juice, then with brown sugar and nutmeg. Bake at 350°F. 15 minutes.

Cool and top with warm Mock Melba Sauce and a sprinkling of fine grated coconut.

Melba Sauce: Combine ¾ cup raspberry jam and ¼ cup boiling water; heat over hot water. Makes 4 servings.

Three-Fruit Shortcake

1 cup chopped fresh cranberries	1 cup sugar
1 cup chopped tart apple (unpeeled)	⅛ teaspoon salt
¼ cup crushed pineapple	Shortcake, home made or bought
	1 cup heavy cream

Do ahead. Combine cranberries, apple, pineapple, sugar and salt and let stand two to three hours.

Meanwhile make shortcake from biscuit mix, or buy angelfood or pound cake, or use your favorite shortcake recipe.

Arrange mixed fruits, cake and whipped cream shortcake fashion, at serving time.

Blueberry Pear Crisp

1 can (15 ozs.) pear halves
1 can (15 ozs.) blueberries
   in heavy syrup
½ cup brown sugar
⅓ cup all-purpose flour

⅛ teaspoon salt
¼ teaspoon nutmeg
3 tablespoons butter or
   margarine
Cream or sour cream

Thirty minutes before serving, drain fruit and reserve ⅓ cup of syrup from each can. Arrange pear halves in an 8 x 8 x 2-inch cake pan and top with blueberries. Add reserved ⅔ cup fruit syrup. Heat oven to 400°F.

Sprinkle with a mixture of the sugar, flour, salt and nutmeg. Dot with butter.

Bake in a hot oven (400°F.) 20 minutes. Serve warm with cream.

Tip: Any number of canned fruit twosomes can be used: peaches with bing cherries, pineapple chunks with raspberries and canned fruit salad with purple plums.

Mocha Pie

1 cup crushed chocolate
   cookies
3 tablespoons melted butter
   or margarine

1 package (3⅝ ozs.)
   instant chocolate
   pudding
¾ cup milk
½ pint coffee ice cream

At least three hours before serving, mix together the crumbs and butter. Press mixture to bottom and sides of a greased 7-inch pie plate with the back of a spoon.

Beat the pudding and milk together until thickened, and then beat in the ice cream. Spoon into the pie plate.

Refrigerate at least 3 hours before serving. Makes 4 to 6 servings.

Strawberry Ice Cream Pie

1⅓ cups very fine vanilla
  wafer crumbs (32 wafers)
¼ cup melted butter

1½ quarts strawberry ice
  cream
¼ cup slivered almonds

Blend crumbs and butter. Press firmly on bottom and around sides of 9-inch pie pan. Chill in refrigerator one or two hours.

When ready to serve fill wafer crust with slightly softened ice cream and sprinkle with nuts. Makes 6 to 8 servings.

Fig Bar Freeze

18 fig bars
1 pint orange sherbet

1 pint chocolate ice cream

Do ahead or an hour before serving. Stand 6 fig bars on end along each of the two long sides of an ice cube tray. Pack sherbet against one row of fig bars.

Stand 6 figs bars down center of tray and pack other side with ice cream. Place in refrigerator freezing unit 1 hour or until firm. Slice between fig bars to make 6 servings.

Frosty Devil's Food Loaf

1 quart vanilla ice cream,
  slightly softened
1 devil's food cake baked in
  a 10½ x 15-inch pan

1 cup heavy cream,
  whipped

The day before serving, line an ice cube tray with waxed paper. Cut three pieces of cake to the same size as tray. Press one piece into tray.

Cover with half of ice cream. Add second piece cake and then second layer ice cream. Top with third piece of cake.

Freeze for 2 or 3 hours. Turn out onto a chilled platter. Remove waxed paper and frost quickly with the whipped cream. Freeze until served. Makes 8 to 10 servings.

Index